A ONE-YEAR DEVOTIONAL STUDY THROUGH THE BIBLE

SLAY THE DAY

Your Daily Dose of Victory

ALISA HOPE WAGNER

A ONE-YEAR DEVOTIONAL STUDY THROUGH THE BIBLE

SLAY THE DAY

Your Daily Dose of Victory

Scriptures taken from multiple translations of the Bible.

Cover design by Alisa Hope Wagner
Author photo by Lori Stead of www.wetsilver.com
Warrior illustrations by Albert Morales

ISBN-13: 978-0692142837
ISBN-10: 0692142835
BISAC: Christian/Religious/Devotional

Dedication

God—my Creator, Savior and Counselor

Daniel—my high school sweetheart and soul mate

Isaac—my first-born son

Levi—my brown-eyed boy

Karis Ruth—my cherished girl

Christina—my twin

Thank you to my sword-wielding friends, Mark and Jennifer Smith of *RIDE FREE* (https://www.ridefree.today), for coordinating our trip to Israel and bringing the Bible to life in my heart. Also, I want to offer my gratitude to my aunt, Patti Coughlin, and to Faith Wilde and Faith Newton for taking time to proof the final draft. Finally, thank you to Albert Morales for his three gorgeous warrior illustrations.

"Do not suppose that I have come to bring peace to the earth. I did not come to bring peace, but a sword." – Jesus (Matthew 10.34 NIV)

Forward

The Bible is our only offensive weapon to live victoriously in Jesus Christ each day (Ephesians 6.17). This daily devotional covers every book in the Old Testament and New Testament, equipping you with the biblical insights to overcome all obstacles and to wield God's authority in your life. Don't live in defeat. Unsheathe your sword. Slay your day.

"But thanks be to God! He gives us the victory through our Lord Jesus Christ" (1 Corinthians 15.57 NIV).

OLD TESTAMENT

Part 1 of a 366-Day Devotional

DAY 1
The Light in Darkness

"And God saw the light, that *it was* good; and God divided the light from the darkness" (Genesis 1.4 NKJV).

God spoke light into existence on the first day He created the heavens and the earth. He divided the light from the darkness, but Scripture never says that He created the darkness. Because God created the light, the absence of light came into existence – darkness. God did not create Evil, but since God is Good, the absence of Good exists – Evil. Because Adam and Eve used their free will to taste from the Tree of Knowledge of Good and Evil, humans are now exposed to the presence and absence of God. God is all Good, and by His nature, He cannot dwell with anything less than perfectly Good. Our free will causes us to walk through the dark valleys of this world, so we are now separated from God. However, Jesus died to give us His perfection and to take our imperfection. When our faith and God's grace collide, we are made perfect and holy before a perfect and holy God, and we are no longer separated from Him. God gives us the light of His Spirit, which not even the darkest valley can snuff; and we become followers of Jesus through the power of His Word – the Bible.

"This is the message which we have heard from Him and declare to you, that God is light and in Him is no darkness at all" (1 John 1.5 NKJV).

DAY 2
The Taste of Sin

"Then the eyes of both of them were opened, and they knew that they were naked; and they sewed fig leaves together and made themselves coverings" (Genesis 3.7 NKJV).

The Tree of Knowledge of Good and Evil is symbolic of our free will to eat of fruit, which embodies the absence of God. God is the Tree of Life. We taste of Him and find life. We find God in our prayers, the Bible and the Holy Spirit, which dwells among us in this imperfect world corrupted by sin. The Tree of Knowledge of Good and Evil only offers us death. The more we eat of its fruit, the further into a pit of darkness we fall. When Adam and Eve used their free will to defy God's loving command to stay away from the Tree of Knowledge of Good and Evil, they opened their eyes and saw their nakedness, their shame. Today, every time we defy God's loving commands, we take bites of the fruit of this tree, and we expose our Spirits to shame. Thankfully, though, Jesus took our shame – past, present and future – and we are forever made clean if we have accepted His gift of salvation. However, our minds, hearts and souls are subjected to the *knowledge* of sin we have freely consumed. But if we determine ourselves to continue eating from the Tree of Life, the effects of our sin-knowledge will dwindle and lose potency.

"I will obey your decrees. Please don't give up on me!" (Psalm 119.8 NLT).

DAY 3

Righteousness Found in Hell

- • — • — ⁕ — • — • -

"Then the Lord said to Noah, 'come into the ark, you and all your household, because I have seen that you are righteous before Me in this generation'" (Genesis 7.1 NKJV).

The Bible never said Noah was perfect, but he found grace in God's eyes because he was righteous in *his generation*. The Bible says that the wickedness of humans was so great during Noah's time that God was sorry He ever made them (Genesis 6.6). Obviously, Noah grew up in an extremely corrupt and perverse family, culture and generation. Some Christians may have a preconceived notion of righteousness based on the trending culture of Christianity existing today. These Christians incorrectly judge others based on outward appearance and/or conduct that does not fit into their world-view of righteousness. However, like Noah, the circumstances surrounding these people may be extremely corrupt and perverse; and God sees the heart of those who are trying to trudge by faith through the swamps of ungodly experiences, upbringings and legacies. God gives grace to people who are fighting against the darkness they've come to know and understand and who are trying to live for God in a Christian world totally foreign to them. Because of the cross, God attributes righteousness in the center of their struggles, and the Holy Spirit transforms them from differing levels of glory into the image of His Son. Jesus reaches down into the individual hells of all His children and pulls them into His love, mercy and forgiveness; and as they cling to Him, they find grace and strength to loosen the strong-holds of sin.

"Because of his grace he declared us righteous and gave us confidence that we will inherit eternal life" (Titus 3.7 NLT).

DAY 4
Rooted Belief

"And he believed in the Lord, and He accounted it to him for righteousness" (Genesis 15.5 NKJV).

Abraham believed God. God promised him that he would be the father of many nations, yet Abraham and his wife had not conceived a baby yet. Years passed after God gave Abraham this promise, and God blessed him with protection, prosperity and prominence; but the kingdom-promise of an heir with his wife, Sarah, seemed hopeless. However, it is in this season of impossibility that God tests the legitimacy of our faith. Will we believe God at His Word or will we be persuaded by the physical evidence in our lives? Our true allegiance is uncovered when we find ourselves in a desert land of doubt, and God quietly watches our resolve either strengthen or disintegrate. When circumstances mount against our kingdom-promise, we must rise up carrying the weight of our hope and shout to all who will listen that we still believe. And in our free will decision to stay rooted in our faith, we will stand righteous before a Holy God.

"The father instantly cried out, 'I do believe, but help me overcome my unbelief!'" (Mark 9.24 NLT).

DAY 5

Grace in Strongholds

"I am not worthy of the least of all the mercies and of all the truth which You have shown Your servant…" (Genesis 32.10 NKJV).

Jacob's name means *deceiver*, and his family had a legacy of deception. Jacob and his mother deceived his father and his brother into giving him the firstborn inheritance and blessing; and Jacob's father-in-law, also his uncle, continually deceived him for many years. The culmination of this deceit climaxed when God told Jacob to return home and confront the sins he committed because of this familial stronghold. Before God broke Jacob and blessed him (Genesis 32.25-28), Jacob confessed the goodness of God. It is interesting that along with claiming God's mercy, Jacob claimed God's truth. We all have familial strongholds – worry, low self-esteem, lack of self-control, greed, dishonesty, pride and/or selfishness – that cause us to stumble. However, God will never deal with us the way we deserve. Instead of deceiving a deceiver, God showed Jacob great truth. And because Jacob struggled with showing truth all of his life, he was extremely attuned to its absence and presence. God gives us overflowing grace in the areas that we are most weak, and He will continually work with us until the stronghold is broken and He can bless us.

"Deny your weakness, and you will never realize God's strength in you." – Joni Eareckson Tada

DAY 6

Burning Bridges of Blessings

—•———•——※——•———•—→

"So it was, from the time that he had made him overseer of his house and all that he had, that the Lord blessed the Egyptian's house for Joseph's sake; and the blessing of the Lord was on all that he had in the house and in the field" (Genesis 39.5 NKJV).

Joseph found favor in God's eyes, so God blessed him. Not only did God bless Joseph, He also blessed Joseph's entire sphere of influence. Joseph was a slave for Potiphar, an Egyptian officer. Potiphar knew that God was with Joseph, so he made Joseph the overseer of his house. However, Potiphar's wife consistently harassed Joseph to the point that he finally fled from her presence. She was so obsessed with her own selfish desires that she lied and caused Joseph to be taken from her home and thrown into jail. The irony is that she disposed of the very source of her own blessings. Joseph was the main reason that her household had become extremely prosperous. Many people become consumed with their own skewed desires, thoughts and opinions; and they directly fight the people that God is using to bless them. If Potiphar's wife would have loved Joseph in purity and truth, her family would have eventually had an alliance with the second most influential man in all of Egypt during the worst drought in history. Instead, she allowed her selfishness and pride to destroy godly relationships and burn bridges of blessings.

"Unfriendly people care only about themselves; they lash out at common sense" (Proverbs 18.1 NLT).

DAY 7
The Sixth Day

"And Moses stretched out his hand over the sea; and when the morning appeared, the sea returned to its full depth, while the Egyptians were fleeing into it. So the LORD overthrew the Egyptians in the midst of the sea" (Exodus 14.27 NKJV).

Many times a life of faith means obediently walking right into a brick wall, trusting that God will supernaturally make a way through it. This is exactly what happened to the Israelites as they took their first steps out of slavery and into their destiny as the Chosen People of God. They obediently followed their God-appointed leader, Moses, into the vicinity between a rock and a hard place. They had the strongest military force behind them and a large sea in front of them. Needless to say, they were stuck with no way out. However, hopeless conditions–according to our natural standards–are God's moving grounds for His miracles–according to His supernatural standards. Not only did God split the waters so the Israelites could walk through the center of the sea, He also used that same water to sweep away the army bent on destroying them. God used what seemed to be an obstacle as their ticket to freedom from tyranny and defeat. God has a purpose for each of us, and we will find that our paths will be riddled with obstacles. Instead of complaining about the obstacles, we need to pray that God uses them to wipe away our enemy and to move us forward into our destiny.

"Jesus looked at them intently and said, 'Humanly speaking, it is impossible. But with God everything is possible'" (Matthew 19.26 NLT).

DAY 8

Blaze a Path

"But the children of Israel had walked on dry land in the midst of the sea, and the waters were a wall to them on their right hand and on their left" (Exodus 14.29 NKJV).

When we imagine the fledgling nation of Israel walking through the middle of the Red Sea with a wall of water on their right and left, we get a glimpse of what it means to walk by faith. God has an extremely specific purpose for each of us. We are all one-of-a-kind planted in this section of life for a definitive and essential purpose. Our insecurities may prompt us to try to blend into what everyone else is doing, but we can't do that! We can appreciate the faith-steps of those on our right and our left and learn from their individual journeys, but we must always remember that our paths (though intertwined) are completely separate from theirs. We may be walking the same direction in God's divine plan, but we each carry our very own piece of His Kingdom's fulfillment. The worst thing we can do is to covet someone else's design and purpose and sacrifice our own to be exactly like them. God's imagination and glory are so deep and wide that He is able to create endless expressions of His will, which allows each of us to blaze our own paths. We all find our salvation through Jesus; however, the display of Jesus in each of our lives is individually beautiful, unique and important!

"But the gateway to life is very narrow and the road is difficult, and only a few ever find it" (Matthew 7.14 NLT).

DAY 9
God's YES!

"Now the LORD had told Moses earlier, 'Pharaoh will not listen to you, but then I will do even more mighty miracles in the land of Egypt'" (Exodus 11.9 NLT).

Has God put a fire of truth into your spirit that ignited a burning passion to do His will? Has He given you a glimpse of His Kingdom Purpose that filled you with excitement to take your faith to the next level? Have you waited patiently–allowing God to teach you, shape you and grow you into His image–but now you know it's finally time for your breakthrough? However, the only problem is that no one will give you the time of day! Moses must have been frustrated when God commanded him to bring the Israelites out of Egyptian slavery only to hear Pharaoh tell him, "NO!" Pharaoh used his earthly power to thwart Moses' vision at every turn. But this was no surprise to God. In fact, God used Pharaoh's dissonance to display the strength of His glory. Every time Pharaoh ignored Moses' request, God did an even greater miracle! If you feel like your vision is being ignored–like the passion God has given you is unable to run its course–you are in a perfect atmosphere to receive a miracle. When all the people around you tell you "no," they are adding fuel to the power of God's "YES!"

"For all the promises of God in Him are Yes, and in Him Amen, to the glory of God through us" (2 Corinthians 1.20 NKJV).

DAY 10
An Altar of Earth

"An altar of earth you shall make for Me, and you shall sacrifice on it your burnt offerings and your peace offerings, your sheep and your oxen. In every place where I record My name I will come to you, and I will bless you" (Exodus 20.24 NKJV).

God told the Children of Israel to make altars out of the earth, so they could use them to burn their offerings to Him. Earth is symbolic of the material realm, which is separate and distinct from the spiritual realm. The Bible describes God creating us out of the earth (material realm), but He also breathed His Spirit into us (spiritual realm). Like Jesus, we are creatures of a temporal existence and eternal existence. Our bodies will die, yet our spirits will live forever. Therefore, the earthen altar, which is used as a platform for offerings, can allude to our earthly lives, which can also be used as a platform for offerings. God gives us a profound and amazing promise about the sacrifices we make on earth to further His eternal agenda! Every time we sacrifice the substance of our earthly lives—our time, our money, our energy, our control, our resources, our ministries, our bodies, our families, etc.–as an offering to God, He will write His name on it. And the offerings written with the *King of Kings and the Lord of Lords* across them will have God's presence and His blessings! So don't hold anything back from God. Freely and joyfully sacrifice everything to His will and believe that the substance of who He is and His glory will manifest in and around you.

"Then the LORD God formed the man from the dust of the ground. He breathed the breath of life into the man's nostrils, and the man became a living person" (Genesis 2.7 NLT).

DAY 11

Understanding the Darkness

"So the people stood afar off, but Moses drew near the thick darkness where God was" (Exodus 20.21 NKJV).

Finally, the freed people of Israel get to stand before the presence of God. They've seen His miracles and followed the instructions of His prophet, Moses; but now they are confronted with an awe-inspiring outpouring of His glory! Thunder, lightning, sounds of trumpets and smoke fill the atmosphere, and the Children of God are afraid to the point of trembling. Only Moses leaves the security of the group to walk into *the thick darkness where God was*. Isn't it interesting that Moses had to go to the dark to gain an intimate encounter with God? God is light (1 John 1.5), but we must remember that our light (understanding) is nothing like His. We have to let go of our understanding, so we can confidently walk in God's understanding. Everything might seem confusing and dark at first; but soon our eyes will adjust, and we will behold the beauty and majesty of God. If God is calling you to follow Him into the darkness, do not fear. Leave the comforts of the crowd and seek Him, and watch your life become flooded with His light.

"When we tell you these things, we do not use words that come from human wisdom. Instead, we speak words given to us by the Spirit, using the Spirit's words to explain spiritual truths" (1 Corinthians 2.13 NLT).

DAY 12

Crazy Vision

———————✻———————

"Now therefore, I pray, if I have found grace in Your sight, show me now Your way, that I may know You and that I may find grace in Your sight. And consider that this nation is Your people" (Exodus 33.13 NKJV).

The one thing that will cause you to cling onto God the most is committing to a task that is way beyond your scope of talent, ability and understanding. God asked Moses to prepare the entire nation of Israel – composed of millions of people – for their Promised Land. Talk about daunting! Moses knew that he was inadequate to get the job done. Not only did he ask God for some reassurance and assistance, he also reminded God that these people were *His people*. God gives all of His children a purpose that they could never achieve alone, so they will learn to lean on Him and grow into the image of Christ. God cares about the fruition of His Kingdom and all of His people; and because of His great love, He wants to give each of us a chance to make an eternal difference. He doesn't need our ability, talent or understanding; He simply needs our obedience. If God is sending you on a journey that scares you to death, you are in good company. Now, let go of your excuses and take a blind leap of faith. Trust that God will accomplish His purpose through you, and don't let fear stop you from your destiny.

"Never be afraid to trust an unknown future to a known God." – Corrie Ten Boom

DAY 13

Holy and Common

"You shall make a distinction and recognize a difference between the holy and the common or unholy, and between the unclean and the clean" (Leviticus 10.10 AMP).

As Christians, we should be in the forefront of deciphering between holy and common and clean and unclean. The Old Testament Levites (priests) were called to teach others the difference; however, Christians today are the New Testament priests (1 Peter 2.5). God is calling us to be on the cutting edge of what is holy and clean, so we can proclaim it to our generation. The world loves to explore "new" and enticing territories of sin in their books, movies, television shows, Internet sites, music and magazines; and before we consume any of it, we need to ask ourselves, "Is this holy or common?" The Bible says that wisdom is the fear of God and understanding is the shunning of evil (Job 28.28). Therefore, wisdom will help us to decipher holiness and understanding will help us decipher cleanliness. The more we put value on God's commands and shield our hearts from the knowledge of darkness (the absence of God), the better we will become at identifying and filtering what has become "common" in our society. Once we have a firm feel for holy (wisdom) and clean (understanding), we can create our own books, movies, television shows, Internet sites, music and magazines for His glory.

"Finally, brethren, whatever things are true, whatever things are noble, whatever things are just, whatever things are pure, whatever things are lovely, whatever things are of good report, if there is any virtue and if there is anything praiseworthy—meditate on these things" (Philippians 4.8 NKJV).

DAY 14

Trending Ordinances

———•———•———✦———•———•———

"According to the doings of the land of Egypt, where you dwelt, you shall not do; and according to the doings of the land of Canaan, where I am bringing you, you shall not do; nor shall you walk in their ordinances" (Leviticus 18.3 NKJV).

It is extremely difficult not to walk in the same direction as the people around us. We can go into a situation thinking that we'll be strong and we won't change, but slowly and surely, we acclimate to the crowd. It takes diligence and resolve to swim against the current, and it's easier just to let go and get taken under by the tide of culture. After a time, we don't even recognize that there is river of indifference towards God's law and His love sweeping us away from achieving our full eternal purpose. Our families, actions, words, efforts and lives may start to emulate the world's attitude, and the fear of God and the pursuit of holiness start to take a backseat. And when we come to the end of our lives, we'll wonder if we took the easy road or the road less traveled. We'll wonder if we missed out on the amazing plan that God has prepared for us using His boundless imagination. God warned His Chosen People not to live like the people around them; but sadly, before their sins finally caused their destruction, they turned their backs on God (Isaiah 1.4). They chose to walk in the ordinances of the world, instead of the ordinances of God.

"I believe our brief life here on Earth is all about legacy: What memory will you leave in the wake of your 70 or 80-odd years of living? If you are still drawing breath, then it's not too late to build the legacy of a champion." – Kenneth Ulmer

DAY 15

Unopened Doors

"Do not defile yourselves by turning to mediums or to those who consult the spirits of the dead. I am the LORD your God" (Leviticus 19.31 NLT).

God dwells in the spiritual realm – a realm more powerful than our physical world because it is eternal. Since God breathed the physical (3rd dimension) from the spiritual (4th dimension), our temporal lives are bound within the sphere of the eternal, like a baby encased in the mother's womb. The spiritual realm is real, powerful and not to be taken lightly. Both good (God and the angels) and evil (Satan and the demons) dwell in the spiritual realm. As Christians, we are to receive spiritual insight from the Holy Spirit, Bible and prophets (God's tried, tested and chosen Christian leaders). God commands His children implicitly not to consult, condone or connect with any other spiritual guides, resources or experiences. This indeed is a tall order in our culture today because many seemingly benign spiritual gateways have become so popular and accessible. Although there are many man-created spiritual doors available to walk through, Christians must not open them. Not all supernatural occurrences are of God, even if they seem useful at first. If we keep our eyes on God, He will unlock His supernatural authority in our lives when He chooses. Until then, we can find fresh insight from His Word, His Spirit and His chosen prophets.

"Someone may say to you, 'Let's ask the mediums and those who consult the spirits of the dead. With their whisperings and mutterings, they will tell us what to do.' But shouldn't people ask God for guidance? Should the living seek guidance from the dead?" (Isaiah 8.19 NLT).

DAY 16

The Fullness of God's Love

"You shall therefore keep all My statutes and all My judgments, and perform them, that the land where I am bringing you to dwell may not vomit you out" (Leviticus 20.22 NKJV).

The fullness of God's love is expressed in His law and grace, and His judgment and mercy. Jesus said He came not to abolish the law but to fulfill it. Any good parent knows that there are times you give grace to a child, but there are also times that child must feel the consequences of his/her actions. We want our children to understand simultaneously the law and grace of our love because they are both necessary to achieving a God-centered presence in our families. Similarly, Christians must follow God's direction in their lives AND accept ample amounts of His grace if they desire to victoriously accomplish their God-given purpose. Before bringing His Chosen People into their Promised Land, God warned them that their ungodly decisions would eventually catch up with them and their land (purpose) would spit them out. God poured out His grace numerous times; but after a time, God's children were faced with a disturbing harvest of all the sins they planted and cultivated. In an instant, God could have transformed their harvest of despair into a harvest of hope, but the people had already forsaken their God and all the good He embodies.

"Don't suppose for a minute that I have come to demolish the Scriptures— either God's Law or the Prophets. I'm not here to demolish but to complete. I am going to put it all together, pull it all together in a vast panorama.... Long after stars burn out and earth wears out, God's Law will be alive and working" (Matthew 5.17-18 MSG).

DAY 17

Cheap and Easy

—·—————·——✦——·—————·—

"The land must never be sold on a permanent basis, for the land belongs to me. You are only foreigners and tenant farmers working for me" (Leviticus 25.23 NLT).

We've all heard the expression, "Hold on Loosely," which we say to remind ourselves that everything ultimately belongs to God. He chooses when to give us stewardship over different landscapes (e.g. people, possessions, talents and callings); and He chooses when to reposition or release us from the various areas we cultivate. However, we tend to focus on the word "loosely" and forget that we are called to "hold on." Many people jump from one stewardship to the next because they are not willing to stay the long haul. Cultivating land is not easy. Often times we will find ourselves frustrated with people, burdened by possessions, lazy in our talents and timid in our callings; and we may be tempted to move to greener pastures. We'll begin to jump from one pasture to another without any real purpose, hoping for a harvest that will come cheap and easy. But that is not how God designed life. He purposefully created land that would take our sweat, strength and sacrifice to cultivate; so we would achieve our highest calling – serving selflessly in love like Jesus. Before you give up and try to sell the "land" God has placed you in, seek the Holy Spirit's approval. If you don't have peace, encourage yourself in the Lord and get back to work! Your diligence will pay off!

"Being forced to work, and forced to do your best, will breed in you temperance and self-control, diligence and strength of will, cheerfulness and content, and a hundred virtues which the idle will never know." – Charles Kingsley

DAY 18

God Shaped Faith

"I will send you rain in its season, and the ground will yield its crops and the trees their fruit" (Leviticus 26.4 NIV).

Wouldn't it be great if we knew when God's season of rain would come? Many people would give up once they saw how long it would take, unable to overcome the idea of waiting so many years. The rest of us—after getting over our shock—would resolutely mark our calendars and prepare for the wait. With our "breakthrough" date set in stone, we would look forward to it, daydream about it and make plans for it. The date would become our heart's obsession, and we would pour our energy, resources and time into preparing our land (purpose) for it. We would carefully organize and execute our steps until the day the rain spilled down from heaven, blessing all of our hard work. There would be no need for faith, no need for hope and no need to trust God. However, we serve a God who has a divine agenda filled with unseen dates; and He has given us power in our words to speak by faith the hope we are trusting Him for. The more we speak by faith—with no cloud in sight—the more we show our belief in our God. If God has promised you rain, do not doubt it for a second. If the air is hot and dry and your land is parched and thirsty, claim God's promises even louder. Let everyone around you hear the hope you have in Him; so that when the downpour is unleashed, they will see our God and give Him all the glory.

"Faith is not believing in my own unshakeable belief. Faith is believing an unshakable God when everything in me trembles and quakes." – Beth Moore

DAY 19

The Standard of Serving

❋

"He shall consecrate to the LORD the days of his separation, and bring a male lamb in its first year as a trespass offering; but the former days shall be lost, because his separation was defiled" (Numbers 6.12 NKJV).

When God sets up a leader to teach, feed, serve and care for His children, that leader is now accountable to God for the welfare of others. God has trusted that leader with the responsibility of influencing people with His heart, movement and will. Much like the Old Testament Nazarite, this leader is called to be separated from the crowd, so he/she can receive, consume and share fresh insights from God. As a symbol of a Nazarite's ministry, he was to never cut his hair. The longer his hair, the longer he has served God in ministry. However, when the Nazarite's separation was "defiled," he had to shave his head. All of his former days of ministry were lost, and he had to begin again on a clean slate. Today when Christian leaders defile their ministry by committing a string of ungodly choices that lead to a devastating fall, God is completely able to give them a fresh start. However, much of their credibility is lost since trust was broken with the people they served. God can restore a fallen leader's ministry and influence, but it will take time for healing and restoration to take place. The weight of influence is extremely heavy, and it comes with both blessings and burdens. It is important that we allow God to establish our ministries, instead of trying to establish our own authority. We may never be perfect, but we can remain faithful to God, serving others with love and humility.

"Don't be in any rush to become a teacher, my friends. Teaching is highly responsible work. Teachers are held to the strictest standards. And none of us is perfectly qualified. We get it wrong nearly every time we open our mouths. If you could find someone whose speech was perfectly true, you'd have a perfect person, in perfect control of life" (James 3.1-2 MSG).

DAY 20

Full-Face Prayers

"The LORD bless you, and keep you; the LORD make His face shine on you, and be gracious to you; the LORD lift up His countenance on you, and give you peace. So they shall invoke My name on the sons of Israel, and I then will bless them" (Numbers 6.24-27 NASB).

God told Moses to give a blessing to the priests, which they could then give to the rest of God's children. In this blessing there is a promise that if we "invoke" God's name, He will respond to our words. In essence, our words leave the physical world, penetrating into the spiritual world with the ability to affect circumstances, lives and hearts. God gave us creative license in this beautiful act of free will to shape and adorn His divine plan. However, there is another part to this promise: "the LORD lift up His countenance on you." When we are hiding nothing from the Lord—with all of our sins, secrets and selfish motives exposed to His care—we are able to fully receive the countenance of God. With our minds and hearts completely bare and focused on Him, we become powerful mirrors from which His face can shine and reflect. And the prayers coming from the lips of a person who is filled with the shining glory of God cannot help but be dominating, robust and influential. The words invested by people completely yielded to God are absorbed into His all-encompassing glory and transformed into a mighty tool to change the world for Christ. If we are going to pray, let us make "full-faced prayers," so our words will display the authority and glory of God.

"For the eyes of the Lord are on the righteous and his ears are attentive to their prayer, but the face of the Lord is against those who do evil" (1 Peter 3.12 NIV).

DAY 21

Heart Evidence

"And Moses said to them, 'Stand still, that I may hear what the Lord will command concerning you'" (Numbers 9.8 NKJV).

Life is messy and circumstances are often times not what they seem. That is why God says He judges our hearts and not necessarily the outlook of our situations. The world is corrupted by sin, and its influence elbows its way into even the best of ministries, families and lives. The Israelites were about to celebrate their second Passover to commemorate when God's judgment passed over them in Egypt. However, some of the people were unable to observe this holiday because they were either far away or ceremonially unclean. Instead of going strictly by the book, Moses told these people to "stand still," so that he could ask the Lord what to do. God lovingly allowed these people to celebrate Passover a month later. He looked past the external evidence and into the hearts of people desiring to honor Him. It is easy as Christians to put our view of God's standards above the movement of His Holy Spirit. However, God sees what we do not, and we must always "stand still" and pray before moving on any assumptions formed by our limited viewpoints. Once we realize how dim our eyes are compared to the bright eyes of Christ, we will never presume to act until we have sought the will of God.

"…For the Lord sees not as man sees; for man looks on the outward appearance, but the Lord looks on the heart" (1 Samuel 16.7b AMP).

DAY 22

Time to Go!

"Whether the cloud stayed over the tabernacle for two days or a month or a year, the Israelites would remain in camp and not set out; but when it lifted, they would set out" (Numbers 9.22 NIV).

The nomadic Nation of Israel is slowly making its way through the wilderness, and the uncharted course makes absolutely no sense. They are following God—represented in a fire at night and a cloud by day—with complete reliance on Him (besides occasional complaining and disobedience). The fire provides warmth and light during the night, and the cloud offers coolness and shade during the day. Sometimes the cloud and fire would stay in one spot for a year, but sometimes they would stay only a few days. The people followed the cloud and fire closely because their protection and direction were dependent on them. Today we don't need a cloud or fire to lead us. The New Testament Chosen People (Christians) have the Holy Spirit dwelling inside of them. God's Spirit is our protection and direction, guiding us to God's best in this life. However, we must be totally reliant on His movement. We get into trouble when we start trying to chart our own course. We might have well-meaning intentions, but we will eventually discover that we journeyed into our own selfishness, which leads to a shallow, self-serving existence. Only God knows the perfect path that ensures our submission to His will, which leads to joy, peace and eternal purpose. Although God's direction may not be known, He does put a passion in us that draws us to His promises. And if we trust our God-given passion and promises, we'd be willing to journey anywhere with Him.

"So don't you see that we don't owe this old do-it-yourself life one red cent. There's nothing in it for us, nothing at all. The best thing to do is give it a decent burial and get on with your new life. God's Spirit beckons. There are things to do and places to go!" (Romans 8.12-14 MSG).

DAY 23

Hauling the Eternal

"Then Moses said to him, 'Are you zealous for my sake? Oh, that all the Lord's people were prophets and that the Lord would put His Spirit upon them!'" (Numbers 11. 29 NKJV).

When you get a fuller understanding of God's divine plan, it may scare you a little. You stand before this amazing eternal development in awe of all its intricacies and impossibilities, and you realize that you could be crushed under the weight of such a vision. You are then confronted with the definite conclusion that there is no way you can bring this vision into fruition alone. In fact, you know that all of your efforts are futile unless God wields some serious supernatural power on your behalf. Once the bigger picture of what God wants to accomplish reveals itself, you might be tempted to throw up your hands and claim defeat. You're smart. You know your limitations. You know that the path before you is hopeless, ridiculous and implausible. Yet, your heart is drawn to the horizon because your spirit senses God's glory like the sun just about to dawn. So you take a few steps and pray for God's provision. But the thing is that God enjoys allowing His children to make an eternal difference. He can easily carry the burden, but He wants His sons and daughters to live a life of purpose, so He allows His perfect plan to be shouldered by imperfect people. How He loves seeing us make a difference no matter how messy we are! When God's Spirit fell on seventy people of Israel and they started to prophesy (communicate God's heart and will), Joshua – Moses' assistant– was upset. He told Moses to make them stop. But Moses saw the eternal plan of God and knew its weight, and he longed to see all of God's children help carry their unique load. So when you see someone living his/her purpose in this life, praise God. And pray for everyone else who seems lost and distracted. Pray that they find their place on the path to God's best, so we can all haul God's plan across the finish line together!

"Trust in the Lord with all your heart and lean not on your own understanding; in all your ways acknowledge Him, and He will make your paths straight" (Proverbs 3.5-6 NIV).

DAY 24

Mocking the Obedient

"And Moses said: 'By this you shall know that the LORD has sent me to do all these works, for I have not done them of my own will'" (Numbers 16.28 NKJV).

God leads us to do crazy things sometimes that make no sense to the world. Whether giving financial, flying our families to another continent for mission work, offering our time and resources in an endeavor that seems fruitless and thankless or risking our own comfort and control in a sacrifice that scares us–we commit ourselves to the ridicule and judgment of others. Moses knew how it felt to walk in obedience to God only to have an entire nation–his own people–mock and ridicule him. How beautiful we must look to God when we stand firm in His Word even when the world pelts us with their stones. Our actions of steadfast perseverance pronounce clearly the unwavering trust and belief we have in a mighty God. We can claim the cross with our words, but the testimony of our lives speaks even louder. Moses told the people of Israel that his actions were in agreement with God's will, and God supernaturally proved Moses' obedience by opening up the earth. Therefore, we don't have to prove or explain ourselves to anyone when we are ridiculed for His namesake. If we continue clinging onto God and do everything in our natural means to follow Him, God will supernaturally pour out His glory and there won't be any question of who's in charge.

"The Lord gives righteousness and justice to all who are treated unfairly" (Psalm 103.6 NLT).

DAY 25

Ignorant Complaining

"You complained in your tents and said, 'The Lord must hate us. That's why he has brought us here from Egypt—to hand us over to the Amorites to be slaughtered'" (Deuteronomy 1.27 NLT).

It is obvious when people do not know the character of God. They call God unjust and cruel, and they say He's a tyrant who mistreats His people. Much like the 1-talent servant in Jesus' parable who accused his master of being a "harsh" man (Matthew 25.24-25 NLT), people use this misconception of God to bury their gifts and talents. They have not allowed themselves to freely receive and embrace God's love, favor and grace; so they fear making the tiniest mistakes which paralyze them from walking in confidence by faith. However, God never asked us to be perfect. In fact, He knows we can't! That is why He sent His perfect son, Jesus, to die for our sins. Although we will never be perfect, we can be faithful–faithful to use the gifts and talents He gave us as we obediently follow His will. The people of Israel falsely accused God of hating them and leading them on a journey that would end in their ruin. But that was not true! God led them away from slavery, protected them in the wilderness and prepared them for their Promised Land. He adored His people and performed many miracles on their behalf. If we firmly hold onto the truth that God is for us (Romans 8.31) and desires the best for us (John 10.10), we would stop complaining and boldly use our gifts and talents to fulfill our purpose and unlock His promises.

"'For I know the plans I have for you,' declares the Lord, 'plans to prosper you and not to harm you, plans to give you hope and a future'" (Jeremiah 29.11 NIV).

DAY 26

Immovable yet Movable

———————————————————

"Therefore circumcise the foreskin of your heart, and be stiff-necked no longer" (Deuteronomy 10.16 NKJV).

Spiritual growth is a choice. A person can be surrounded by the best Christian resources, people and experiences; but unless that person's heart is circumcised and his neck pliable, he will not mature. In order to be circumcised, a man must stay absolutely still for the procedure to be performed properly. God wants to trim our hearts of sin, selfishness and pride; but when we are not disciplined to stand firm, we indirectly shake His hand away. God has given us many commandments in the Bible, and if we remain immovable in them, He is able to shape us into the awesome image of Christ. Also, we must ensure that our necks are not stiff. When farmers plowed their fields, they couldn't use stiff-necked oxen. These obstinate oxen could not be led; therefore, they could not be trained and used. God wants to lead us into His best. He wants to train us up as Christian leaders. However, if we are not humble, we will be stubbornly stuck in our sin, selfishness and pride. If we allow God to guide and move us, we will walk in victory in His favor and grace. Christians have the choice to stay immovable in God's Word but movable in God's Will, so they will experience amazing spiritual growth and be used as a powerful tool for God's kingdom.

"A man who is eating or lying with his wife or preparing to go to sleep in humility, thankfulness and temperance, is, by Christian standards, in an infinitely higher state than one who is listening to Bach or reading Plato in a state of pride." — C.S. Lewis

DAY 27

MORE: A Four-Letter Word

• — • — ※ — • — • —

"For the LORD your God has blessed you in all the work of your hand. He knows your trudging through great wilderness. These forty years the LORD your God has been with you; you have lacked nothing" (Deuteronomy 2.7 NKJV).

Too many Christians think the word, *MORE*, is a "four letter word." They believe that as Christians, we should be satisfied with what we have, where we are at and who we have become. There is no need to have crazy, big dreams because that would be greedy and a little risky. However, our God is a big God, and His favor, grace and goodness are limitless. We stop the fruition of His work in our lives when we believe that wanting more is wrong. All throughout the Bible, people have desired more while learning to stay content in God's timing. We can appreciate where we are at, yet keep our eyes focused on where we want to go. God led the people of Israel through the wilderness where they lacked nothing. Even though God made sure that they had everything they needed, He was not planning on leaving them there. God wanted to give them *MORE*! God had a Promised Land waiting for them! The wilderness looks different for all of us, and God will make sure that our needs are met. But He doesn't intend for us to stay there–He wants our God-given passions to drive us to our Promised Land! When we become open to *MORE*, we will begin to have a hunger and a thirst for God that can't be quenched. We will crave, seek and claim *MORE* of His goodness, and we will willingly sacrifice all that hinders us from greedily taking *MORE* of Him!

"The greatest enemy of hunger for God is not poison but apple pie. It is not the banquet of the wicked that dulls our appetite for heaven, but endless nibbling at the table of the world. It is not the X-rated video, but the prime-time dribble of triviality we drink in every night." – John Piper

DAY 28

Moral Decay

———————————————————

"You shall not worship the LORD your God with such things" (Deuteronomy 12.4 NKJV).

The Old Testament Chosen People lost their Promised Land because they completely erased God and His Word from their lives and nation. Assyria conquered the Northern Kingdom (Israel) starting in 740 BC and Babylon conquered the Southern Kingdom (Judah) starting in 587 BC. The sad truth is that the Children of God were still worshiping God, but they were worshipping God like the pagan people worshipped their Gods. When God's people stopped sitting with Him every day and seeking His Word and Will, the fiber of their purity, beauty and righteousness slowly deteriorated. God warned them not to worship Him with the things of this world, but they allowed the weeds of sin to flourish in their lives. As the New Testament Chosen People, the nation of the United States of America is the New Testament Promised Land. It is extremely obvious to the rest of the world that we are a blessed and favored people. But we must take care not to allow the world to dictate to us how we worship God in our churches, lives, families, relationships, government, etc. If we don't continually sit with God and obey His Word and Will, our nation will begin to morally decay. When we compartmentalize God in His own creation to justify our disobedience, it's only a matter of time until we completely forsake Him. And once we lose His blessing and His favor, we will realize just how much we sinned and how good we truly had it.

"When we have a new heart, we become new people, and then we have a new society, then we have a new nation." – James Yen

DAY 29

The Blameless Talk

"But the prophet who presumes to speak a word in My name, which I have not commanded him to speak, or who speaks in the name of other gods, that prophet shall die" (Deuteronomy 18.20 NKJV).

It is very important that we sit with God every day and consciously submit our spirits to His, so that our spirits and the Holy Spirit may blend and become one. When we try to compartmentalize God in our lives, we divide our intentions from His. If this happens, we may speak His Words in certain capacities, but in others–where our spirits dominate–our words will speak the will of our flesh. We may feel safe in our words because in most areas we know we are submitted to His will, but the enemy won't attack the submitted areas of our lives. He'll attack the areas that we grope at for control. If the Holy Spirit does not claim complete authority, we walk a tight line of being true and false prophets. At any moment our fleshly intentions can rear up and profess the will of God falsely. As Christians and leaders in God's Kingdom, we stand accountable when we speak words that are absent of the heart of God. God tells us in His Word that a prophet "shall die" if he/she speaks in the spirit of the flesh. Although we are saved by grace and have assured forgiveness, we do strangle the amazing purpose God has planned for us with each false self-spoken word. It is no small matter to claim insight and wisdom of God if we are not daily sitting with Him. False prophets are not the loudest voices making the biggest commotions against Christ; they are the whispers and nuances of average Christians claiming faith but not aiming to achieve complete surrender to the Holy Spirit.

"Now may the God of peace make you holy in every way, and may your whole spirit and soul and body be kept blameless until our Lord Jesus Christ comes again. God will make this happen, for he who calls you is faithful" (1 Thessalonians 5.23-24 NLT).

DAY 30

Overtaken

- • ———— • —— • ☀ • —— • ———— • -

"And all these blessings shall come upon you and overtake you, because you obey the voice of the LORD your God" (Deuteronomy 28.2 NKJV).

God is the creator, maker and giver of everything good. He is an unending tap of love, hope, peace and joy in a world corrupted by sin. He bestowed us with free will knowing we would sabotage His perfect creation with our godless choices, so He prepared a redemption plan by sending Himself to take the punishment for our sin through Jesus Christ—God clothed in flesh. Although God did not create sin, He allows it to exist in this world as a tool to cut away the sin in our own lives and hearts. Christians can grin and bear the painful process of transforming into the image of Christ or we can be so enraptured by the favor of God that we find joy in the center of our breaking and healing. The Bible says that if we follow the voice of the Lord, His blessings will "come upon and overtake" us. Can our enjoyment and enthusiasm of living for Christ be so great–so overwhelming–that we barely notice the bumps and bruises along the way? Can we recognize just how fleeting our time is on earth that our view of the finish line–heaven–prevents us from dwelling on our stumbles in this life? We have a promise: If we obey the voice of the Lord we will be overtaken by His blessings. Though heartache and pain will continue until our deaths, we can diminish their weight by receiving the unlimited favor and blessings God has for each of us. All we have to do is obey His voice and tap into the source of all that is good.

"Though you have not seen him, you love him; and even though you do not see him now, you believe in him and are filled with an inexpressible and glorious joy, for you are receiving the end result of your faith, the salvation of your souls" (1 Peter 1.8-9 NIV).

DAY 31

New Testament Priests

— • — — • — ✳ — • — — • —

"Since you have never traveled this way before, they will guide you. Stay about a half mile behind them, keeping a clear distance between you and the Ark. Make sure you don't come any closer" (Joshua 3.4 NLT).

The Nation of Israel wandered in the wilderness for forty years, but now they are about to take their first steps into their Promised Land. They have never been this way before, so God chose His priest to carry the Ark of the Covenant a small distance away from the people. The people then followed in the wake of God's chosen leadership into this new area and chapter of their lives. Sometimes we are called to be the "people." God appoints leaders in our lives who guide us into further intimacy with Christ. We learn by their example and find strength in their confidence to live a life pleasing to God. However, God also calls us to be the "priests." As Christians, we are chosen by God to be New Testament Priests; and many times God will choose us to be the first in our families, churches or spheres of influence to walk a unique path with God. Others will follow in our wake, so we need to make sure that we cling tightly to the "Ark of the Covenant," which symbolizes the presence of God. If God has given us authority and influence, we are now responsible for the people who follow our leadership. So when we feel unsure and nervous about the new direction God is leading us, we can find strength in God and hold firmly to His Word, Promises and Presence. We'll never know how many people find guidance and confidence by watching our walk with Christ and who may step out in faith because of our example.

"If you have achieved any level of success, then pour it into someone else. Success is not success without a successor." – T. D. Jakes

DAY 32

Reminders

◆•———•——※——•———•◆

"Tell them that the flow of the Jordan was cut off before the ark of the covenant of the Lord. When it crossed the Jordan, the waters of the Jordan were cut off. These stones are to be a memorial to the people of Israel forever" (Joshua 4.7 NIV).

People are influenced by our realities, especially those who are under our authority and influence. When those people trust and respect us, our experiences will alter their fundamentally rooted perceptions of life. Our hang-ups and strongholds will affect them just as much as our victories and triumphs. It is so easy to allow our mistakes to take precedent in our thoughts, words and actions. Little do we know, though, that our focus on the negative will cause those we influence to focus on the negative. But we forget that the ugliness of our lives has been washed clean by the blood of Jesus. We are rehashing things that no longer exist, and we are teaching others that GRACE isn't strong enough–but the truth is that our FAITH is what's not strong enough. Instead of repeating our failure, pain and bitterness over and over again, we need to speak of what God has done in our lives. Then those who look up to us will begin to see the beautiful movement of God, and their realities will have a firm grasp of how amazing He truly is. We may not have stones of memorials like Israel had after crossing the Jordan, but we can write a list of all of God's blessings and favor. Instead of professing the corrupting sin of this world, we can use our list to start professing all the good God has done.

"'No, go back to your family, and tell them everything God has done for you.' So he went all through the town proclaiming the great things Jesus had done for him" (Luke 8.39 NLT).

DAY 33

Clearing the Land

"But the mountain country shall be yours. Although it is wooded, you shall cut it down, and its farthest extent shall be yours; for you shall drive out the Canaanites, though they have iron chariots and are strong" (Joshua 17.18 NKJV).

The children of Joseph — the tribes of Ephraim and Manasseh — want more of the Promised Land. The nation of Israel is dividing their inheritance and establishing their individual tribes, and the children of Joseph explain they are a "great people" who need more room. Israel's anointed leader, Joshua, offers them the mountain, but they insist that they need more land. They also complain that the people who are currently living in the area of interest have "chariots of iron" and suggest that they will need help securing their land. Instead of bowing to their indirect request for help, Joshua tells them that they can have the mountain and the wooded area, but they will have to fight for it themselves and prepare the land on their own. He encourages the two tribes that they are indeed a "great people" who have "great power," but he does not let them off the hook of fighting for their own inheritance. Many people want to expand their Promised Land, but they are not willing to fight for it. They expect others to do the work of clearing the path and establishing their inheritance, but God will only provide us help when we come to the end of our own ability. If we do everything in our power to achieve God's promises, He will provide the additional assistance and resources we need. We must be careful not to burden people with our obligations or allow ourselves to be burdened by the demands of those who are completely capable.

"He that would have the fruit must climb the tree." – Dr. Thomas Fuller

DAY 34

Satan's Minefield

"The men of Israel looked them over and accepted the evidence. But they didn't ask God about it" (Joshua 9.14 MSG).

Joshua is leading the people of Israel into their Promised Land, and they are claiming and securing dominion over the area that God has given them. Since the enemy knows that he can't stop God's chosen people from establishing their nation, he decides to plant as many snares into their land as possible. The enemy can then use these skillfully placed traps to ensnare God's people into sin at a later date. The Hivites deceived Joshua and the leaders of Israel by claiming they were from a distant land. Instead of consulting with God, the people of Israel accepted the false evidence presented to them and made an alliance with a nation that God said He would drive out of their Promised Land (Exodus 34.11). The Hivites would become one of the handful of nations that would test Israel and cause them to forsake God (Judges 3.4-6). For this reason, it is very important that we daily consult God about all of our decisions. The enemy might not be able to stop us from entering our Promised Land, but he will diligently lay out a spiritual minefield in our path. Whether pride, vanity, lust, greed, selfishness, insecurity, lies, deceit, fear, addictions — Satan will plant anything and everything to get our eyes off God so we will wind up "piling up sins." But if we simply consult God first, we will save ourselves loads of trouble, heartache and time.

"'What sorrow awaits my rebellious children,' says the Lord. 'You make plans that are contrary to mine. You make alliances not directed by my Spirit, thus piling up your sins'" (Isaiah 30.1 NLT).

DAY 35

A God that Serves

"And there has been no day like that, before it or after it, that the LORD heeded the voice of a man; for the LORD fought for Israel" (Joshua 10.14 NKJV).

Why did God give us free will knowing that we would abuse it and create evil? Why did He bother creating us when He already knew (God dwells outside the realm of time, so He is able to see past, present and future simultaneously) the damage we would make in His design? Why did He give us dominion in His perfect Kingdom when we ourselves are corrupted by sin? Because He could see the beauty we would create, the strength we would show, and the fierce loyalty we would claim. He saw the possibility of good in each of us, and He washed away our evil by the blood of His Son, Jesus. Although God has designed us with a plan and a purpose (everything with value has a purpose), He allows us creative license to envision and achieve the impossible. He gave us His Spirit (John 20.22) and the mind of Christ (1 Corinthians 2.16), and He wants us to please Him with our words, choices and actions. As long as we keep our focus on Him, God wants to bless us with the desires of our hearts — especially the desires that only He can accomplish! Joshua is obediently leading the Nation of Israel into their Promised Land, and his eyes are on the Lord. When Joshua asks God for the impossible (the sun to stand still), God "heeds" Joshua's requests! When our purest motive is to give God the glory and accomplish His will, He promises to fulfill the desires of our hearts. God wants to fight for us!

"And I will do whatever you ask in my name, so that the Father may be glorified in the Son. You may ask me for anything in my name, and I will do it" (John 14.13-14 NIV).

DAY 36
The Reason for Promises

"Not a word failed of any good thing which the LORD had spoken to the house of Israel. All came to pass" (Joshua 21.45 NKJV).

God plants seeds of wants and desires into each of us. Though these wants and desires can be twisted and tainted by sin in our lives, the foundation of our passion is rooted to the glory of God. Each seed draws us to the God-ordained promises that make up our unique purpose in life. And as we persistently take the difficult steps towards our promises, God is able to break us and mold us into His personally tailored image of Christ for us. God created this system of "religious commerce" as a means to cultivate a relationship with His children. At first our intentions are selfish, but after a time, our love for our Creator blossoms and He becomes our heart's desire. However, it still pleases God that we achieve our purpose, and He enjoys connecting our passions with His promises — not because of our perfection or righteousness, but because of His love and faithfulness. In the *Book of Joshua*, God's Chosen People finally find rest in their Promised Land, and the Bible says that every "good thing which the LORD has spoken" came to pass. Though the people made mistakes and lost their way a few times, God accomplished His purposes for them. If our intimacy with God is to grow, we will have to seek God's promises which create the mosaic of our purpose. When we finally reach our Promised Land, our love for our Creator will be so rich and deep that our selfish motives will have transformed into an eagerness to see His glory established in our lives.

"God has condescended by this *religious commerce*, to bind us to Himself more firmly by means of our wants and our desires." – Le Maistre de Sacy

DAY 37

Thorns of Weakness

"Therefore I also said, 'I will not drive them out before you; but they shall be *thorns* in your side, and their gods shall be a snare to you'" (Judges 2.3 NKJV).

The Nation of Israel are in their Promised Land, but God has allowed people of other nations (thorns) to live among them. God uses these *thorns* to test His people, but He also uses the *thorns* to keep them from becoming proud. It is interesting that during the book of Judges, whenever God blesses His people with peace and prosperity, they forsake Him; but when their weaknesses hinder their lives, they seek Him. God allows us to have our own thorns to expose our limitations, but they should not cause us to claim defeat; rather, they should keep us in constant communication with Jesus when we realize we can't make it in our Promised Land without Him. They break our corrupted sin nature, permitting God's holy nature to shine through our lives. Once we identify our thorns and give them to God's care, He will pour out His strength in our weaknesses, and His love for us will be evident to the world. We will give God all the glory because we know that we couldn't have accomplished our goals without an intimate relationship with our Creator.

"Three different times I begged the Lord to take it [thorn] away. Each time he said, 'My grace is all you need. My power works best in weakness.' So now I am glad to boast about my weaknesses, so that the power of Christ can work through me" (2 Corinthians 12.8-9 NLT).

DAY 38

Faith Might

"Then the LORD turned to him and said, "Go in this might of yours, and you shall save Israel from the hand of the Midianites. Have I not sent you?" (Judges 6.14 NKJV).

When God told Gideon to "go in this might of yours," Gideon's mouth probably dropped wide open. It was obvious to Gideon that he didn't have the "might" necessary to defeat an entire nation. He was from the weakest clan, hiding from his enemy in a winepress. God had to give Gideon many supernatural signs in order to break his inferiority complex and do the great things God had planned for him. However, God didn't prepare Gideon for victory by adding to his confidence or self-esteem; rather, God stripped Gideon of almost everything. Out of obedience, Gideon offended his neighbors by tearing down their shrine, he slimmed down his army to only 300 soldiers, and he devised a battle strategy that would make any military leader laugh. God left Gideon exposed, dependent and vulnerable; which is exactly the best place we need to be. Only when we realize how inadequate we are to achieve God's will for our lives, will we learn to completely surrender to the authority of the Holy Spirit. God breaks our inferiority complex by teaching us to rely solely on His superiority. As God's children and co-heirs with Christ, everything belonging to God is ours — including His might! If we are to accomplish the amazing life God has designed for us, we must learn not to be dependent on our own strength. We need to allow God to strip us of everything that boosts our ego, so we will finally decide to tap into God's might and claim it as our own.

"Our God has boundless resources. The only limit is in us. Our asking, our thinking, our praying are too small. Our expectations are too limited." – A.B. Simpson

DAY 39

Remote Places

"The Lord said to Gideon, 'You have too many warriors with you. If I let all of you fight the Midianites, the Israelites will boast to me that they saved themselves by their own strength'" (Judges 7.2 NLT).

Before God poured His power mightily through Gideon's leadership, He took great care to ensure that Gideon would be the underdog. Gideon obediently handed over his authority to God's hand and watched as God stacked the cards against him. By the world's standard, Gideon would not accomplish the task for which God anointed him. It is interesting that the very same God who called Gideon to victory also put Gideon in a losing position. Gideon would need a miracle to win his God-ordained battle. Many times God leads us into "remote places" in order to perform a miracle. God plants promises in our horizon, but the Holy Spirit seems to lead us into a desert land of obedience. We willingly walk into a wilderness void of our dreams, only to watch God saturate the dry land with His abundance. When we hold onto our hope in Christ even against impossible odds, God will fulfill His promises. And we will give Him all the glory because only He can achieve the impossible–only He can make something out of nothing.

"Late in the afternoon the twelve disciples came to him and said, 'Send the crowds away to the nearby villages and farms, so they can find food and lodging for the night. There is nothing to eat here in this remote place.' But Jesus said, 'You feed them'" (Luke 9.12-13a NLT).

DAY 40

Overcompensating Pride

"Then it will be that whatever comes out of the doors of my house to meet me, when I return in peace from the people of Ammon, shall surely be the LORD'S, and I will offer it up as a burnt offering" (Judges 11.31 NKJV).

Jephthah overcompensates, and he brings unnecessary devastation to his family. He really wants to win the battle against the people of Ammon, and he thinks he can attain God's favor by offering a burnt sacrifice. The Lord has not required a sacrifice from Jephthah, so he does not have the grace that usually accompanies one. Because Jephthah did not seek the Lord when he made his vow, his "good intentions" are rooted in pride, and the peace of victory is replaced by the pain of loss. His daughter was the first to walk out of the doors of his house, probably excited to greet her father after his victory, and she became Jephthah's needless sacrifice. Pride leads to many sneaky sins, including insecurity, lack of faith, lack of self-control and selfishness. Sometimes we are deceived by our own pride to make unsanctioned sacrifices to God. We slave in a yoke not designed for us and then complain to God for making our lives miserable. But if we listen closely to the Holy Spirit, we might hear a still, small voice saying emphatically, "I have not required this sacrifice from you!" God wants our obedience that comes with an intimate relationship with Him; and when He does require a sacrifice from us, He will give us the grace to bear it.

"But Samuel replied, 'What is more pleasing to the Lord: your burnt offerings and sacrifices or your obedience to his voice? Listen! Obedience is better than sacrifice, and submission is better than offering the fat of rams'" (1 Samuel 15.22 NLT).

DAY 41

Small in Our Eyes

"Then Samson prayed to the Lord, "Sovereign Lord, remember me again. O God, please strengthen me just one more time. With one blow let me pay back the Philistines for the loss of my two eyes" (Judges 16.28 NLT).

Samson was destined for greatness even before his birth. The Angel of the Lord appeared to his mother and told her not to drink wine or eat anything unclean because she would give birth to a Nazarite son sent to delivery God's people from their enemy. Samson was blessed with good looks, strength, a sense of humor and a fire for life. He was a celebrity everywhere he went — people either loved or hated him. The only problem was that he didn't honor God by obeying His commands. God designed specific standards for Samson that would launch him into God's extraordinary plan for his life, but Samson decided to do his own thing. Samson was so full of himself that there was little room left for God. Finally, Samson's selfish and careless decisions lost him both his eyes. He was stripped of his honor and humiliated before his enemy, but God in His love and mercy still used Samson mightily before his death. It is a difficult discipline to learn to be small in our own eyes, but this ability is necessary if we want our eyes to be full of God. There is room for only one master: One leads us to destruction; the Other leads us to honor (Proverbs 18.12).

"Oral, obey God and stay small in your own eyes." – Priscilla Roberts to her son, Oral Roberts

DAY 42

One Voice

"And all the people arose as one man, saying, Not any of us will go to his tent, and none of us will return to his home" (Judges 20.8 AMP).

A man was traveling home with his wife. The day grew dark, and he needed to find a place for his family to stay overnight. The man's servant suggested they lodge with foreigners, but the man was determined to stay in a town of his own people, the Israelites. Finally, an elderly man offered to house them, but certain people of Israel took the man's wife during the night and raped her until she died. God's Chosen People had slowly forsaken their God and were following the whims of their own lust and immorality. The man was so devastated by his loss that he sent a sign to the twelve tribes of Israel, and the Bible says that Israel people "arose as one man." The united nation sought God and obediently rooted out the sin that had spread in their people. There is power in unity and chaos in discord, and that is why the enemy would like nothing better than to divide God's people, churches, ministries, families or any corporate voice testifying to the glory of God. When God's people arise as one in obedience to the movement of the Holy Spirit, the force of their progress will be unstoppable. Our nation needs to hear a United Voice, declaring the Way to eternal life through Jesus Christ.

"How wonderful and pleasant it is when brothers live together in harmony!" (Psalm 133.1 NLT).

DAY 43

Empty to Full

"I went out full, and the LORD has brought me home again empty" (Ruth 1.21 NKJV).

A drought hit Bethlehem, so Naomi traveled with her husband and their two sons to a foreign town to live. By the time Naomi returned to her hometown, she was empty. Her husband and two sons had died, and only one daughter-in-law, Ruth, remained with her. Naomi changed her name to Mara (bitter) because she believed God was dealing negatively with her. But what she didn't realize was that she was being adopted into the royal line of David and eventually Jesus. God allowed Naomi to lose everything she held dear because He was about to bless her with His abundance, including the Messiah who died for us. God will empty us when He's ready to fill us. The process of emptying is different for each of us, but we can remain joyful and confident that we will be filled with more of God's Spirit (the Holy Spirit), the Giver of all things — power, guidance, comfort, health, strength, understanding, wisdom, freedom, love, acceptance, peace, grace, glory, resources, purpose, fellowship, blessings and eternal life.

"And may he be to you a restorer of life and a nourisher of your old age; for your daughter-in-law, who loves you, who is better to you than seven sons, has borne him" (Ruth 4.15 NKJV).

DAY 44

Why Wealth?

"Now behold, Boaz came from Bethlehem and said to the reapers, 'The LORD be with you!' And they answered him, 'The LORD bless you!'" (Ruth 2.4 NKJV).

We know two things about Boaz before he walks into the Story of Ruth. 1) He is related to Naomi, Ruth's mother-in-law. 2) He is wealthy. The scene opens up to him walking through his fields among his trove of employees, and the first words he speaks give us a glimpse of this man's life and heart: He shouts, "The Lord be with you!" Obviously, his employees have a high regard and much respect for their employer because they roar a blessing back to him: "The Lord bless you!" One of Boaz's main purposes in life is to be a kinsman-redeemer (a relative who redeems a widow and her family). In order to fulfill his purpose, Boaz needs monetary wealth and the spiritual gift of giving, and Boaz has both of these. Boaz's entrepreneurial integrity and success will maintain the financial support of the royal and anointed blood line of King David and the Messiah, Jesus Christ. Boaz allows God to infiltrate his life to the point that even his servants and reapers proclaim God's blessings on him (which have a profound effect!). Though we might not all be called to have great wealth like Boaz, we can infuse the Lord's presence into our spiritual giftings whatever they may be, so we can fill the need that God created us to fill – so we can achieve our purpose!

"Get up every day, love God, and do your best. He will do the rest." – Joyce Meyer

DAY 45

Pleasant and Beautiful

"So the servant who was in charge of the reapers answered and said, 'It is the young Moabite woman who came back with Naomi from the Country of Moab'" (Ruth 2.6 NKJV).

Naomi comes back to her hometown of Bethlehem very bitter after losing both her sons and her husband, and she tells the town's people to call her "Mara," which means *bitter*. Even though Naomi gives herself another name, it does not stick. Throughout the rest of the *Book of Ruth* and all of history, she is known as Naomi, which means *pleasant* and *beautiful*. Many times we (and others) try to give ourselves very negative names – fat, ugly, stupid, lazy, weak, worthless, insignificant, used-up, hopeless, angry, hurt and ruined. However, these names do not stick because the blood of Jesus continually washes us clean — not by our effort but by His sacrifice. Not because we deserve, but because God loves us. God has named us His children and co-heirs with Christ (Romans 8.17 NIV), and the value of those names cannot be shaken. No matter our circumstances, He sees us as He saw Naomi — pleasant and beautiful in how He designed each of us. When we get to know our Creator and daily seek His Spirit, we will be filled with His many precious thoughts concerning us and finally embrace how He sees us!

"How precious also are Your thoughts to me, O God! How vast is the sum of them! (Psalm 139.17 AMP).

DAY 46

Kanaph

"May the Lord repay you for your kindness, and may your reward be full from the Lord, the God of Israel, under whose wings you have come to take refuge" (Ruth 2.12 AMP).

When Boaz first meets Ruth, she is gleaning grain from his land in accordance to the gleaning laws (Lev 19.9), which allow the poor to harvest from the corners of a field. Not only does Boaz acknowledge her, but he praises her for leaving her entire life behind in order to take care of her mother-in-law, Naomi, in a land where she is a foreigner. He then proclaims a blessing over her that the Lord will reward her for her sacrifice because she has found refuge under the Lord's wings. The Hebrew word for wings is *kanaph*, which also can mean *shirt* or *corner of a garment*. *Kanaph* is found in many verses, including Psalm 91.4 NIV and Ezekiel 16.8 NIV, and it alludes to something of a covenant protection–like that of marriage. What Boaz may not realize at this point is that he will literally fulfill his own blessing to Ruth. God is going to use Boaz to provide Ruth His divine protection. Ruth eventually is able to remove Boaz's covering (protection), and she asks him to "spread the corner of your garment [*kanaph*] over me." Essentially, Ruth is proposing to Boaz (a form of protection), and he accepts her proposal by fighting for her hand in marriage. God blesses us each with resources to bless, protect and care for those around us. It is one thing to speak a blessing, but it is another to be that blessing. Whether we are serving the people in our home, church, community and/or other nations (and everyone in between), we can spread the corners of our wings over others and use the resources God has given us to fulfill their needs.

"'Who are you?' he asked. 'I am your servant Ruth,' she said. 'Spread the corner of your garment [*kanaph*] over me, since you are a guardian-redeemer of our family'" (Ruth 3.9 NIV).

DAY 47
The Right Time

"And now, my daughter, don't be afraid. I will do for you all you ask. All the people of my town know that you are a woman of noble character" (Ruth 3.11 NIV).

Boaz completely redeemed Ruth and her family. Not only did he marry Ruth, but he also fought for her hand in marriage. There was another kinsman-redeemer of closer relation to Ruth, but Boaz showed great wisdom and patience when dealing with this man. He also demonstrated a wonderful concern for more than just his own welfare. What spawned Boaz's intense desire to provide for Ruth? What caused him to tell her, "I will do for you all you ask"? The answer is simple: he knew that Ruth was a "woman of noble character." Ruth could have gone to Boaz the first day she arrived in town, pleading her case and begging for help, but she didn't. She understood that it is far better to encourage loyalty, rather than force obligation. If she would have coerced Boaz's marriage proposal without waiting on God's perfect timing, Boaz would have never seen her "noble character." And she would have found herself stuck with the other kinsman-redeemer who obviously did not care for her well-being. God has created a system of reliance in His people — we all need each other to further God's plan in our lives. However, we can't demand people's help; but we can encourage it by the integrity of our words, actions and lives. If we daily give our hopes and dreams to God and live in obedience to the Holy Spirit, at just the right time, God will redeem our sacrifice, work and heartache in ways we could never imagine. We just have to be patient.

"So humble yourselves under the mighty power of God, and at the right time he will lift you up in honor" (1 Peter 5.6 NLT).

DAY 48

Divide to Multiply

"And the close relative said, 'I cannot redeem it for myself, lest I ruin my own inheritance. You redeem my right of redemption for yourself, for I cannot redeem it'" (Ruth 4.6 NKJV).

The closest kinsman-redeemer to Ruth is eager to redeem Ruth and her family's land, but he is not so eager to redeem Ruth and her family's lineage. When the kinsman-redeemer realizes that he has to redeem Ruth by incorporating her family into his, he quickly changes his mind. This man doesn't want to divide his inheritance with others, so he clings tightly to what is his. Little does he know, however, that he is missing out on the most amazing adventure in all of eternity. Instead of being part of the lineage of Jesus Christ Himself, this selfish man remains nameless and an example of how not to live. Instead, Boaz gets to redeem Ruth, and he weaves himself into the beautiful scarlet thread of Jesus' introduction and coronation into the history pages of human life. God wants to multiply His blessings in our lives, but we must be willing to let them go. When we selfishly cling tightly to our resources, talents, time and money; we limit the fullness He has for us. When God asks us to divide that which we desire, He is preparing to multiply it. God knows that our arms are too weak to hold the enormity of His blessings. We must lay our incapable hands into His, so He can uphold us under the weight of His bounty. But the arms of those who try to take everything for themselves shall be broken.

"For the arms of the wicked shall be broken, but the Lord upholds the righteous" (Psalm 37.17 ESV).

DAY 49

Tainted Vision

"Do not consider your maidservant a wicked woman, for out of the abundance of my complaint and grief I have spoken until now" (1 Samuel 1.16 NKJV).

Hannah is barren, and she is desperately praying at the tabernacle for a child. Her heart is overwhelmed with sorrow, and she is crying out to God. She places her grief and misery at God's feet, and she fervently prays for God to answer her prayers. The acting priest sitting at the doorway of the temple at this time is Eli. Eli is a large man, undoubtedly eating the sacrifices that his corrupt sons steal from God (1 Samuel 2.16-17). Eli's sons, Hophni and Phinehas, not only steal the offerings from God, they also sleep with the women who gather at the temple (1 Samuel 2.22). Because Eli honors his sons over God and takes what belongs to God (1 Samuel 2.29), God says that He would no longer allow Eli and his family to serve Him (1 Samuel 2.31). So when Eli watches Hannah cry out to God at the tabernacle, he accuses her of being drunk (1 Samuel 1.14). His eyes may be tainted with his own sin and disregard for God's commands that he sees wickedness in Hannah instead of humility. It is very easy for people to view others through eyes that have been tainted by sin, hurt, bitterness, jealousy, greed, selfishness, lust, anger, judgment, pride, etc. Although we can continue to love these people, we can't allow corrupt opinions to define us and destroy what God is doing in our lives. Moreover, we must take great care to constantly renew our minds in Christ and lean on His understanding, so we don't let our tainted eyes discolor the beauty of others.

"So we have stopped evaluating others from a human point of view. At one time we thought of Christ merely from a human point of view. How differently we know him now!" (2 Corinthians 5.16 NLT).

DAY 50

God's Powerful Arm

———————— ※ ————————

"And when they arose early the next morning, there was Dagon, fallen on its face to the ground before the ark of the Lord. The head of Dagon and both the palms of its hands were broken off on the threshold; only Dagon's torso was left on it" (1 Samuel 5.4 NKJV).

The Ark of God is the physical representation of God's presence and glory in Israel, and it is taken by the Philistines (an oppressive nation to Israel). The Philistines put the Ark into their temple next to their idol, Dagon. Dagon is a god of fertility, which they worship in order to have abundance in every area of their lives. However, when the Ark and Dagon share a temple, Dagon is found the next morning lying face down in the dirt. The Philistines put Dagon back up, and the next morning it is found face down again; but this time, Dagon's hands and head are severed from its body. This is very encouraging for us today! As Christians, we constantly struggle with having idols in our lives. But instead of focusing on them, we can seek God and allow His presence and glory to fill our temples (body, mind and soul). And when God dwells next to an idol in our temple, the idol will fall. If it comes back up, God's presence will break its hands and head, which means that God will break the idol's work, influence and stronghold over us. We don't have to tear the idol down in our own weak efforts; we simply need to give God His rightful place as King in our lives and watch His mighty arm move!

"Powerful is your arm! Strong is your hand! Your right hand is lifted high in glorious strength" (Psalm 89.13 NLT).

DAY 51

Sixth Sense

"Nevertheless the people refused to obey the voice of Samuel; and they said, 'No, but we will have a king over us, that we also may be like all the nations, and that our king may judge us and go out before us and fight our battles'" (1 Samuel 8.19-20 NKJV).

The people of Israel were demanding a lineage of kings like the other nations around them. Although they had the Supreme Supernatural King, who manifested Himself in many physical ways to His people; the people wanted a king that they could see, touch, hear, smell and feel. It didn't matter that this line of imperfect kings, no matter how good or well-intentioned, would be nothing compared to their amazing Father-God who created them and loves them. This temporal, physical earth has a very strong hold over its inhabitants, and we find it extremely difficult to esteem our unseen God more than the people we can define with our five senses. But we have a sixth supernatural sense who is the Holy Spirit inside of us, and one of the Holy Spirit's purposes is to give us discernment to distinguish between what is holy and what is common (Leviticus 10.10). We don't have to rely on the world's standard or our own understanding to dictate a version of "truth" to us. God knows that we would have difficulty looking beyond our physical world, so He wisely placed His Spirit in each Born-again Believer who wears the righteousness of Christ (John 3.6-8). However, we must grow this sixth sense and follow and trust its promptings of eternal Truth. It might be difficult at first, relying on this supernatural sense; but we have Jesus' example, His prayers and His Word to help us cultivate discernment. And once we esteem our God as King; no person, circumstance or problem will stop us from serving our purpose in His Kingdom!

"But solid food is for the mature, for those who have their powers of discernment trained by constant practice to distinguish good from evil" (Hebrews 5.14 ESV).

DAY 52

A Second Glance

———————※———————

"When Saul saw David going out against the Philistine, he said, to Abner, the commander of the army, 'Abner, whose son is this youth?'" (1 Samuel 17.55 NKJV).

It is interesting that Saul did not recognize David. Just a few verses previously, Saul had tried to put his armor on David. When David killed Goliath and started going out after the Philistines, Saul had no clue who the young man was. Maybe David was too far in the distance, so Saul couldn't see him clearly. No, because Saul's military leader, Abner, went and fetched David, bringing him face to face with his master. And still King Saul asked, "Whose son are you, young man?" David had played the harp for King Saul many nights and even became his armor bearer (1 Samuel 16.21-22); yet when King Saul witnessed David fighting in war, he did not know him. He couldn't perceive the anointing of God in David's life. This is exactly what happens when people finally step into their anointing. God's power and authority will be so great in them that the family and friends who know them intimately will not recognize them. We do not want to live our lives in our own strength; we want to live in God's supernatural strength. People will have trouble connecting who we are with God's movement in our lives because they will no longer see us; rather, they will see God's glory being displayed in us. We must learn to stay patient in God's timing. At just the right time, when we are completely submitted to God's will, He will unleash us into the purpose for which we were born. And the people around us will have to take a second glance, because they are now perceiving God's glory.

"When Jesus finished telling these stories, he left there, returned to his hometown, and gave a lecture in the meetinghouse. He made a real hit, impressing everyone. 'We had no idea he was this good!' they said. 'How did he get so wise, get such ability?' But in the next breath they were cutting him down: 'We've known him since he was a kid; he's the carpenter's son. We know his mother, Mary. We know his brothers James and Joseph, Simon and Judas. All his sisters live here. Who does he think he is?' They got their noses all out of joint" (Matthew 13.53-57 MSG).

DAY 53

Stepping Aside

"And Jonathan took off the robe that was on him and gave it to David, with his armor, even to his sword and his bow and his belt" (1 Samuel 18.4 NKJV).

Many times God will allow us to assist in a vision that is not our own. This can be a very precarious situation, especially if our own desires, thoughts and conditions get in the way. God gives us the resources, knowledge and influence to help a person or ministry, and He watches our actions and decisions to see whether we will serve in humility or control in pride. Jonathan had the resources that David needed to fulfill his purpose as a great king over Israel. Jonathan gave his robe, armor, sword, bow and his belt (in essence his future kingship) willingly to David with absolutely no strings attached. When God gives us the resources to help others, and the Holy Spirit is prompting us to commit, we can stay humble to God's will and not try to take control of a vision that is not ours. We are stewards of God's resources, not owners. If God can trust us to be conduits of His glory, we'll find ourselves at the center of action in His unfolding supernatural plan on the earth. We can give in humility and push others to achieve God's best in their lives, while keeping our hope and trust in a God who will accomplish all He has promised in our own lives.

"Don't be selfish; don't try to impress others. Be humble, thinking of others as better than yourselves" (Philippians 2.3 NLT).

DAY 54

Accepting the Whisper

———————————✦———————————

"So she fell at his feet and said: 'On me, my lord, on me let this iniquity be! And please let your maidservant speak in your ears, and hear the words of your maidservant'" (1 Samuel 25.24 NKJV).

The Bible is filled with stories of strong, wise women; and Abigail (David's future wife) is one of them. Abigail's current husband, Nabal, is a very rich but an extremely foolish man. Nabal is so full of his own selfish merriment that he knows nothing of God's movement that is unfolding on his own front porch, and his self-absorption will cause his untimely death. However, his wife, Abigail, is aware of God's promises to David as Israel's future king; so, she is able to intercede on behalf of her husband and his household. Abigail finds herself in a very tricky situation. She has immense respect for David as God's anointed one, but she also must prevent David from sinning and taking God's justice into his own hands. What does Abigail do? She whispers! She humbles herself to David, and pleads, "Let your maidservant speak in your ears," and she confirms God's promises to David and privately corrects his unsanctioned intentions. Also, she makes it clear that she loves her God, her people and her future king, which is why her rebuke from the Lord is appropriate. David rejoices in her admonition, because he is humble and wise enough to know that he has received a word from the Lord. Instead of allowing his insecurity to take offense, David embraces Abigail's advice and his respect and gratitude become apparent when he marries her after Nabal dies. God will use His devoted people to declare His Word to others with love; and we can stay humble enough to accept God's loving rebuke when it is a whisper, so it doesn't have to become a deafening roar.

"Whoever stubbornly refuses to accept criticism will suddenly be destroyed beyond recovery" (Proverbs 29.1 NLT).

DAY 55

Pregnant with Destiny

"Therefore return now, and go in peace, that you may not displease the lords of the Philistines" (1 Samuel 29.7 NKJV).

God gave David a very precious and profound promise: David would be king over Israel. However, this promise seemed to take forever to come to pass. God put David in the flames of persecution from King Saul in order to purify David's leadership, life and heart before he became king. David learned to be a king after God's own heart while hiding in caves with the weight of his growing military on his shoulders. Before David became king–at the climax of King Saul's demise–David forged a loose union with Israel's enemy, the Philistines. David's heart was so full of destiny, but he had no place to claim it. Therefore, he willingly went after any fake substitute that came close to quenching his need to serve his purpose. Luckily, though, he was rejected; and David found himself void of a platform for his kingship even though he had all the wisdom, people and resources necessary to successfully achieve it. Many times, when our purpose-fulfillment comes close, the enemy sends us fake substitutes to divert our attention from God's amazing plan for our lives. God knows our hearts and understands that we are yearning for purpose, so He lovingly allows us to be rejected by the adulterers to our destiny. Don't be dismayed by rejection; instead, rejoice because God is protecting our paths and shepherding our patience.

"Be faithful in small things because it is in them that your strength lies." – Mother Teresa

DAY 56

Stand Firm

"All the people took note and were pleased; indeed, everything the king did pleased them" (2 Samuel 3.36 NIV).

Saul died, and David became the king over one tribe of Israel — Judah. He was king for this single tribe for 7 & 1/2 years. During this time the house of David and the house of Saul fought. The kingship of David became stronger as the kingship of Ish-bosheth, Saul's son, became weaker. Finally, Abner, the commander over Saul's army, decided to help King David reign over all of Israel; but one of David's leaders killed Abner. David mourned Abner's death and proclaimed that he would not eat before the sun set, but the people urged him to eat. David stood firm, though, and he would not let others sway him from fulfilling his promise to the Lord. Were the people upset that David wouldn't listen to them? No! They were actually "pleased" that David kept his word to God. People will knowingly or unknowingly try to get us to disobey God's commands in our lives, and God will test our hearts to see if they are fully committed to Him. When we care too much about other people's opinions; our words, actions and motives will try to twist God's commands to make people happy. However, if we truly fear God and trust His will, nothing or no one will be able to detract us from standing firm in our faith. We must stay rooted in God and His Word and guard ourselves from the well-meaning intentions of others.

"Be on guard. Stand firm in the faith. Be courageous. Be strong" (1 Corinthians 16.13 NLT).

DAY 57

Humble Strength

* — · — · — ✳ — · — · — *

"And I am weak today, though anointed king; and these men, the sons of Zeruiah, are too harsh for me. The LORD shall repay the evildoer according to his wickedness" (2 Samuel 3.39 NKJV).

David found himself in the middle of a big mess that he did not create. God called David to be king over Israel, usurping the previous king's rule, and the transfer of power spawned a ton of drama! However, David never tried to establish his kingship by his own authority. God worked His will through the repercussions of those who did not submit to His sovereignty, and David learned to rest in God's strength, power and timing. Many times David could have claimed the throne for himself, but he learned to trust God's ways even though they didn't always make sense. When David realized that he was "weak" and confronted by men who were too "harsh" for him, he didn't fear. David had already achieved the difficult discipline of complete trust and reliance on God, and he believed with all his heart that God would take care of the situation for him. When we as Christians fear and worry, we are letting God and others know that we do not truly believe that God is on our side. Complete reliance on God is a challenging but necessary discipline to learn; but if we practice it enough, it will become more instinctual and less forced. Once we see how God works everything for good in the little things, we will start to trust Him in the big things. We'll be able to humbly acknowledge when we are at our wits' end, which will open the path for God to take charge and redeem the situation. We can save ourselves a lot of sleepless nights if we would only put our trust in God.

"'My thoughts are nothing like your thoughts,' says the LORD. 'And my ways are far beyond anything you could imagine'" (Isaiah 55.8 NLT).

DAY 58

Kindness Attacked

"But the princes of the Ammonites said to Hanun their lord, 'Do you think that it is because David honors your father that he has sent comforters to you? Has he not rather sent his servants to you to search the city, spy it out, and overthrow it?'" (2 Samuel 10.3 AMP).

God's promise to David had come to pass: He was now the King of Israel! David was so overwhelmed with joy that he had finally reached his Promised Land that he decided to bless certain people and their families who had helped him along the way. The man David wanted to show kindness to was Hanun, the son of Nahash, the Ammon King who had recently died. David sent his servants to Hanun to give his condolences for his father's death, but Hanun and his princes falsely accused David of having ulterior motives. Although David's intentions were pure and right; these men's words and actions asserted that David was a heartless man who lied, deceived and cheated. David's sincere offering of friendship was thrown back at his face, and his peace offering was twisted into something ugly. There are some people who—no matter what we do or say—will always see us in a negative light. We can offer them everything that is good within us, and they will take it, twist it and throw it back at our face. Sometimes we are tempted to change or prove ourselves, but this will only leave us feeling disappointed, insecure and bitter. However, if we concentrate on how God sees us and place our self-worth on His estimation of who we are in Christ, we will be better able to rise above the pettiness and forgive as Jesus forgives. Our feelings won't be affected by other people's negative opinions of us because we are so consumed by how much God loves and values us.

"The Lord your God in your midst, The Mighty One, will save; He will rejoice over you with gladness, He will quiet *you* with His love, He will rejoice over you with singing" (Zephaniah 3.17 NKJV).

DAY 59

Giving Mercy

"'No!' the king said. 'Who asked your opinion, you sons of Zeruiah! If the Lord has told him to curse me, who are you to stop him?'" (2 Samuel 16.10 NLT).

David is fleeing from his son, Absalom, who is trying to steal his kingdom. As David is running for his life, he is openly cursed by Shimei, a descendant of Saul. Shimei accuses David of being bloodthirsty and evil. David's servant wants to kill Shimei for speaking lies, but David prevents him. David explains that if God has allowed this man to curse him, he won't stop the will of God. Later, God redeems David, and Shimei begs for forgiveness. Against his advisers, David forgives Shimei and spares his life. In this one situation, God was able to reveal the substance of David's heart. When chaos occurs, the inner nature of people is exposed. It's very easy to have strong Christian character when life is going our way; but when everything falls apart, it's all too simple for us to dive right back into our default setting of selfishness. David demonstrated love, grace and mercy when he chose to ignore and forgive Shemei's insults. Many times we will be lied about, cursed, deceived, treated unfairly and persecuted; and we must choose to rely on God to be our redeemer. It is hard to give mercy when we are hurt, but we can trust that God is rooting for us to do the right thing–even when we don't feel like it. But when we finally let go of the pain, God will fill us with His comfort, peace and joy.

"But He [Jesus] turned and rebuked them, and said, 'You do not know what manner of spirit you are of. For the Son of Man did not come to destroy men's lives but to save them.' And they went to another village" (Luke 9.55-56 NKJV).

DAY 60

Swallowed Up Inheritance

───────◆◆───◆◆※◆◆───◆◆───────

"I am among the peaceable and faithful in Israel. You seek to destroy a city and a mother in Israel. Why would you swallow up the inheritance of the LORD?" (2 Samuel 20.19 NKJV).

It seems that everyone is jumping on the bandwagon to dethrone King David. David's son, Absalom, tries to get rid of David, and now the covetous desires of others are starting to seep through. After Absalom's death, Sheba, a man from the mountains of Ephraim, decides that he is going to lead Israel into anarchy. David's men go after Sheba and besiege the city in which he hides. As the soldiers are attempting to tear down the city wall, a wise woman asks David's commander, Joab, why the army is trying to "swallow up the inheritance of the LORD." Joab explains that they are looking for one man; and if the people give him up, they will leave the city alone. The city quickly cuts off Sheba's head and gives it to David's men, and the soldiers leave the city in peace. One corrupted man almost caused the Lord's inheritance to be *swallowed* up. This truth is the same for every Christian. God has an inheritance and purpose for us, but one tainted stronghold in our lives can prevent us from claiming God's fullness. God wants to take whatever is robbing us of His best in our lives, so He can accomplish all that He has planned for us. However, we need to be wise enough to realize how damaging the stronghold is and willing to let God prune us and cut away all that holds us back.

"He cuts off every branch in me that bears no fruit, while every branch that does bear fruit he prunes so that it will be even more fruitful" (John 15.2 NIV).

DAY 61

Buying the Filed

"But the king replied to Araunah, 'No, I insist on buying it, for I will not present burnt offerings to the Lord my God that have cost me nothing.' So David paid him fifty pieces of silver for the threshing floor and the oxen" (2 Samuel 24.24 NLT).

King David needs to make a sacrifice using an altar and field that do not belong to him. The owner, Araunah, wants to give the land and the wood for the altar to David for free, but David insists on paying. He will not let his burnt offering to the Lord be diminished by taking the easy way. Our "burnt offerings" to the Lord are never cheap. Instead, the work and sacrifices we lay at God's altar usually take everything we have to give. God knows when we are giving Him the minimum. He knows when we are easing through life, making very few risks and taking many shortcuts. Nothing worthy of God comes easy. Many times we are confronted with two roads. The first road looks easy and has very little roadblocks. The other road looks difficult and is riddled with roadblocks. Almost always God is calling us down the harder path. He wants to refine our character and mold us into the image of His Son, and the trials and tribulations of this world do a great job of whittling away our flaws. It takes faith and obedience to willingly choose the more difficult path, but God sees our dedication and He will be pleased with our offering. We must never let people talk us into taking shortcuts. Instead, we can give God our best, knowing that He will reward every shred of effort that we give Him.

"Therefore, my dear brothers and sisters, stand firm. Let nothing move you. Always give yourselves fully to the work of the Lord, because you know that your labor in the Lord is not in vain" (1 Corinthians 15.8 NIV).

DAY 62

The Father's Sheep

"When David saw the angel about to destroy the people, he prayed, "Please! I'm the one who sinned; I, the shepherd, did the wrong. But these sheep, what did they do wrong? Punish me and my family, not them" (2 Samuel 24.17 MSG).

David's kingship and life are coming to a close, so David decides to take a census of Israel. God judges the hearts of people, and He knows that David is acting in pride. David wants to see just how great *his* kingdom has become, but he has forgotten that everything belongs to the Lord. David realizes he has acted foolishly and repents, but God still demands justice for David's transgression. Through a prophet, God gives David three punishments. Two punishments are on the people of David's kingdom; however, only one punishment is on David and his family. After hiding from enemies most of his life, David does not choose the punishment where he and his family must run for three months. Instead, David allows a plague to hit his country for three days, killing 70,000 people. Finally, David remembers the days of his youth when he spent years caring for his father's sheep, and he understands that he was born to be a shepherd for God's sheep–His beloved children. David stops focusing on himself and his accomplishments and starts paying attention to the people that God has called him to serve. Many times Christians can get caught up in numbers, accomplishments and influence, which can take our eyes off the real reason we are here: We are here to love God and others and accomplish the purpose He has established for us before time began.

"Don't copy the behavior and customs of this world, but let God transform you into a new person by changing the way you think. Then you will learn to know God's will for you, which is good and pleasing and perfect" (Romans 12.2 NLT).

DAY 63

Rebuke Me, Please!

"Then Adonijah the son of Haggith exalted himself, saying, 'I will be king'; and he prepared for himself chariots and horsemen, and fifty men to run before him" (1 Kings 1.5 NKJV).

It seems that King David had a little problem rebuking his sons. After Absalom tried to take his father's throne, Adonijah (Absalom's younger brother and David's oldest living son) declares that he will take the throne. The Bible says that King David never once corrected his son's behavior (1 Kings 1.6). Adonijah did what the flesh constantly desires to do: exalt itself. Adonijah was very good looking, and he was next in line (according to the world's standard) to be king; so, it was easy for him to justify his motives for power and self-glory. However, one word from his father could have prevented the mass chaos, heartache and death that transpired from Adonijah's unsanctioned decisions. Rebuking others is uncomfortable and difficult because we ourselves are imperfect; but as outsiders, we can have a clearer perspective untainted by emotions that could prevent chaos, heartache and death (sin) in someone else's life. If the Holy Spirit is prompting us to intercede, we need to get over our discomfort and fear and say the truth no matter how it hurts. Pride punctures easily; and once it deflates after the initial sting, a humble perspective is gained. Moreover, as Christ-followers, we must achieve a healthy habit of allowing people to burst our bubbles every so often. We can gratefully receive every rebuke done in love because we know that only God is to be exalted. In the end, we will save ourselves a lot of trouble by accepting criticism from people we trust.

"A single rebuke does more for a person of understanding than a hundred lashes on the back of a fool" (Proverbs 17.10 NLT).

DAY 64

The Treason of Flattery

"Then he said, 'Please speak to King Solomon, for he will not refuse you, that he may give me Abishag the Shunammite as a wife'" (1 Kings 2.17 NKJV).

Adonijah is still trying to steal the throne from his brother, Solomon; but instead of taking it outright this time, he tries to scheme his way onto the throne by using flattery. Adonijah goes to the king's mother, Bathsheba, to ask if she will influence young Solomon to give him Abishag as his wife. This request seems innocent enough, but it is chock-full of indecency, trickery and deceitfulness. Abishag is a young, beautiful woman who was part of King David's harem before his death, and now she is one of his widows. Right off the bat, Adonijah breaks one of God's commandments by desiring his deceased father's wife (Leviticus 18.8). This entire request parallels King David's oldest son, Absalom, who tried to take the throne and slept with King David's concubines as a symbolic statement to that effect (2 Samuel 16.22). Bathsheba should have caught Adonijah's deceit instantly since it was her son's kingship he was trying to destroy, but two emotions probably distorted her thinking. First, Adonijah flattered her. She was now the mother of a king–which could actually be better than being the wife since there were many wives but only one mother– and he pumped up her pride by flattering her new position and the control it entailed. Second, Adonijah ignited her jealousy. Abishag was young and beautiful and more than likely stole King David's attention away from Bathsheba while he lived. Bathsheba might have been tempted to flaunt her new-found control over the young widow by dictating who she could marry. Therefore, flattery and jealously caused Bathsheba to attack the very source of her pride and authority: her son's kingship! We must be very careful not to allow flattery and jealousy to wreak havoc on our thinking, decisions and actions. Instead of acting on an emotionally foolish impulse, we can use wisdom in deciphering the best way to handle a tricky situation.

"Are you faced with a major decision or need a solution to a challenge? Let God's wisdom give you the inspiration and insight that you need to succeed." – Joseph Prince

DAY 65

Established

"But King Solomon shall be blessed, and the throne of David shall be established before the LORD forever" (1 Kings 2.45 NKJV).

When King Solomon moves into his kingship, he must clean "house" in order to have one of the most prosperous reigns in all of history. Before God securely establishes Solomon as the anointed king over Israel, He gives Solomon time to rid his "Promised Land" of unresolved issues that would prevent King Solomon from achieving the full extent of his kingdom-vision. The process of ridding a God-anointed territory of sin is very important to the establishment of a calling or vision. Each hidden seed of sin left behind after a person is established with God's authority can cause that person to stumble in the future. The enemy loves it when we sweep things under the rug because he knows he can use that dirt to make us trip up in the future. For this reason, the young King Solomon was very wise not to declare that his royal line "shall be established before the LORD forever" until after he pulled out every root of wickedness that he knew existed. We must be patient in God's timing and not be too eager for God to establish our callings so quickly. If we withdrawal from the Holy Spirit's leading and establish ourselves too soon, we may find that the "little" things we chose to ignore will become big things that seek to destroy our witness in Christ. Taking time to do some housecleaning before we set out to change the world for Christ will prove essential to achieving our purpose in the Kingdom of God!

"People who conceal their sins will not prosper, but if they confess and turn from them, they will receive mercy" (Proverbs 28.13 NLT).

DAY 66

High Places vs. Church

———————✳———————

"And Solomon loved the Lord, walking in the statutes of his father David, except that he sacrificed and burned incense at the high places" (1 Kings 3.3 NKJV).

"High places" become a major stronghold for the kings and people of God's chosen nation–Israel. The fact that Solomon allowed this one sin to slip by him had major ramifications; one of which was that he started worshiping other gods at these high places. His intent and the desire of the people was to worship God, but Leviticus 17.3-5 specifically tells the Chosen People to bring their offerings (worship) to the Tabernacle or House of God. By the time the divided nation of Israel was completely destroyed, they were worshipping other gods and committing all kinds of sin at these high places. The high places essentially became flesh-contrived religious substitutes used to justify the selfish and ungodly desires of the people. When Christians decide not to join a church and instead worship God on their own terms, they are creating a high place in their lives. This may seem innocent at first; but without the authority and anointing of a local church, the corrupted heart of human nature will begin to twist the truth and use this high place as an excuse to satisfy the flesh. We can worship God anytime and anywhere; but along with our individual worship, we are each called to a specific and profound purpose in the Body of Christ. We will completely miss the fullness of our destiny if we are living our lives void of a faithful church. The Church is the Bride of Christ (Revelation 19.7-9 NLT): a harmonious collection of righteous (albeit imperfect) people, caring and serving others while glorifying their Creator; and we each have our important part to play.

"Just as our bodies have many parts and each part has a special function, so it is with Christ's body. We are many parts of one body, and we all belong to each other" (Romans 12.4-5 NLT).

DAY 67

Godly Connections

"So it was, when Hiram heard the words of Solomon, that he rejoiced greatly and said, 'Blessed be the LORD this day, for He has given David a wise son over this great people!'" (1 Kings 5.7 NKJV).

King David was both greatly loved and hated by many people. Hiram, king of Tyre, is an example of someone who loved David (1 Kings 5.1). King David must have influenced those who admired him with a great understanding and respect for God, since King Hiram so easily blessed the Lord for giving David a wise heir. During Solomon's early years as king, he had to rid his kingship of many unresolved issues that could possibly damage his rule in the future. However, King Solomon also inherited many powerful and important connections that would enhance his leadership–like the one with King Hiram. King Solomon could have balked at this relationship and let it die, but he didn't. Instead, he grabbed hold of his father's connection and used it to foster a peaceful and extremely profitable relationship between the two nations. We don't need to search outside our realms of influence to find exactly what we need to fulfill the calling God has prepared for us. Like never before, we are surrounded by godly connections eager to deepen our relationship with Christ and enhance our Kingdom Purpose. Godly books, sermons, movies, music, blogs, devotionals, conferences, artwork and other resources are all waiting to feed us with insight, encouragement and growth. We just need to realize that they are there and grab hold of them.

"Whoever walks with the wise becomes wise, but the companion of fools will suffer harm" (Proverbs 13.20 ESV).

DAY 68

Budding King Fruit

———————※———————

"And in the eleventh year, in the month of Bul, which is the eighth month, the house was finished in all its details and according to all its plan. So he was seven years in building it" (1 Kings 6.38 NKJV).

King Solomon started building the Temple of God in the month of *Ziv* or *Zif,* which means "brightness" or "splendor" because the flowers budded in this month (April-May). He completed building the Temple seven years later in the month of *Bul,* which means "increase" and "produce" because the fruit became ripe in this month (November-December). Seven years of transformation–of buds blooming into fruit– had to transpire for the Temple to be completed. And when the work was done, the Temple was dedicated to God and His glory came down so thick that people could not enter it (2 Chronicles 7.1-2). Today, we have the amazing privilege of the Holy Spirit dwelling inside of us. But God wants more than to simply reside in us, He wants to fill us so completely that nothing but His glory can be seen. His Spirit desires to reign so supremely in our lives that sin and the forces of evil can't even come close to touching, influencing or stopping us. Only when we are solely submitted to God will we be able to produce Kingdom Fruit, which is fruit birthed out of the sacrifice of Jesus and not the work of our own flesh. God has buried supernatural seeds of destiny in all of our lives. But we must learn to let go of our efforts, be patient in His timing and trust the shaking of His hand in our lives, so His "increase" and "produce" will manifest.

"I will shake all the nations, and the treasures of all the nations will be brought to this Temple. I will fill this place with glory, says the Lord of Heaven's Armies" (Haggai 2.7 NLT).

DAY 69

Concessions

"On the Mount of Olives, east of Jerusalem, he even built a pagan shrine for Chemosh, the detestable god of Moab, and another for Molech, the detestable god of the Ammonites. Solomon built such shrines for all his foreign wives to use for burning incense and sacrificing to their gods" (1 Kings 11.7-8 NLT).

The main difference between King David and his son, King Solomon, was that King Solomon made concessions for the false gods of other nations. Not only was he tolerant of these demonic forces clothed in royal robes, he used the resources God blessed him with to build them their own temples of worship! Instead of influencing his foreign wives with the revelation of the One True God, he gave into their desires and allowed them to influence him. Whether he was trying to keep the peace, interested in their religious ideologies or simply eager to have a good time; he dove headfirst into the Tree of Knowledge of Good and Evil and away from the Tree of Life. His seemingly little compromise caused his entire heart to eventually turn from the Lord, and his God-blessed nation began its rapid course to destruction. Many times we take for granted the blessing and protection of God. We make concessions for the false beliefs of others because we fear them more than we love them. If we truly loved others, we would do everything possible to share with them the love, redemption and purpose found in Jesus Christ. People may mock and persecute us, but we must follow the Holy Spirit's leading and stay rooted in the Truth. Life is too short to compromise. We only have a set number of days to rescue people from the sinking ship of this world and get them onto the Life Boat of Jesus. They might not see the water rising all around them, but we do. We can't tell them everything is fine when they're about to drown into eternity without their Creator. Jesus is the only way to heaven, and this Truth is worthy to be shared.

"To go to heaven, fully to enjoy God, is infinitely better than the most pleasant accommodations here." – Jonathan Edwards

DAY 70

The Third Captain

"Again, he sent a third captain of fifty with his fifty men. And the third captain of fifty went up, and came and fell on his knees before Elijah, and pleaded with him, and said to him: "Man of God, please let my life and the life of these fifty servants of yours be precious in your sight" (2 Kings 1.13 NKJV).

God sent his most powerful prophets when the moral decay of Israel was at its greatest. One of these prophets was Elijah. Elijah was a notorious man of God. A single description of him, "A hairy man wearing a leather belt," was all Israel's evil king, Ahaziah, needed to identify him (2 Kings 1.8). King Ahaziah fell through the lattice of his home and injured himself, so he sent his servants to inquire of a false god if he would recover from his injury. Therefore, God sent Elijah to intercept the servants to reprimand the king for seeking counsel from a source other than God Himself and to let the king know that he would die from his fall. Obviously, King Ahaziah didn't like the godly discipline, so he sent a captain with fifty men to confront Elijah. If the king had valued the lives of his men, he would never had sent them on this suicide mission; and if the captain had valued the lives of the men, he would have never had confronted Elijah, God's representative, with such disrespect and disdain. All fifty men and the captain were consumed by fire. King Ahaziah continued sending men to Elijah, knowing very well what the outcome would be. Finally, however, the third captain stopped the bloodshed. He fell on his knees before Elijah and pleaded with him to see his life and the lives of his men as "precious." Because this captain feared God and valued the lives of his men, they were all saved. The ultimate sign that a society has lost its moral plumb line is when human life is no longer precious in the eyes of its citizens. The only way to combat the moral decay and prevent our society from being swept away is to humble ourselves and base our lives on the *precious cornerstone* of all life, Jesus Christ.

"Therefore, this is what the Sovereign Lord says: 'Look! I am placing a foundation stone in Jerusalem, a firm and tested stone. It is a precious cornerstone that is safe to build on. Whoever believes need never be shaken. I will test you with the measuring line of justice and the plumb line of righteousness....'" (Isaiah 28.16-17 NLT).

DAY 71

A Cut Above

"Now the sons of the prophets who were at Bethel came out to Elisha, and said to him, 'Do you know that the LORD will take away your master from over you today?' And he said, 'Yes, I know; keep silent!'" (2 Kings 2.3 NKJV).

The prophets in Israel know that Elisha's master, Elijah, is about to be taken up by the Lord. The prophets approach Elisha in excitement with their revelation. Elisha becomes irritated. He yells in frustration: "Yes, I know; keep silent!" If Elijah's awesome flight to heaven is known by all the prophets, what makes Elisha so special that he receives the double portion of Elijah's spirit? Why does Elijah's mantle go to Elisha and not the hundreds of other prophets who also have the gift of prophecy? The answer is in the Journey! Elijah traveled from Gilgal, to Bethel, to Jericho and to the Jordan River. At every stop before the Jordan, Elijah tells Elisha to stay; but Elisha insists on continuing the journey—a journey that parallels the intimacy of our Christian walks of faith. First, they begin in Gilgal. This is the place that the nation of Israel followed Joshua miraculously across the Jordan River and where all the men were circumcised and the 12 stones (tribes) were established. Second, they went to Bethel. Bethel is where Jacob saw God in a dream and where he received God's blessing and purpose (Genesis 28.13-15). Third, they went to Jericho. Jericho was the "mountain" that blocked the nation of Israel from entering their Promised Land. God's Chosen People demonstrated faith in the face of a mocking world, relying solely on God's hand to tear down the walls (Joshua 6). Finally, they ended in the Jordan River. The Jordan River is where Jesus Himself was baptized, which is symbolic of dying to sin and resurrecting in new life with God (Matthew 3.13 & Romans 6.3-6). As Christians, if we want to be a cut above the crowd, we need to be willing to travel with the Holy Spirit on this journey. We must be willing to wait, abide in Him, have faith in His Hand and make God the master of our lives. The further we go on this journey, the more powerful our anointing will be.

"And so it was, when they had crossed over, that Elijah said to Elisha, 'Ask! What may I do for you, before I am taken away from you?'" (2 Kings 2.9 NKJV).

DAY 72

Bitter Gourd

—•————•——❋——•————•—

"So he said, 'Then bring some flour.' And he put it into the pot, and said, 'Serve it to the people, that they may eat.' And there was nothing harmful in the pot" (2 Kings 4.41 NKJV).

The ignorance, carelessness and bitterness of one man caused a pot of death to be served to many people. This man went looking for herbs to flavor the stew that all the prophets would be eating later. As he wandered, he found some gourds and decided to chop them up and add them to the pot. He did not ask anyone's opinion about the gourds–whether they would be beneficial to the soup or not. Instead, he took it upon himself to tamper with the soup, ruining it for an entire group of hungry souls. Some gourds can be eaten, but others are so bitter that they will cause the consumer to throw up. A handful of gourds have toxins that have been known to kill animals and humans. Thankfully, Elisha knew how to turn a bitter situation into a testimony of God's amazing grace. Elisha threw a little flour into the pot, turning the putrid stew into savory sustenance for everyone. Sometimes bitter people will try to throw their toxins into a situation that affects entire groups of people. We must be careful who we allow to add their "flavor" to the mix; however, as long as we ensure that Jesus (the Bread of Life) permeates the pot, we can trust that God will turn even the sourest of circumstances into an awesome stew of His glory.

"For the bread of God is the bread that comes down from heaven and gives life to the world" (John 6.33 NIV).

DAY 73

The Power of Belief

"So an officer on whose hand the king leaned answered the man of God and said, 'Look, if the LORD would make windows in heaven, could this thing be?' And he said, 'In fact, you shall see it with your eyes, but you shall not eat of it'" (2 Kings 7.2 NKJV).

Belief is the telltale sign if we really trust in God. Many times we don't realize our disbelief until it is tested. God will reveal if we truly put our faith in Him when we are confronted with impossible situations that are completely out of our control. Joram, King of Israel, was confronted with an impossible situation. His kingdom was on the brink of collapse from the devastation of war and famine. The starvation got so bad that women were eating their children (2 Kings 6.28-29). Finally, the king had had enough, and he demanded that the prophet, Elisha, pray for the kingdom. At this time, a donkey's head was sold for over 80 shekels of silver and a portion of dove droppings (which may also mean carob beans) was five shekels of silver (2 Kings 6.25 NKJV). Since 5 shekels was about one month's worth of wages, this was a small fortune for such measly items. However, Elisha (speaking under the influence of the Holy Spirit) declared that by the next morning 1 seah of fine flour (31 cups) and 2 seahs of barley (62 cups) would be sold for one shekel! King Joram's officer spoke incredulously of such an impossibility. He said that even if God would put windows in the sky, this prophecy could not happen. The officer's disbelief caused him to see God's miracle, but he wasn't able to partake in it. Our disbelief in God's promises has major ramifications. If the Holy Spirit gives us a desire, we must believe it even when our faith is tested. When things look impossible, we know the fulfillment of our promise is near. If we truly have faith that God sent His Son, Jesus, to save our souls from eternal separation, we can rejoice in the face of impossibility for all the promises along the way!

"Then Jesus told them, 'I tell you the truth, if you have faith and don't doubt, you can do things like this and much more. You can even say to this mountain, '*May you be lifted up and thrown into the sea,*' and it will happen. You can pray for anything, and if you have faith, you will receive it'" (Matthew 21.21-22 NLT).

DAY 74

Hanging on by a Thread

"And Hezekiah received the letter from the hand of the messengers, and read it; and Hezekiah went up to the house of the LORD, and spread it before the LORD" (2 Kings 19.14 NKJV).

King Hezekiah was a good king; but because of the sins of previous kings and the people, the second half of God's chosen nation, Jerusalem, was hanging on by a thread. The first half, Israel, had already been absorbed by the powerful kingdom of Assyria. Tiny Jerusalem was surrounded by enemies; however, the Assyrians were dominating the world at this time; and they boasted about their victories. The Assyrian king, Sennacherib, wrote a letter to Hezekiah describing his strength and mocking King Hezekiah for having faith in the One True God. Hezekiah's first plan of action when receiving this letter was to go straight to the House of the Lord and to spread the letter before God. Almost two hundred thousand Assyrian soldiers were at Hezekiah's doorstep, and there was absolutely nothing he could do. Although this situation seemed bleak, it was actually the best place to tap into the supernatural power of God. Many times we dip into our own abilities, resources and strengths; but when we do, we bypass the abilities, resources and strengths of our perfect God. King Hezekiah went to God, and God supernaturally dominated Jerusalem's enemy. When we learn to bring everything before the Lord first—both big and small situations— we begin to develop a discipline of relying on God's abundance instead of our insignificant stockpile of fragments. When we expose our lack, God pours out His grace.

"The LORD himself will fight for you. Just stay calm" (Exodus 14.14 NLT).

DAY 75

Professional vs. Personal Work

"But they paid no attention, and Manasseh seduced them to do more evil than the nations whom the LORD had destroyed before the children of Israel" (2 Kings 21.9 NKJV).

Manasseh had the longest and one of the most evil reigns in Judean Kingdom history. His sins compiled in the Bible make a very shocking and depressing list, imprinting humanity's imperfection on God's Holy Word. Although we are called to respect our leaders and their positions, we should not let their personal choices alter our commitment to God's commands. The people of Israel allowed Manasseh's loose lifestyle to affect their obedience to God. The Bible says that they "paid no attention" and that they were "seduced" to commit more evils than the corrupt nations surrounding them. Today, we have many influential people who do not have the authority of the Holy Spirit correcting and leading them. Although we can respect these people's talents, positions and work, we must pay careful attention not to let their personal choices justify our own acts of disobedience. Also, our children may perceive these actions as normal if we are not aggressively staying aware of the influences feeding their young minds and being proactive about pointing out diversions from God's Word. We can implement mercy while distinguishing between what is Holy and what is Common (Lev. 10.10), so our lives and our families are not seduced to live as though we were not the righteousness of Christ (Romans 3.22).

"So practice and obey whatever they tell you, but don't follow their example. For they don't practice what they teach" (Matthew 23.3 NLT).

DAY 76

Attributes of a Mighty Person

"Now these were the heads of the mighty men whom David had, who strengthened themselves with him in his kingdom, with all Israel, to make him king, according to the word of the Lord concerning Israel" (1 Chronicles 11.10 NKJV).

God cultivated David's future kingship and molded his heart while David hid in caves and ran from the injustice of Saul. During this time, David collected quite an interesting group of followers who formed a motley crew of an army. According to 1 Samuel 22.2, these men were "distressed," "in debt," and "discontented." However, they were also "bold," "mighty," "trained for battle," and had "faces of lions" (1 Chronicles 12.8). Although the focus is on David's transformation into a man after God's own heart, the men fighting and living alongside David also transformed and "strengthened themselves" with David in the kingdom. In fact, the valor of these men is recorded in the Bible, and their exploits would impress even the most fervent connoisseur of patriotic action films. As Christian leaders, we shouldn't feel a need to surround ourselves by people who have it all together. In fact, God may give the messiest of lives to the strongest of leaders! On the contrary, we should be looking for people who are willing workers, eager to learn, ready to grow and loyal to the vision. No one will ever be perfect, and leaders shouldn't fear the flaws of others because they themselves will never be perfect. However, a heart for God, devotion to the cause and a determination to see things through to the end are all attributes of a mighty person; and an individual with such tenacity will be a strong force in God's Kingdom.

"So let's not allow ourselves to get fatigued doing good. At the right time we will harvest a good crop if we don't give up, or quit. Right now, therefore, every time we get the chance, let us work for the benefit of all, starting with the people closest to us in the community of faith" (Galatians 6.9-10 MSG).

DAY 77

Keeping Ranks

"All these men of war, who could keep ranks, came to Hebron with a loyal heart, to make David king over all Israel; and all the rest of Israel were of one mind to make David King" (1 Chronicles 12.38 NKJV).

After King Saul died, David became king over Judah for seven years while King Saul's lineage lingered in Israel. Civil unrest between the two political houses was fierce, and disputes ending in death multiplied. Finally, after seven years, King David was anointed by a nation with a unified voice and heart. There are many reasons why God allows our promises to tarry, but two of them are crucial to establishing our God-given dreams. First, it took a few more years for the infrastructure of David's vision to solidify. The Bible says that the men who helped establish David's kingship "could keep ranks." This ability shows that they embraced their niche in the group, they were obedient to authority and they were willing and strong pillars of the vision. Once they could "keep ranks" in a smaller Promised Land (Judah), they were ready to bear the weight of a larger Promised Land (the entire Nation of Israel). Second, it also took a few years for the loyalty of hearts to be sifted. The human heart (inner person, soul, mind, will, understanding, etc.) is extremely complex. Many times people need a season of reckoning to figure out where their allegiance lies. By the time God was ready to establish David's promises, the founding people of his government had "loyal hearts" and the people of the nation were of "one mind" to make him king. This is why people must not attempt to rush the fulfillment of their dreams; it takes time to establish something great. We can remain patient and faithful and trust God's timing, so we won't choose to abandon, adulterate or abate our dreams.

"For the vision is yet for an appointed time, but at the end it shall speak, and not lie: though it tarry, wait for it; because it will surely come, it will not tarry" (Habakkuk 2.3 KJV).

DAY 78

Uzza's Hand

"And when they came to Chidon's threshing floor, Uzza put out his hand to hold the ark, for the oxen stumbled. Then the anger of the LORD was aroused against Uzza, and He struck him because he put his hand onto the ark; and he died there before God" (1 Chronicles 13.9-10 NKJV).

David, his commanders and almost all of Israel were celebrating the beginning of David's kingship over the entire kingdom of Israel (previously, David ruled only Judah). King David sent out men to go find and invite all the people who weren't with them celebrating in Jerusalem. Once everyone was in attendance, David commanded music to be sung and played on a variety of instruments because they were going to bring the Ark of the Covenant (God's presence and glory) back to the Chosen People! However, on the way one man, Uzza, touched the Ark and died from the consequences. Although not much is known about Uzza, two things can be gleaned. First, Uzza did not have reverence for the Lord and His commandments. He directly disobeyed God's rules on how to move the Ark of the Covenant as listed in Numbers 4.5-6 and Numbers 15. The priests built poles, so that the Ark could be transported without being touched by human hands. Second, Uzza's name means *strength* and the word "hand" comes from the Hebrew word, *Yad*, which also means *strength*. Therefore, Uzza represents a person walking in his own authority using his own strength to steer the presence and glory of God. As Christians, we desire the fullness of God's presence and glory in our lives, but this yearning must be anchored to our obedience to His commands and our submission to His authority. We can't expect God's fullness in our lives when we disobey His Word and walk in our own strength. If we want to taste all the good that God has for us, maybe we should start embracing the Protection of His laws and the Provision of His Sovereignty.

"That's the whole story. Here now is my final conclusion: Fear God and obey his commands, for this is everyone's duty" (Ecclesiastes 12.13 NLT).

DAY 79

I've Got Your Back

"Then he said, 'If the Syrians are too strong for me, then you shall help me; but if the people of Ammon are too strong for you, then I will help you'" (1 Chronicles 19.12 NKJV).

King David's men were about to go to war; however, David's military leader, Joab, discovered that "the battle line was against him before and behind" (1 Chronicles 19.10). In a nutshell, the army of God's Chosen People was surrounded. Instead of running away in fear and declaring defeat, Joab divided his soldiers into two units, and each division fought a different enemy. Before the soldiers began their campaign, however, Joab commanded that if one division of soldiers fell behind, the other division would help them. In life, God leads us into battles and calls us to overcome difficult situations. Many times these battles are so overwhelming that we can't fight victoriously alone. We use up all our strength, willpower, resources and faith; but still we feel like we are falling behind. We need a Holy Spirit inspired person, group or resource to come along side of us and help us defeat our enemies. Sometimes the world looks down on people who ask for help. Somehow, seeking outside guidance and/or assistance is seen as weakness or faithlessness. But the truth is that if we are doing God's will, admitting when we need help is a sign of strength and understanding. Life is too short to live in constant defeat. Instead of feeling like we have to overcome every obstacle ourselves, we need to look around us at the people and resources God has provided to help us claim our victory.

"Be of good courage, and let us be strong for our people and for the cities of our God. And may the LORD do what is good in His sight" (1 Chronicles 19.13 NKJV).

DAY 80

Diligent Work

"Now Ornan turned and saw the angel; and his four sons who were with him hid themselves, but Ornan continued threshing wheat" (1 Chronicles 21.20 NKJV).

King David's reign had become mighty, and he decided to take a census of Israel against God's wishes. Since censuses have been done in the past without dire consequences, it could be assumed that David's motives instigating this particular census found in 1 Chronicles 21 and in 2 Samuel 24 were not pure. Pride was probably the main motivator of this census, and God sent an angel to destroy Israel (1 Chronicles 21.15). David wasn't the only one who saw the angel standing between heaven and earth with his sword drawn over Jerusalem (1 Chronicles 21.16). Ornan the Jebusite (Jebusites originally built Jerusalem before they were conquered by the Israelites) saw the angel. Ornan (aka Araunah) was threshing wheat (separating the edible grain from the inedible chaff) on his threshing floor upon the top of Mount Moriah (the place that Abraham took Isaac for the foreshadowing sacrifice of Jesus). Ornan's four sons who were threshing with him ran and hid from the angel, but Ornan continued his work of threshing. He didn't let fear stop him from what he was called to do. Since Ornan was threshing, he was able to offer David the wood, the animals and the location for the sacrifice that would eventually sheath the angel's sword. Ornan was paid greatly for his land (that eventually would become the site for God's temple built by Solomon) and his name would be recorded in history. Our lives are intertwined by the lives of others; and we may see and feel the consequences of their mistakes. However, if our motives and hearts are pure, we do not have to hide from God. God will protect us within life's storms; and if we diligently continue the work that He has called us to, trusting His will for our lives and not fearing the storms around us, our work will be rewarded.

"Such love has no fear, because perfect love expels all fear. If we are afraid, it is for fear of punishment, and this shows that we have not fully experienced his perfect love" (1 John 4.18 NLT).

DAY 81

Do Not Fear

"Then you will prosper, if you take care to fulfill the statues and judgments with which the LORD charged Moses concerning Israel. Be strong and of good courage; do not fear or be dismayed" (1 Chronicles 22.13 NKJV).

King David is dying, and he is passing on the plans of building God's temple to his son and heir, Solomon. In his speech to the people and leaders of Israel, he repeats a twofold command that is seen all throughout the Bible: 1) Take care to fulfill God's statutes and judgments. 2) Be strong and courageous and do not fear or be dismayed. New Testament Christians no longer need to go to a man-made temple to hear from God. Because of Jesus' sacrifice on the cross, our lives (body, mind and spirit) have become God's Temple and the Holy Spirit dwells within each of us. However, when we accept Jesus as our Savior and Lord and allow the presence of the Holy Spirit into our lives, the work of a life of faith has only begun! Some Christians easily adhere to God's statues (plans, laws, tasks, portions, etc.) and obediently follow His judgments (discerning between what pleases and displeases God), but they are weak in their faith, have little courage to accomplish God's will and live in constant defeat. On the other hand, other Christians seem fearless and full of courage, yet they do not obey the parameters that God has set for their lives. In order to experience the fullness of the Holy Spirit overflowing in our Temples, we must have both obedience and faith! Only when these two demonstrations of our love and belief work together will our lives be overcome with the awesome power, glory and anointing of God.

"Do you not know that your body is the temple (the very sanctuary) of the Holy Spirit Who lives within you, Whom you have received [as a Gift] from God? You are not your own, You were bought with a price [purchased with a preciousness and paid for, made His own]. So then, honor God and bring glory to Him in your body" (1 Corinthians 6.19-20 AMP).

DAY 82
Supernatural Intervention

"Give me now wisdom and knowledge to go out and come in before this people, for who can govern this people of yours, which is so great?" (2 Chronicles 1.10 ESV).

King David has died, and his son, Solomon, is about to take his place as king. King Solomon correctly understands his inadequacies of running the kingdom. He doesn't have the experience or knowledge to govern such a great people. David learned to lead while hiding in caves from King Saul. Through the years in the wilderness, David cultivated a heart for the Lord and a great ability of leadership. But King Solomon's road to kingship is vastly different than his father's, and he doesn't have the time to allow the hardships of life to teach him. He will need to gain the wisdom his father learned through the years in a different way. God comes to Solomon in the middle of the night and says, "Ask what I shall give you" (2 Chronicles 1.7). Solomon asks for wisdom, and God gives Solomon a supernatural abundance of it. In fact, King Solomon's wisdom is so well known that kings and queens across the world visit him during his life just to meet him. Some things in life we will learn through time and hardships. But there will be some things that we learn through the supernatural intervention of God. When God gives us a destiny, He will ensure that we are prepared to be victorious in it. And when the world and circumstances haven't prepared us, He will give us a supernatural endowment that we didn't earn. When we are humble about our limitations, God's grace will supply us with everything we need.

"And God is able to bless you abundantly, so that in all things at all times, having all that you need, you will abound in every good work" (2 Corinthians 9.8 NIV).

DAY 83

Solomon's Wise Words

"…and if they turn back to you with all their heart and soul in the land of their captivity where they were taken, and pray toward the land you gave their ancestors, toward the city you have chosen and toward the temple I have built for your Name; then from heaven, your dwelling place, hear their prayer and their pleas, and uphold their cause. And forgive your people, who have sinned against you" (2 Chronicles 6.38-39 NIV).

King Solomon had finally completed the temple that his father, King David, had envisioned. God's presence filled the entire congregation of people so thickly that the priest couldn't enter the temple. Such a beautiful experience this must have been for the entire kingdom of God's people! However, Solomon was very wise in his words. He had dealt with people long enough to know that the human heart is deceitful, and its actions cannot be understood (Jeremiah 17.9). Even though the people were right in the presence of God, Solomon knew that a time would come that the people would turn their hearts away from God. Repentance is the only cure to our wandering hearts. In our lives, there will be times that we are tempted to turn away from God. Whether by disappointment or distraction, our eyes will focus on lesser things that rob our attention from the Lord. But the Holy Spirit does not give up on us! He will continue to pursue us because He knows that only in Him do we find all that our heart desires. When we realize that we have been taking God out of His rightful place as King in our lives, we can quickly repent and be consumed by His mighty presence once more.

"See to it, brothers and sisters, that none of you has a sinful, unbelieving heart that turns away from the living God" (Hebrews 3.12 NIV).

DAY 84

Bad Advice

"But Rehoboam rejected the advice of the older men and instead asked the opinion of the young men who had grown up with him and were now his advisers" (2 Chronicles 10.8 NLT).

King Solomon's son, Rehoboam, began to rule over of the kingdom after his father's death, but he lost over half the kingdom in record time. Because Rehoboam didn't listen to the advice of the elders, he lost the northern tribes of Israel, keeping only Judah and Benjamin. Talk about bad advice! Instead of keeping his father's wise advisors, he enlisted all of his buddies to give him counsel. What did his friends know about running a country? Rehoboam didn't understand the weight of his rash decisions, and he obviously didn't know what he was doing. Instead of just acting on his limited understanding, he should have listened to the words of people that had experience and knowledge. This is a great example of what not to do. When we have a big decision to make, we need to count the cost and seek understanding. We can glean guidance from others, but today we have what the people in the Old Testament didn't have. We have the indwelling of the Holy Spirit. Whenever we are at a crossroads, our first inclination should be to pray and seek God's help. He can see the finish line. He knows the best path to take. We may not understand His movements, but we can definitely choose to be obedient. God always leads us on paths of righteousness, and if we would keep our ears attentive to His direction, we will make the right decision.

"I instruct you in the way of wisdom and lead you along straight paths" (Proverbs 4.11 NIV).

DAY 85

A Nice Looking Evil

"And he did evil, for he did not set his heart to seek the Lord" (2 Chronicles 12.14 ESV).

King Solomon's son, Rehoboam, did evil because his heart was not dedicated to the Lord. This is the curse of so many of God's people today. Sometimes we deceive ourselves, thinking that our hearts are set on God, but when our every thought, intent and action is done in obedience to our own will, our hearts are truly set on ourselves, not God. Moreover, many of us think that if our hearts are not set on God, then we fit into some kind of neutral zone. We're not living for God, but we believe that we are still doing good. Are we doing evil just because we are not doing God's will? The answer is yes. The truth is that anything done outside of God's will—no matter how good, pretty and acceptable it looks to us—is evil. The only way our actions can be furthering God's Kingdom is when they are rooted in the vine of Christ. And the only way they can be rooted in the vine of Christ is if they are done in obedience to God's commands and the movement of His Holy Spirit in our lives. We are vessels, and we will be filled with the things of the Lord or the things of Satan. There is no other option for us. If we are not seeking the Lord in everything we do, we can be sure that there is an enemy working through our seemingly innocent actions.

"I am the vine; you are the branches. If you remain in me and I in you, you will bear much fruit; apart from me you can do nothing" (John 15.5 NIV).

DAY 86

Outward Robes

"Now the king of Israel and the king of Judah were sitting on their thrones, arrayed in their robes. And they were sitting at the threshing floor at the entrance of the gate of Samaria, and all the prophets were prophesying before them" (2 Chronicles 18.9 ESV).

The image of two kings, sitting on their thrones with their royal robes pooling out onto the threshing floor leaves quite an impression. King Jehoshaphat ruled over Judah and King Ahab ruled over Israel. God's Chosen People had long since been divided into two kingdoms, but they joined together to fight a common enemy. Though the two kings look similar outwardly—both with their robes seated on their thrones—they looked very different inwardly. Jehoshaphat, though far from perfect, sought God and tried to stay sensitive to God's commands. On the other hand, Ahab ignored God and didn't listen to His prophets. Finally, when the Prophet Micaiah declared the downfall of their united war, Ahab thought he could fool God. Before charging into battle, Ahab changed out of his royal robes, but a random arrow still found its mark in his chest and he died. Jehoshaphat, however, cried out, and the Lord saved him. God does not respond to the outward appearance; rather, He responds to the heart. When we earnestly seek Him, it doesn't matter if we look the same as everyone else. Eventually, God will move His hand and separate what belongs to Him from what does not. The inward dealings of our heart will spill out into the natural world, and God will bless those who have stayed sensitive to Him.

"'Consider carefully what you hear,' he continued. 'With the measure you use, it will be measured to you—and even more'" (Mark 4.24 NIV).

DAY 87

The Willing Levites

"But there were too few priests to prepare all the burnt offerings. So their relatives the Levites helped them until the work was finished and more priests had been purified, for the Levites had been more conscientious about purifying themselves than the priests had been" (2 Chronicles 29.34 NLT).

All priests were Levites, but not all Levites were priests. The priests had the distinct honor of making the sacrifices at the altar, sprinkling the blood and burning the portions of meat. The Levites that were not priests did other duties around the temple, like cooking, cleaning, singing, teaching, etc. For years, the kings of Judah had forsaken the temple and had neglected the offerings. Finally, King Hezekiah begins to make massive changes during his reign, and he reestablishes the holy rituals that his predecessors had long forgotten. However, there was a lack of priests who had readied themselves for the occasion. While the other priests hurried up to purify themselves, God allowed the other Levites—who normally don't get the privilege of making the sacrifices—to prepare the offerings unto the Lord. This is a great reminder for us today! As we keep our hearts pure before the Lord, He will call us to serve Him in situations that are not part of our normal duties. God's kingdom is being established on this earth whether people are ready or not. If someone is called to a task but is not ready with a pure heart, God will give that task to someone else who is ready and willing. Our disobedience will not stop God's perfect plan from coming into fruition. We must be careful that we stay available to the leading of the Holy Spirit, so we don't miss out on the amazing opportunities that God has for us!

"For God is working in you, giving you the desire and the power to do what pleases him" (Philippians 2.13 NLT).

DAY 88

Hearts Moved

"Then the family heads of Judah and Benjamin, and the priests and Levites–everyone whose heart God had moved–prepared to go up and build the house of the LORD in Jerusalem" (Ezra 1.5 NKJV).

The prophecy foretold by Jeremiah that God's Chosen People would be released by King Cyrus after 70 years of captivity finally comes to pass. King Cyrus gives a proclamation to his entire kingdom that the surviving people of the once great nation of Israel can return home to Jerusalem and rebuild their temple and their city. The Bible explains that God "moved the hearts" of His people to undertake this amazing yet difficult task. As the story unfolds with one struggle after the other, it becomes apparent that this rebuilding vision brings everyone involved to the brink of giving up. For this reason, the hearts of the people had to be supernaturally moved by God's Spirit or else they wouldn't have the devoted stamina to bring God's plan to fruition. In the world today, there are many, many worthy causes to which we can devote our time, energy and resources; however, we must feel a heart movement first. God has a person in mind to fulfill every need that exists today, and if we are listening, He will move each of us in the direction that is stamped with His highest blessing. We must rely on God's Spirit to guide us, so we know that we will have the "heart" to see the vision to the end. Otherwise, we may jump from one vision to another, wondering why we don't feel God's mighty arm move with our faith steps.

"God will meet you where you are in order to take you where He wants you to go." – Tony Evans

DAY 89

Altars to God

‒•————•—·—※—·—•————•‒

"Despite their fear of the peoples around them, they built the altar on its foundation and sacrificed burnt offerings on it for the LORD, both the morning and evening sacrifices" (Ezra 3.3 NIV).

The remnant of God's Chosen People are reclaiming their land. They have one mind to rebuild the temple of the LORD, so they begin with building the altar and making sacrifices. The only problem is that everyone around them wants to see the Israelites fail. Their sacrifices provoke rage in people who do not know or honor God, and the last thing these people want to see is smoke filling the skies, symbolizing the flame of faith that has been rekindled in the hearts of God's people. However, "despite their fear," God's people continue in obedience and make sacrifices to the Lord day and night. Today, there is much darkness in our world, and many people do not want to see the light of Christ in us. But God asks us to live out our faith on platforms–work, school, home, social media, etc.–surrounded by people who do not know or honor Him. And if we are to claim our land for God, we must not fear the people around us. Though we may be scorned or ridiculed, we can continue to build our lives as altars to God, and allow Him to offer up the ultimate Sacrifice, Jesus, to a world that desperately needs Him.

"The next day John saw Jesus coming toward him and said, 'Look! The Lamb of God who takes away the sin of the world!'" (John 1.29 NLT).

DAY 90

When God Moves

"The joyful shouting and weeping mingled together in a loud noise that could be heard far in the distance" (Ezra 3.13 NLT).

As God's purposes are brought to fruition, shouts of joy and sorrow can be heard simultaneously. A family mourns the death of their daughter, but another family rejoices over a donated organ that saves a child's life. A man cries out to God because he did not get the job, while another man excitedly tells his wife of his new employment. The rain ruins a long-planned family vacation, yet it feeds the crops of a farmer's land desperate for water. In the Book of Ezra, the foundation of the new temple is formed. The young people shout for joy, but the older crowd who remember the glory of the first temple weep with sadness. When God moves, we will never know if we'll be standing with the mourners or the rejoicers. We live in a corrupted world pulled to shreds by the free will of humanity. Our lives on earth will echo with cries of joy and sorrow. Both sounds inhabit God's heart because He too grieves and rejoices with us. And though we will experience the devastation of sin during our short time on this earth, God promises that nothing can snatch our eternal spirits from His hands. We have heaven guaranteed through Jesus Christ.

"I give them eternal life, and they shall never perish; no one will snatch them out of my hand. My Father, who has given them to me, is greater than all; no one can snatch them out of my Father's hand" (John 10.28-29 NIV).

DAY 91

The Decree

"May God, who has caused his Name to dwell there, overthrow any king or people who lifts a hand to change this decree or to destroy this temple in Jerusalem. I Darius have decreed it. Let it be carried out with diligence" (Ezra 6.12 NIV).

The building of the temple has been halted for about 14 years. King Cyrus who helped the construction to begin is now gone, and his predecessor, King Artaxerxes, does not know the decree that King Cyrus made. The local Samaritans, upset by the rejection of their offer for help, set out to stop the rebuilding of the temple and succeed for a time. The Samaritans' false niceties and dishonest intentions to help are exposed, and their desire for power and control becomes obvious. Finally, the prophets of God encourage the Jewish people back to their rebuilding efforts, and the Samaritans once again try to stop them. However, King Darius is in control now, and after a little research, he finds the decree made by King Cyrus. King Darius not only encourages the rebuilding, but he demands the Samaritans help pay for it out of their treasury. And he gives a warning to anyone who tries to stop it. Finally, he offers a divine blessing over the project. We learn two valuable lessons from this story. First, we must allow time to expose the evil intentions of "well-meaning" people, including ourselves. The human heart is corrupt and very few people realize that they are working out of selfish desires for control and power (Jeremiah 17.9). Second, sometimes God's pauses actually put us on the fast track to our destiny. After the Israelites waited a few years, God revitalized their work with much need resources, protection and divine blessing; and the temple work was finally finished.

"Wait for the Lord; be strong, and let your heart take courage; wait for the Lord!" (Psalm 27.14 ESV).

DAY 92

A Christian Writer

"This is what was written in the letter which King Artaxerxes gave to Ezra the religious leader, the writer, who had much learning in the Laws of the Lord and His Laws for Israel" (Ezra 7.11 NLV).

The term "Christian writer" is a well-known and often used description in today's culture. Adding the proper adjective, "Christian," before any noun, distinguishes that word as separate, distinct and special somehow. We like to use this modifier when using certain terms to set them apart, like "Christian movies," "Christian music," "Christian literature," and "Christian counseling." There should be a marked difference within the movie, song, book and/or counselor that makes the effort to highlight the difference necessary. King Artaxerxes called Ezra a "writer," but with that term he added a very special description: "who had much learning in the Laws of the Lord and His Laws for Israel." There should be an imprint of God's law—to love God and to love others—when we add the label, "Christian," to our lives (Matthew 22.37-39). Our thoughts, actions, relationships and creations should start with a love for God and His people, and that love will encourage us to continue "working out our salvation" by reading God's Word, praying to Him and staying obedient to His Spirit. Replacing selfishness with a supernatural love that is only accomplished in the spirit will be the fastest and most lasting signifier that we are indeed Christ-followers.

"Therefore, my beloved, as you have always obeyed, so now, not only as in my presence but much more in my absence, work out your own salvation with fear and trembling" (Philippians 2.12 ESV).

DAY 93

A Wall of Protection

"They said to me, 'Things are not going well for those who returned to the province of Judah. They are in great trouble and disgrace. The wall of Jerusalem has been torn down, and the gates have been destroyed by fire'" (Nehemiah 1.3 NLT).

The wall around Jerusalem is symbolic of protection. The problem with the actual physical wall, however, is that it caused the Children of God to find safety in anything manmade instead of God alone. As God's people relied more and more on this wall, they walked away from true protection that comes from obedience to God. God provides us with safety within His laws (Leviticus 25.18). God's commandments are written for our benefit, granting us protection, prosperity, blessings and abundance (Deuteronomy 30.15-20). Nehemiah is distressed because the remnant of Israel is living in Jerusalem without a wall. Their lack of a wall is symbolic of their lack of knowledge of God's laws and how to live holy and set apart. Nehemiah, Ezra and the other community leaders are going to help them build a wall, while simultaneously teaching them how to come under the authority and protection of God's law. As Christians, we find our true protection in obeying God's laws. His commandments are sweet and provide us with God's eternal best (Psalm 119). We don't have to worry or have fear because God promises that He alone will be a fire of protection around the fullness and beauty of our lives.

"'Then I, myself, will be a protective wall of fire around Jerusalem,' says the Lord. 'And I will be the glory inside the city!'" (Zechariah 2.5 NLT).

DAY 94

But I Replied

- • ———— • — • —— ❋ —— • — • ———— • ◄

"Then I was terrified, but I replied, 'Long live the King! How can I not be sad? For the city where my ancestors are buried is in ruins, and the gates have been destroyed by fire'" (Nehemiah 2.2-3 NLT).

Nehemiah, King Cyrus's cupbearer and trusted servant, had never looked sad before the king during his work of service. The king instantly knew that Nehemiah was "deeply troubled." King Cyrus asked Nehemiah, "Why are you looking so sad?" And with all eyes on him, Nehemiah was "terrified" to answer. Although it is not stated, Nehemiah most likely knew that he was staring into the face of the man who the prophet Isaiah prophesied 150 years earlier would help Israel rebuild their nation. A single, little conversation with so much at stake was about to change history. One prophecy, one request, one king – the weight of the moment must have been unbearable! But through his fear, Nehemiah simply writes, "…but I replied…" When Christians gain a promise from God, we do not have to fear the people, situations and obstacles that are in the way. God's "yes" is the only ticket we need to enter our destiny, and He will ensure that people's hearts and life's circumstances will be swayed for our benefit when the time is right. So instead of allowing fear and doubt deter us from making our claim in faith, we need to fearlessly "reply" with our assurance in God's faithfulness.

"I will raise up Cyrus to fulfill my righteous purpose, and I will guide his actions. He will restore my city and free my captive people—without seeking a reward! I, the Lord of Heaven's Armies, have spoken!" (Isaiah 45.13 NLT).

DAY 95

Before the Storm

- • ———— • ———— ✦ ———— • ———— • -

"I slipped out during the night, taking only a few others with me. I had not told anyone about the plans God had put in my heart for Jerusalem. We took no pack animals with us except the donkey I was riding" (Nehemiah 2.12 NLT).

Nehemiah does not tell any of the Israelites his plan to rebuild the wall around Jerusalem. He seemingly comes as a spokesperson from King Cyrus, but no one knows about the support and resources that the king has bestowed upon Nehemiah to rebuild the city. Instead of coming into Jerusalem with pomp and haughty declarations of grandeur, Nehemiah remains silent and secretly scopes out the situation at night. Only a few men go with him to analyze the damage and neglect of Jerusalem, and Nehemiah takes no other supplies with him beside the animal in which he rides, as a safeguard from suspicious thoughts of others. The rebuilding of the wall will create a firestorm of attack and difficulty, and Nehemiah rightly takes time during the silence of the storm to ready himself for the mountain climb ahead of him. Many times when God gives of us a promise, the fruition of it becomes increasingly clear. Much like a chess game reaching the climax of a checkmate—every circumstance opens up like a stair-step into our destiny. But instead of jumping in face-first without a plan, we can prepare our hearts for the work and reward that from our promise. We'll have our entire life to dwell in our Promised Land, but we will only have a moment to show God our gratitude and adoration by faith and to root our lives in peace before the waves of change hit us.

"Don't worry about anything; instead, pray about everything. Tell God what you need, and thank him for all he has done. Then you will experience God's peace, which exceeds anything we can understand. His peace will guard your hearts and minds as you live in Christ Jesus" (Philippians 4.6-7 NLT).

DAY 96

Against All Odds

"When all our enemies heard about this, all the surrounding nations were afraid and lost their self-confidence, because they realized that this work had been done with the help of our God" (Nehemiah 6.16 NIV).

Against all odds the Israelites finally finished building a wall around Jerusalem. Even though God's people sacrificed much and poured all their energy, strength and resources into the work; there was no doubt that God had supernaturally intervened. All the nations surrounding the city were afraid because they realized a supernatural presence was involved. Today, even when Christians pour all of their strength, energy and resources into a promise, there will still be great lack, especially if the promise is big. God knows this and purposefully orchestrates our lack, so He can come through for us in a supernatural way. When God pours His abundance, favor and blessing into our promise, there will be no doubt of His mighty existence in our lives. God will claim the glory and the people surrounding us will have a fresh and undeniable sense of His presence reigning on this earth. Only God can do the impossible, but we must believe in our lack and wait for Him to provide abundantly.

"The Lord reigns, let the earth be glad; let the distant shores rejoice" (Psalm 97.1 NIV).

DAY 97

Administration

"Then my God put it into my heart to assemble the nobles and the officials and the people to be enrolled by genealogy. And I found the book of genealogy of those who came up at the first…" (Nehemiah 7.5 ESV).

Nehemiah is doing a lot of administrative work. He is reestablishing God's people in their Promised Land, and there is a lot of organizing and restructuring to be done. He is also writing down the names of the people who have returned back to the Promised Land. Administrative work is definitely not the most appealing task to many people. And a lot of it seems a waste of time when we could be going out and changing the world for Christ. However, when God "puts it in our hearts" to do administrative work, it becomes a priority. In fact, if we ignore God's command to stop our work in the trenches and take the role as a pen-pusher for a moment, we will be in stark disobedience to God. The truth is that nothing takes precedence over God's will. The world might arrange our actions in order of most effective to least effective, but God sees beyond what we see and His plans will not make sense to us. Sometimes God will tell us to "go and do" and other times He will tell us to "sit and write." And they are equally important when done in obedience to the Holy Spirit.

"For everything that was written in the past was written to teach us, so that through the endurance taught in the Scriptures and the encouragement they provide we might have hope" (Romans 15.4 NIV).

DAY 98

Safety of God

"Now the leaders of the people lived in Jerusalem. And the rest of the people cast lots to bring one out of ten to live in Jerusalem the holy city, while nine out of ten remained in the other town." (Nehemiah 11.1 ESV).

It is interesting to note that before Jerusalem was conquered by the Babylonians, the Prophet Jeremiah kept warning the people to leave the city because Babylon would destroy it (Jeremiah 37.9). Jeremiah told the city folks that Jerusalem would fall in total devastation, but his warnings went onto deaf ears. The people felt protected and invincible within the city walls, and the ones who stayed in their false security perished. Now as the People of God return to their Promised Land, they didn't want to go back to the city. They had to draw lots in order to get 1 out of 10 men to go back to Jerusalem and make their home there. The once invincible city of Jerusalem had fallen, and the people no longer felt safe in man-made structures. When we find safety in anything other than God, He can easily tear down our false sense of security. There is no true safety outside the protection and will of the Lord. God is our only unshakable fortress and our only true source of strength!

"God is our refuge and strength, an ever-present help in trouble" (Psalm 46.1 NIV).

DAY 99

Honor the King

"But Queen Vashti refused to come at the king's command delivered by the eunuchs. At this the king became enraged, and his anger burned within him" (Esther 1.12 ESV).

Vashti means "beautiful." Queen Vashti had obviously taken her husband, the most powerful man alive at this time, King Ahasuerus of Persia, for granted and put too much stock in her own beauty. The king's courts were filled with guests, and he wanted to honor his bride by praising her beauty before the people. However, the queen was so wrapped up in her own selfishness that she not only missed out on the chance to be celebrated, she also shamed her husband in front of everyone. She couldn't be bothered to submit to her husband's simple request to be with him. Today, we have a King that wants to honor and praise us before the world as His special bride, yet many times we shun God's every effort to spend time with us. What a shame! We are so occupied with ourselves that we can't even take a moment to speak with God in prayer and listen to His voice. We become angry with God because we are not living in His promised abundance as His special and beloved creation. In actuality, we are our own problem! How can the King honor His bride when she doesn't submit to His requests? How can we possibly hear the King's call when we are so absorbed in our own self-interest, feelings and desires? Let us show honor to God by dropping everything when He calls. Let us keep our hearts attentive to the King, so we can live in the full beauty He has for us!

"…But now the Lord declares: 'Far be it from me! Those who honor me I will honor, but those who despise me will be disdained'" (1 Samuel 2.30 NIV).

DAY 100

Trusting the Helper

"When the turn came for Esther the daughter of Abilhail the uncle of Mordecai, who had taken her as his own daughter, to go into the king, she asked for nothing except what Hegai the king's eunuch who had charge of the women advised" (Esther 2.15 ESV).

After a year of preparation, it was finally time for Esther to present herself before the king. She had one shot to stand out above all the other young ladies to win the king's heart and be the next queen. However, a little subtle test stood between her and the throne. Before each lady went before the king, she was allowed to take anything from the palace treasury with her, as her own reward and possession. Instead of acting on her own instincts, Esther wisely relied on the suggestion of the king's eunuch, Hegai. Esther could have grabbed for herself treasure to her heart's content, but she would have undoubtedly passed up the prize of being queen and obtaining the influence that saved her people, the nation that birthed our Messiah and King. Many times God asks us to give up the chance to lay hold of certain immediate treasures because He has a bigger and better prize in store for us. The prize will not only greatly exceed the other treasures we denied ourselves, but it will also allow us to have great and eternal influence in the everlasting Kingdom of God. Before we are enticed by the quick or easy road to our destiny, we need to ask our guide, the Holy Spirit, for His guidance and expertise. He will help direct us away from our selfish desires and ensure that we stay on the path that leads to God's best in our lives.

"Do not store up for yourselves treasures on earth, where moths and vermin destroy, and where thieves break in and steal. But store up for yourselves treasures in heaven, where moths and vermin do not destroy, and where thieves do not break in and steal. For where your treasure is, there your heart will be also" (Matthew 6.19-21 NIV).

DAY 101

Unwavering Reliance

"And when they spoke to him day after day and he would not listen to them, they told Haman, in order to see whether Mordecai's words would stand, for he had told them that he was a Jew" (Esther 3.4 ESV).

The king made Haman the head over all his kingly officials. Every official, including Mordecai, Esther's uncle, was commanded to bow down before Haman and pay homage to him. However, Mordecai would not do this. The other officials did not like the fact that Mordecai would not bow, and they pressured him day in and day out to pay homage. But Mordecai explained that he was a Jew, and the Jewish people only bow down to God. The Bible says that Mordecai would not heed the officials' words, so they tested Mordecai to see if he was all talk and no follow through. It's easy for Christians, especially in America, to say that we only serve the One True God, but the world will test our words. The world wants to see if we will stick to our guns and stay faithful to God even when we will lose something we desire – popularity, promotion, influence, friends, gifts or even our lives. It's beautiful to have a desire to serve God, but our desires need to be quickly followed by our obedience, steadfastness and resolve. We can't buckle under pressure just because someone says they don't like our beliefs or they think we are fools. Just like Mordecai, we can stay faithful to God even when the circumstances are threatening, because God is faithful to redeem our unwavering reliance on Him in powerful and amazing ways.

"If you listen to your fears, you will die never knowing what a great person you might have been." – Robert H. Schuller

DAY 102

A Bothered Mind

"On that night the king could not sleep. And he gave orders to bring the book of memorable deeds, the chronicles, and they were read before the king" (Esther 6.1 ESV).

It is no coincidence that the King Ahasuerus (King Xerxes) couldn't sleep. Esther had obediently followed God into a tricky situation. In her efforts, she had done everything to help save her people. However, she still had lack. She was just a young woman with very little power or influence. God would have to do something supernatural to help save His Chosen People from complete annihilation by the hand of Haman. And that's just what God did. God was able to use a seed that Mordecai had planted a long time ago. Mordecai had warned the king of an attack on his life, yet the faithful deed had never been rewarded. God purposely put the reward on hold, so He could use it when the time was right. Many times we obediently follow God's will only to end up in lack, but we must trust as Esther did that God will come through for us supernaturally. Also, we should never forget that any seed we plant by faith in God's kingdom is never forgotten. It may seem like the Lord will not reward it, but He is saving it for His perfect time and perfect will.

"For still the vision awaits its appointed time; it hastens to the end—it will not lie. If it seems slow, wait for it; it will surely come; it will not delay" (Habakkuk 2.3 ESV).

DAY 103

Transformed light

"For [at this time] the Jews had light [a dawn of new hope] and gladness and joy and honor" (Esther 8.16 AMP).

God allowed the Jewish people to face complete annihilation from the Persian king. Seduced into Haman's evil plan, the king proclaimed a day that commanded everyone to kill and plunder all the Jewish people—young and old—living in the kingdom. The energy of fierce hatred and greed must have been so thick in the weeks leading up to the day of death. Bullying, mistreatment and evil thoughts would have been rampant among the people planning the destruction of the Jewish people. However, with His mighty arm, God turned the tide, and the energy that was meant for evil became a blessing of good upon the Jews. Today the Jewish holiday that celebrates this blessing is called Purim, and it is one of the most joyous of all Jewish occasions. Through Jesus Christ, the sin of this world was transformed into grace. All the hate that nailed Jesus onto the cross morphed into an abundant love that exploded across space and time. Nothing surprises God. When He allows us to face dark times, our faith in His promises is tested. When we stand firm in obedience, God is able to transform that darkness into His light shining onto the world. We can claim peace in the fiercest storm, knowing that God is in control and His Kingdom has the final word.

"Peace I leave with you; my peace I give you. I do not give to you as the world gives. Do not let your hearts be troubled and do not be afraid" (John 14.27 NIV).

DAY 104

Good for Evil

"…on the very day when the enemies of the Jews hoped to gain the mastery over them, the reverse occurred: the Jews gained mastery over those who hated them" (Esther 9.1 ESV).

The reverse occurred. What the enemy meant for evil, God used for good. When we read the entire story of Esther, the mind cannot comprehend how extremely delicate the plan of reversal turned out. God used every little detail of the situation to His advantage, and there were so many elements that the people in the story did not see. Each person had to do his/her part in obedience to the Lord, trusting that God saw the bigger picture. Esther went to the king, risking her life. Mordecai had to tell a young woman dear to his heart to stay obedient to the Lord even unto death. God had to supernaturally disturb the king's sleep. And Haman's pride and deceit had to reign for just a moment while God put all the pieces of the puzzle in place. The heroes of the story (Queen Esther and her uncle, Mordecai) had to walk in absolute blind faith! They had to trust each other and trust that God would work everything out for His good. The greatest stories come with the biggest tests of faith. God will only use people whom He can trust with great plans of reversal that involve very subtle details. If we are to be used by God to do great and mighty things, we need to be able to walk out blindly on faith, trusting that God sees the bigger picture.

"As for you, you meant evil against me, but God meant it for good, to bring it about that many people should be kept alive, as they are today" (Genesis 50.20 ESV).

DAY 105

A Heritage of Blessing

"And when the days of the feast had run their course, Job would send and consecrate them, and he would rise early in the morning and offer burnt offerings according to the number of them all" (Job 1.5 ESV).

Job was an extremely wealthy man. The Bible says he had "very many servants," which is important because he had thousands of animals that needed to be cared for. The Bible goes on to say that Job "was the greatest of all the people of the east." Even though Job was obviously busy and most likely did much for his community, he still carved out a large chunk of his day for his family. He would rise up early in the morning and personally make burnt offerings for each of his children. Making burnt offerings was extremely time-consuming and very much a task of solitude, especially when doing an offering for ten kids; but Job's zeal and passion for his children moved him to sacrifice his time, energy and resources for their eternal wellbeing. Job's love for his children and his eyes on heaven dictated the events and order of his daily schedule. As parents, caring for our children with the same attitude as Job means much of what we do every day is for their benefit and eternal good. When we pour time, energy and resources into our kids, we are emulating a man that God considered "blameless and upright." We can gladly make sacrifices for our children every day because we know that they are a blessing from the Lord and He is well pleased with our offerings of love and care.

"Children are a heritage from the Lord, offspring a reward from him" (Psalm 127.3 NIV).

DAY 106

Why Do Bad Things Happen?

———————————✴———————————

"And the LORD said to Satan, 'Behold, he is in your hand; only spare his life'" (Job 2.6 ESV).

The story of Job reaches into the heart of every believer in every season, faith-walk and circumstance. The Book of Job tackles many difficult questions, and one of the most essential themes is *if God is sovereign, why does He allow bad things to happen?* Just like Satan was allowed into the Garden of Eden to tempt Adam and Eve and cause the ultimate fall of man, Satan was allowed into Job's life to destroy everything Job held dear. Even Jesus was "led" into the wilderness to be tempted for 40 days. We must then come to the conclusion that God allows Satan to attack every aspect of our lives. But why? Adversity forces our faith to strengthen and grow. We are only on this earth for a very short time, and once we look at this life through the lens of eternity, our perspective of Satan's purpose changes. Satan has been allowed by God to challenge and attack us and to create chaos in our lives; however, God always has the final word. We are born naturally underdeveloped spiritually, and it is both the good times and the hard that mature us. God allows just enough adversity into our lives to change us into mature souls before we reach heaven's gates. God's eyes are on eternity, and He knows the growth, understanding and Christ-likeness we achieve on this earth will last forever. So when hard times hit, we must not be smothered by questions of "why?" Instead, we can dig in our heels, lean on God and allow Him to strengthen us, so that in our perseverance we lack nothing.

"Consider it pure joy, my brothers and sisters, whenever you face trials of many kinds, because you know that the testing of your faith produces perseverance. Let perseverance finish its work so that you may be mature and complete, not lacking anything" (James 1.2-4 NIV).

DAY 107

If Only a Mediator

───────◆─•─────•───────✳───────•─────•─◆───────

"If only there were someone to mediate between us, someone to bring us together, someone to remove God's rod from me, so that his terror would frighten me no more" (Job 9.33-34 NIV).

Job knew that he could not speak to a holy God without God's rod of judgment being against him. Obviously, Job had a good degree of wisdom when it came to his understanding of the lowliness of humans compared to an awesome, supreme God. But in Job's heartache, he still had questions for God. He still needed to wrestle through his devastating situation, so his understanding of God would deepen and become more meaningful. It's hard as Christians to bring our case to a God who is supernaturally divine beyond comprehension. When we having a clearer vision of how truly magnificent God is, our notions of entitlement quickly dissipate. And we are stuck between a rock and a hard place. How can we—a creation steeped in imperfection—defend our case to a perfect God? That is why Job begged for a mediator. The prophets wished they could live in the time that we find ourselves today. The Bible is full of joyful prophecies about a Messiah who would become our Mediator. Jesus Christ is the Mediator that Job longed for, and we have the true privilege and honor to have Him with us today. Because Jesus died for our sins, shedding His redemptive blood on the cross, we can boldly go to the throne of God. We must not take this amazing gift for granted! Let us go to God, knowing that Jesus mediates between an imperfect world and a perfect God.

"For there is one God and one mediator between God and mankind, the man Christ Jesus, who gave himself as a ransom for all people. This has now been witnessed to at the proper time" (1 Timothy 2.5-6 NIV).

DAY 108

Eyes that See

———※———

"I loathe my life; I will give free utterance to my complaint; I will speak in the bitterness of my soul" (Job 10.1 ESV).

Job has literally lost everything but his life. His children have all died. His livelihood has been completely destroyed. His health has been seriously afflicted. The respect of his friends has been compromised. And his wife has walked out on him. Life could not possibly get any worse, and Job begins to wrestle with God. Much like a snake sheds its old skin, there is a shedding process that Job must endure. God is bringing Job to a greater awareness of Him by stripping Job of everything he holds dear. Job complains in every way, but he never once curses God. He doesn't understand God's ways and he struggles to gain wisdom, but the purest form of faith roots Job to his God. Finally, Job breaks through his previous awareness of God and receives a deeper and more intense revelation of God's presence. And on the other side of the major struggle, God has laid out a redemptive path that multiplies everything Job had lost. God desires to uncover the deep layers of His revelation in our lives. He is not content to allow our understanding of Him to become stagnant. Seasons of stripping are opportunities to forge a more intimate relationship with God. When we wrestle through the difficult moments with Him and find our strength in His presence, we gain a deeper awareness of God's character and receive a clearer understanding of His love for us.

"I had heard of you by the hearing of the ear, but now my eye sees you" (Job 42.5 ESV).

DAY 109

Not Inferior

"But I have understanding as well as you; I am not inferior to you. Who does not know such things as these?" (Job 12.3 ESV).

It's hard to understand why bad things happen to good people. We know from the Bible that all of us have fallen short of the glory of God (Romans 3.23). However, we also know that we will reap what we sow (Galatians 6.7). If we sow disobedience to God, we will reap negative circumstances. If we sow obedience to God, we will reap positive circumstances. Even though we live in a time where our sins are forgiven through the Finished Work of Jesus Christ, God still has given us each the ability to choose blessings or curses. Therefore, we do have some control over many of the hardships that we face in our lives (Deuteronomy 30:19). But what Job was facing and what his friends couldn't understand is that he was under spiritual attack, which had nothing to do with Job's choices. God allowed the enemy to touch Job's life in order to strengthen him and test his resolve for God. The negatives circumstances surrounding Job were completely out of his control, and all he could do was wait out the storm and press into God. God made sure to bless Job abundantly once the spiritual attack was over. The spiritual attack we occur in our lives does not make us inferior to others. In fact, our hardships (that aren't circumstantially related to disobedience) show that God is fortifying our strength and building our character. We should not be ashamed of our spiritual attack; rather, we can wait out the storm knowing that God's victory and blessing will be there for us when it blows over.

"The thankful heart sees the best part of every situation. It sees problems and weaknesses as opportunities, struggles as refining tools, and sinners as saints in progress." – Francis Frangipane

DAY 110

Prayer for Friends

"And the LORD restored the fortunes of Job, when he had prayed for his friends. And the LORD gave Job twice as much as he had before" (Job 42.10 ESV).

Job's friends did a great job of knocking Job down when he was already low. Job had lost everything; and instead of encouraging Job with the truth that God was refining his already stellar character, they accused Job of having sin and claimed that he deserved what was happening to him. Instead of praying for Job, they sat and had theological debates with him, making the extremely difficult situation even worse. God was not happy with Job's friends. In fact, the Bible says that God's anger burned against them and their self-righteous actions. Once Job prayed on their behalf, the Lord accepted his prayer and did not react to Job's friends according to their foolishness. In this life, we will be persecuted, and many times those attacks will come from people closest to us. However, it is in our best interest to humble ourselves and not take offense because in our humility, we will be most like Christ who gave up everything to become a servant for us (Philippians 2.7). We can call on God to redeem us and pray for those who persecute us, so God will shine His glory through our lives and reap honor in our humility.

"If we don't risk being hurt, we cannot give unconditional love. Unconditional love gives others the right to hurt us." – John Bevere

DAY 111

The Gentleness of God

"You have also given me the shield of Your salvation; Your right hand has held me up, Your gentleness has made me great" (Psalm 18.35 NKJV).

It seems odd that the terms "gentleness" and "greatness" should be used in the same sentence. God has just rescued David from the murderous hands of King Saul again, and David is singing a Psalm of praise and appreciation to God. Even though David has been promised the throne by God, David must wait many years, hiding and running from his predecessor, before the promise comes to fruition. God has allowed King Saul to torment David because God is using the fires of persecution to transform David into a king after God's own heart. David reacts by submitting to the process of refining instead of resisting it. God loves and cares for each of His children. He allows a level of persecution to come into our lives in order to mold us into the image of His Son, Jesus. Even so, in the middle of the storm, God has His abundance of "gentleness" waiting for us if we simply submit to the process of our refining, choosing to abide in the Spirit and wait on the Lord. The hardest part of the storm is our reaction to it. Once we surrender to God's hand, we'll find the "gentleness" of God that shall make us "great."

"So I advise you to buy gold from me—gold that has been purified by fire. Then you will be rich. Also buy white garments from me so you will not be shamed by your nakedness, and ointment for your eyes so you will be able to see" (Revelation 3.18 NLT).

DAY 112
The Fool Wise

"The law of the Lord is perfect, reviving the soul; the testimony of the Lord is sure, making the wise simple" (Psalm 19.7 ESV).

God makes the fool wise. All of us begin our lives in a selfish state and ignorant of eternal things, thinking mainly of the fleeting trivialities that our world deems important. It is the Holy Spirit's job to infiltrate the hearts, minds and wills of God's people, steadily changing us from glory to glory unto the likeness of Christ. The Bible is the testimony of our Lord. Jesus is the Word, and He was made flesh to walk among us over two thousand years ago. Jesus' legacy lives on through the proclamation of the disciples, the inspiration of the Holy Spirit and the revelation of the Bible. God's commandments and promises walk side-by-side through the pages of the Bible, allowing us to daily live in the grace and love of Jesus Christ. The Bible flows like liquid salve, healing the soul and igniting the spirit. To neglect the reading of God's Holy Word is to ignore the purest gold and disregard the sweetest honey. When we view the Bible as it truly is, the Living Water of True Life, we will drink from it daily with thirsty hearts eager for more!

"The Word became flesh and made his dwelling among us. We have seen his glory, the glory of the one and only Son, who came from the Father, full of grace and truth" (John 1.14 NIV).

DAY 113

Multiplied Thoughts

"You have multiplied, O Lord my God, your wondrous deeds and your thoughts toward us; none can compare with you! I will proclaim and tell of them, yet they are more than can be told" (Psalm 40.5 ESV).

King David had a healthy understanding of God's love for him. Even though David was running for his life from enemies that were all around him, He knew that God's deeds and thoughts are always good because God is good. In fact, David says in this Psalm that God's deeds and thoughts are too many to be told. Many times Christians struggle in their current difficult situations with holding onto the truth that God is always good. Our focus is blocked by the natural world, and we don't have a clear view of eternity. Yes, there is evil in this world and people are allowed to wield their free will, whether for good or for bad. But God uses all things for His great purposes (Romans 8.28). Even when it doesn't feel like it during difficult times, we must claim the truth that God's deeds are wondrous and His thoughts for us are good! It may take a while, but if we stand resolutely on that Truth, it will begin to seep into the very core of us. And we will begin to walk in strength during those hard times empowered by the knowledge that God is good and His thoughts towards us are good. He is not trying to condemn or punish us during hard times, but He will use them to make us complete in Him.

"Not only that, but we rejoice in our sufferings, knowing that suffering produces endurance, and endurance produces character, and character produces hope, and hope does not put us to shame, because God's love has been poured into our hearts through the Holy Spirit who has been given to us" (Romans 5.3-5 ESV).

DAY 114

Tiresome Pride

* * *

"Behold, you delight in truth in the inward being, and you teach me wisdom in the secret heart" (Psalm 51.6 ESV).

Pride prevents God's Truth from penetrating the inward parts of our being. Our pride works tirelessly to protect our self-interest, and we are void of the rest that is found in humility and brokenness to our God. We will never face our sins if the thick blanket of pride covers our hearts. And we will never know we are walking in darkness if the light hasn't exposed the secret places of our souls. God does not delight in a heart that is constructed of its self-established works and self-confirmed glory; rather, He delights in a heart fully aware of its sin, choosing to walk outside of the corrupted flesh in the complete peace of the spirit. God will aggressively attack our pride, and the process of killing it is very painful. We may feel like we are not being valued, but the truth of the matter is that we have no value outside of Christ. All our worth comes from God, and the sooner we come to grips that we are nothing without Him, the quicker we will gain freedom from our tiresome pride. So instead of resisting the chance to humble ourselves, we should jump at the opportunity to slay pride and its sneaky devastation. Humility is the only gateway to receiving God's honor in our lives, and pride seeks only to steal the wisdom we inherit from God's unchangeable Truth.

"Before destruction the heart of a person is proud, but humility comes before honor" (Proverbs 18.12 NET).

DAY 115

A Cheer within Despair

"Unless the Lord had helped me, I would soon have settled in the silence of the grave. I cried out, 'I am slipping!' but your unfailing love, O Lord, supported me. When doubts filled my mind, your comfort gave me renewed hope and cheer" (Psalm 94.17-19 NLT).

There are times when we will find ourselves on the verge of slipping into a dark place of despair. With all hope lost and our dreams crushed, the silence of the grave seems more alluring than the ugliness of our situation. The ache in our heart penetrates to the farthest corners of our souls, and the heavyweight of confusion, disappointment and defeatism becomes thick like water in our lungs. We can't breathe. We can't think. We can't move. We are sinking in a deep pit and there is no more strength within us to claw our way out or to cry for help. However, it is at our darkest moments that God's help shines the brightest. If only we would believe in the truth that He loves us, we could stand firm on His promise to bring us His comfort and restore our hope. Even when the circumstances surrounding us reek with doubt and death, we can offer a sliver of faith to an unseen and loving God; and that tiny speck of trust will unleash the abounding faithfulness, love and peace of God into our lives. And just maybe, we will find a supernatural portion of "renewed hope and cheer" in our most desperate hour of need.

"I will lead blind Israel down a new path, guiding them along an unfamiliar way. I will brighten the darkness before them and smooth out the road ahead of them. Yes, I will indeed do these things; I will not forsake them" (Isaiah 42.16 NLT).

DAY 116

God's Light in the Shadows

———————※———————

"Even the darkness is not dark to you; the night is bright as the day, for the darkness is as light with you" (Psalm 139.12 ESV).

God allowed David to live in the darkness of caves for many years. David ran for his life from King Saul, a reckless leader appointed by God to shape David into a man after His own heart. In the darkness, David poured out his distress to God through music, and he finally came to the understanding that the darkness does not change God's goodness. King David learned that even in the confusion and the concealment of the shadows, God's light shines brightly in his mind, heart and will when he surrenders himself to the hope of God's faithfulness. When Christians walk through those shadowed times scattered along our brief life on this earth, we need to remember that God is right here with us. Though our circumstance is shrouded in darkness, we can trust that God's presence continues to dwell inside of us, lighting our path and working all things into His greater good. When we stand firm on the promise that God loves us and He is always faithful, we can let go of fear and cling tightly onto our hope in Him. And once we walk out of the shadows into the light, we will realize that our faith has grown stronger and we have become more like Jesus.

"Jesus spoke to the people once more and said, 'I am the light of the world. If you follow me, you won't have to walk in darkness, because you will have the light that leads to life'" (John 8.12 NLT).

DAY 117

Transformation of Rebuke

"Repent at my rebuke! Then I will pour out my thoughts to you, I will make known to you my teachings" (Proverbs 1.23 NIV).

God doesn't rebuke us to shame us but to transform us. The Bible says that Jesus came to this world not to condemn us but to save us. We will always be flawed, and those imperfections become plainly visible in the light of a perfect God. As we draw near to God, He will highlight our sin in order to perfect us into the image of Jesus. However, if we do not "respond" to God's rebuke, we will learn nothing and the process of our glorious transformation will stagnate. We must throw off the guilt of this world and walk in the truth and love of our relationship with God. And the truth is that God loves us, and His correction does not have to sting. Our pride is the only thing that is wounded when God continues the process of pruning us; but when we decide to walk with Him in humility, the grace and mercy of God overflows. When we become open to God's correction, His thoughts and heart flood through us like a river. So let us gladly receive God's rebuke and joyfully humble ourselves to His correction because we know that our intimacy with God will deepen, and the beautiful ramifications of that intimacy will affect every area of our lives with His greater good.

"For God did not send his Son into the world to condemn the world, but in order that the world might be saved through him" (John 3.17 ESV).

DAY 118

First Fruits

—•———•——☀——•———•—

"Honor the LORD with your wealth, with the first fruits of all your crops; then your barns will be filled to overflowing, and your vats will brim over with new wine" (Proverbs 3.9-10 NIV).

The promise of first fruit reaches past our finances and into every aspect of our lives. We have a first fruit of our time, our day, our energy, our talents, our thanksgiving, our discipline, education, work, home, thoughts, confidence, body, etc. Only until we have God in the center of our lives, will the first fruit of each of our moments be given unto His care. When God is our heart's desire and our mind's preoccupation, we will automatically offer the choicest portion of our existence to Him. God doesn't need our offering. He has an all-consuming perfection in and of Himself. His glory needs no additions or supplements. However, since God has an endless and overpowering love for us, He wants to bless every second of our days on this earth. But He can't bless what is not offered to Him. That is why we must always give Him the first fruits of all our efforts, so He can bless the fullness of our work with His glorious touch. So don't hold back from God. Give up your entire life to Him, knowing that when you lose your life in Christ, you will truly find it.

"For whoever would save his life will lose it, but whoever loses his life for my sake will find it" (Matthew 16.25 ESV).

DAY 119

Resurrected Dreams

"Blessed is the one who listens to me, watching daily at my gates, waiting beside my doors. For whoever find me finds life and obtains favor from the LORD" (Proverbs 8.34-35 ESV).

One of the hardest disciplines as a Christian is to listen and wait patiently for the Lord. The Lord will create in us a desire to do some great and beautiful thing for His kingdom, and it is so tempting to focus on the circumstances and offerings of this world to achieve that dream. But when we obediently seek God's guidance and abide in His timing, we allow His fire to refine our hearts over a lengthy season of waiting. And our lives will become much like Moses's burning bush–lit with the flames of destiny, yet never consumed. It is this unquenchable burning that becomes the focus of our submission, and it is so difficult to surrender to a promise that continues in an endless process of fulfillment. It would be much easier to call it quits and allow the dream to burn up or to satisfy the yearning with a lesser, attainable idol-dream. But the "life" of the dream with eventually take breath in those who daily watch and wait at the door of the Lord. Only the few who allow their dream to die in the natural will see it resurrected in the supernatural glory of the risen Lord. Therefore, don't try to quench the burning that God has placed in you; instead, allow the fires of passion to lead you to the throne of God with an awareness of your absolute need for a Savior.

"Whom have I in heaven but you? I desire you more than anything on earth. My health may fail, and my spirit may grow weak, but God remains the strength of my heart; he is mine forever" (Psalm 73.25-26 NLT).

DAY 120

God's Right Path

"There is a way that seems right to a man, but its end is the way to death" (Proverbs 14.12 ESV).

Satan knows that the surest way to knock Christians off the course of walking in God's promises is to sidetrack them by laying out distractions. Some of these distractions will obviously look like sin (sexual impurity, greed for gain, self-glory, etc.), but many more of them will appear as beauty-glossed good works. However, according to eternity and God's kingdom plan these good works actually become self-willed actions sugar-coated to smell and taste appealing to the eyes of others. Christians who do not walk in humility will chase after these good work morsels, satisfying a standard of perceived holiness until one day they burn out. Walking in self-righteous pride, they never bother to ask God if His will was being accomplished. Just because a certain way seems right to us, does not mean that the path is appointed by God. God speaks in an everlasting love and truth, which is not bound by the niceties of this world. Love is sometimes hard and truth sometimes hurts because we are sinners and God's light continually burns off our pride. We can try to control an outward appearance of perfection; but all the while, our inner spirit is in complete rebellion to God. We must never trust our judgment on what "seems right" unless we are in constant surrender to the Holy Spirit. Only when we are submitted to God's authority will our paths be made straight according to the purposes of God.

"A passion to obey Christ is born out of our relationship with him. The more we love him, the more we want him to be a part of our affairs." – Calvin Miller

DAY 121

The Choice of Love

* * *

"Whoever pursues righteousness and unfailing love will find life, righteousness, and honor" (Proverbs 21.21 NLT).

Love is more than a feeling; it is a choice. Feelings are fleeting and hard to control; however, we have the ability to control our choices. Jesus states that the second greatest commandment after loving God is loving others (Mark 12.31). God would not command us to do something if we were incapable of doing it. Therefore, we have the ability to love even when the emotions to back that love have hidden themselves. Loving others is a choice. The Bible asks us to pursue "unfailing love." The emotional sense of love will always fail us. Romantic words, gestures and trifles will fall short unless the motive of that love is based on an everlasting and unchanging choice to love without fail. And if that love can persevere through temptations, difficulties and changes; it will glow with "life, righteousness, and honor." The world and all its efforts to portray love can only scratch the surface of a love tied firmly to choice. It's easy to love when the romance is swirling and the feelings are igniting, but choosing to love while emotions lie dormant is truly magnificent. Instead of our feelings dictating our choices, our steadfast love will cause our choices to guide our feelings into a supernatural love bathed in God's glory and goodness.

"'And you must love the Lord your God with all your heart, all your soul, all your mind, and all your strength.' The second is equally important: 'Love your neighbor as yourself.' No other commandment is greater than these'" (Mark 12.30-31 NLT).

DAY 122

Faithful Wounds

"Faithful are the wounds of a friend; profuse are the kisses of an enemy" (Proverbs 27.6 ESV).

The hardest thing about being a true friend is telling the truth, especially when emotions are high. It's difficult because 1) no one is perfect, and we all have shortcomings and 2) we don't want to offend our friends. However, we become an enemy to our friends when we gloss over their sin with quick kisses of appeasement. If the Holy Spirit is prompting us to speak up, our words may wound our friend for the moment, but God will pour out His healing, restoration and wisdom onto them. If the wound we offer is not taken well, the friendship might end, but God may be doing a work that is now beyond us. Hopefully, in a new season after God has gotten a hold of our friend, He will restore the broken relationship. He is, after all, the Master at restoration (Jeremiah 30.17). Just like parents correct their children, we can offer and receive correction with grace and truth in our friendships. We can joyfully claim, "I receive that correction," knowing that we are being made into the image of Christ every time the sandpaper of friendship rubs away our hard edges.

"Don't lie to each other, for you have stripped off your old sinful nature and all its wicked deeds" (Colossians 3.9 NLT).

DAY 123

Trust without Control

"...Also, he has put eternity into man's heart, yet so that he cannot find out what God has done from the beginning to the end" (Ecclesiastes 3.11 ESV).

We have eternity set in our hearts. This truth has many implications on our lives today. First, we will never be content in this life. Without reconciliation to our eternal God through Jesus Christ and the presence of the Holy Spirit inside of us, we will always feel an emptiness without God. We will never shake the fact that we have a longing for eternity inside of us. This life on earth will never satisfy our need for an everlasting existence. Second, the understanding of eternity means that we will never understand the fullness of our lives on earth. There is so much more to the ultimate picture, and we will have to resolve ourselves to having childlike faith in order to keep our sanity. We won't know it all. And God will have us take steps of faith that make no sense. Luckily, we can gain a peace that transcends all understanding through the work of the Holy Spirit inside of us (Philippians 4.7). Also, when we understand the power that let loose across the earth at the cross once Jesus finished the work to which God called Him, our trust in God's unknown will strengthen. We will never understand everything on earth, but there will come a time when all of God's kingdom plans will be done on earth as they are done in heaven—and we will finally see the fullness of God's redemption!

"May your Kingdom come soon. May your will be done on earth, as it is in heaven" (Matthew 6.10 NLT).

DAY 124

Idol Sacrifices

"Guard your steps when you go to the house of God. To draw near to listen is better than to offer sacrifice of fools, for they do not know that they are doing evil" (Ecclesiastes 5.1 ESV).

One of the saddest things we can do as Christians is to sacrifice time, money, resources and energy in the name of God but not in true obedience to God. It is sad because we place a burden on ourselves and others that God our loving Father has not required of us. To be sure, God will and does expect our complete surrender to His will, which undoubtedly entails sacrifice. However, God gives us grace to bear the weight of our appointed sacrifice when we are in obedience to the Holy Spirit. He does not give us grace when we walk in our own strength in pure disobedience to His individualized calling in our lives. We can claim to do good works in the name of the Lord; but when our actions are done outside of God's will, we create idols. If we become comfortable in our own preconceived holiness, we might very well cease to cling and depend solely on the Holy Spirit and take matters into our own hands while ignoring and shunning the mighty arm of God. If we commit to actions in the name of the Lord, we better make sure we are attentively listening for the Holy Spirit's direction. Otherwise, we won't realize that our self-motivated sacrifices are evil in the sight of God. Absolutely nothing—no matter how good it appears to us and to the world—is sanctified to the Lord unless it is birthed from His Spirit and dedicated to His Kingdom Plan.

"Dedication is writing your name on the bottom of a blank sheet of paper and handing it to the Lord for Him to fill in." – Rick Renner

DAY 125

The Beauty of a Good Name

"A good name is better than precious ointment, and the day of death than the day of birth" (Ecclesiastes 7.1 ESV).

Living for Christ is a daily challenge. Even when we are filled with God's perfect love and goodness, there is a continual battle between our "old self" and "new self." We can have an amazing time of quiet prayer in the morning, encourage a friend with the words of our testimony during the day, be the hands and feet of Jesus for the poor that evening and yet revert to our old selves that night. We yell an angry word at a family member, covet another person's success or allow our faith to be filled with doubt and, in an instant, we are walking in the darkness of our flesh away from the light of God's Spirit. At any moment, we can fall prey to our old selves and our "good name" is shot. Understandably, we will never be perfect. We are sinners in constant need of a savior. But there is a place where our need will finally be quenched, and where we will never have to struggle again. Birth is a beautiful phenomenon, but death allows our spirits to step past our flesh and into the full presence of God. There will be no more struggle, for the shell of our old selves will be dead, leaving only the lasting legacy of our good name. We will never again have to "put on our new nature." Jesus has washed our old nature clean, and our new nature stands before God's heavenly throne.

"Instead, let the Spirit renew your thoughts and attitudes. Put on your new nature, created to be like God—truly righteous and holy" (Ephesians 4.23-24 NLT).

DAY 126

Spirit of Understanding

———————————————————

"As you do not know the way the spirit comes to the bones in the womb of a woman with child, so you do not know the work of God who makes everything" (Ecclesiastes 11.5 ESV).

One of the worst things a Christian can do is limit God. It is very hard not to perceive the world around us through our own personal perspectives. In fact, God has to monumentally disrupt our lives in order to get us out of our comfort zones, so He can broaden our understanding. But once we experience those moments of glimpsing through God's perspective, we realize that our viewpoints have been restricted by our experience, background and upbringing. No matter how much wisdom we gain and how much we grow in our relationship with God through Christ, we will never know the fullness of God's work. We cannot trust the circumstances around us because God moves in an atmosphere far above our comprehension. Christians can daily lift their eyes to God and allow His understanding and truth to penetrate the darkness of their assumptions. God is doing so much in our lives and in this world that we can't see or comprehend, so we need to rely on the soft leading of the Holy Spirit, especially when we don't understand. When we release our small perspectives to God, we will be freed from the hindrances of our preconceived limitations.

"The unfolding of your words gives light; it imparts understanding to the simple" (Psalm 119.130 ESV).

DAY 127

Youth for God

"Remember also your Creator in the days of your youth, before the evil days come and the years draw near of which you will say, 'I have no pleasure in them'" (Ecclesiastes 12.1 ESV).

The writer of Ecclesiastes highlights a problem that occurs many times in our youth today. As youth mature into adults, the world will try to vie for their attention, drawing them away from their relationship with God. The world is like a flowing stream, following the dictates of the devil, steering people away from God. Today's youth are faced with a decision of faith: will they follow the commands of God taught to them by the Bible, parents and church or will they go down the easy path of moral compromise, which is so celebrated in a world without Christ. When people are young, they tend to forget that they are mortal beings who will eventually stand before God in heaven. When we are young, we sometimes don't comprehend how short life is and that we have only one chance to become the people on earth that we will be for eternity. We have many chances in life, but we only have one life to make a difference for God's kingdom. If we choose to stand strong in our faith and not be seduced by the counterfeit glory of the world, we will age in peace and joy, knowing that we have lived a life pleasing and purposeful to God.

"Don't let anyone look down on you because you are young, but set an example for the believers in speech, in conduct, in love, in faith and in purity" (1 Timothy 4.12 NIV).

DAY 128
Better than Wine

─────────※─────────

"Kiss me and kiss me again, for your love is sweeter than wine" (Song of Solomon 1.2 NLT).

Song of Solomon is about a king (many believe it is King Solomon) who falls in love with a Shulamite woman. The word, *Shulamite*, has the meaning of the "perfect one" in the Hebrew language. However, the woman is far from perfect compared to the standard of her culture at that time. She is a shepherdess who also tends vineyards, which means she is a lower-class worker who definitely is not of royal blood. The song details the beautiful process of these two people falling in love, which is the best romance story ever told! The song also makes a profound spiritual statement. The King represents Jesus, and the Shulamite woman represents the Church. We too have fallen in love with the King! Even though we are not of royal blood, He woos us because of His great love for us. We are mere workers, yet He sees us as "perfect ones," because of the blood He shed on the cross to take away our sin, giving us His righteousness. He wants to bring us into His Great Kingdom for eternity, experiencing an eternal love with Him in heaven! This news should create passion, giddiness and joy in our everyday lives—much like the effects of a supernatural wine. We have the King of the Universe pursuing an intimate relationship with us, and He is scooping us off our feet from our work in the natural world and bringing us into a life of royalty with Him forever!

"And if I go and prepare a place for you, I will come again and receive you to Myself; that where I am, *there* you may be also" (John 14.3 NKJV).

DAY 129

Seeking Him

"I will rise now and go about the city, in the streets and in the squares; I will seek him whom my soul loves. I sought him, but found him not" (Song of Solomon 3.2 ESV).

The Shulamite couldn't find her beloved, so she instantly got up and went searching for him. She finds him only a few verses later, and she holds onto him with a fervent grip. Sometimes in our walk of faith, we will feel like God has left us. We have a choice to make. We can stay where we are at and complain about it or we can get up and go search for God with all our might. God never leaves our side, but sometimes He will move His ever-present hand out of view, drawing us away from what is comfortable and closer into relationship with Him. God wants us to become strong and sure in our walk with Him, so He allows us space to learn and grow. We may stumble or even get lost, but He is always there to help us in our time of need. We can trust God's promise that He will never leave us (Hebrews 13.5). When we feel like He is absent in our life, we can dig in our feet and search for Him until He is found. Then we may wrap our arms around Him with all our need, love and desire.

"You will seek me and find me when you seek me with all your heart" (Jeremiah 29.13 NIV).

DAY 130

Waiting for Perfect

"I had put off my garment; how could I put it on? I had bathed my feet; how could I soil them? (Song of Solomon 5.3 ESV).

The king comes to the woman at night, knocking on the door and calling for her. However, the woman is naked and had already washed for bed, so she hesitates getting the door. She thinks about the robe she just took off and her feet she had just cleaned. By the time she finally gets up, though, he has left. She instantly leaves her home in her nakedness, soiling the very feet she feared to get dirty and exposing her body to others. If only she had gone to the king when he asked, he could have covered and protected her. Many times, Christians hesitate to answer God when He knocks for us. God almost always calls us when we least expect it. Nakedness is symbolic of shame, and we feel like we need to cover our shame before we open the door to Him. Also, we want to stay comfortable in our bed, never getting our feet dirty. But we shouldn't worry about our nakedness because Jesus died to clothe us with the royal robes of His righteousness. We don't have to feel shame anymore! Also, we need to realize that even if we are clean, as we follow Jesus, our feet will get dirty because of our journey with Him. A life of faith will be messy, and we may feel like our feet are walking down strange, dusty paths. But we shouldn't worry about the craziness we walk through as we follow Jesus. Jesus Himself will wash our feet clean as we walk this life with Him.

"Jesus replied, 'A person who has bathed all over does not need to wash, except for the feet, to be entirely clean'" (John 13.10 NLT).

DAY 131

Eyes on the King

"Where has your beloved gone, O most beautiful among women? Where has your beloved turned, that we may seek him with you?" (Song of Solomon 6.1 ESV).

The "Others" are speaking in the song. They are watching the amazing romance between the king and the Shulamite woman unfold. They have become so enraptured in the love affair between these two people that their focus is completely on them. Much like someone reading a book or watching a movie today, the story has become part of their very hearts and minds. The "Others" are even willing to drop the tasks of their everyday life, so they can go with the Shulamite woman to find her beloved! The "Others" are symbolic of the world or people who don't have an intimate relationship with the King. Our love of God and our search for Him can ignite the curiosity of others, getting them involved with the beautiful love affair between the Church and Jesus. Christians don't have to guilt, scare or bribe people into a relationship with Christ. We simply need to let our love for Him shine into the dark world. People will take notice, and many will drop the trivialities of their lives, so they too can be a part of the Divine Romance!

"The Lord your God is with you, the Mighty Warrior who saves. He will take great delight in you; in his love he will no longer rebuke you, but will rejoice over you with singing" (Zephaniah 3.17 NIV).

DAY 132

Marked by Love

"Set me as a seal upon your heart, as a seal upon your arm, for love is strong as death…." (Song of Solomon 8.6 ESV).

A seal was worn from a person's arm, so that any correspondence given by the person could be sealed and/or identified with a mark that shows that the individual's approval has been attached to it. The seal was usually pressed into clay, and the mark transferred to any item the person wished to approve. The Shulamite woman wants to be a seal upon her beloved's heart much like the seal worn around his arm. This way everything that the king approves will bear the image of the woman he loves. His heart—love, care, thoughts and plans—will always have the woman's acceptance and benefit as the focal point. When Jesus died on the cross, He spilled out His blood, leaving His mark of redemption on all of us. His blood became the New Covenant of reconciliation to His Church. He loves us so much that He died on a cross, so we could have the royal seal as co-heirs with Christ in the Kingdom of God (Romans 8.17). God is communicating to the world that He overcame death because of His great love for us, giving us His stamp of approval. Because of the Finished Work of Jesus Christ, we are literally set as a seal upon God's heart. We never have to worry about Him forsaking us because our lives are intertwined with His, and His heart continually seeks our best interests.

"And you also were included in Christ when you heard the message of truth, the gospel of your salvation. When you believed, you were marked in him with a seal, the promised Holy Spirit" (Ephesians 1.13 NIV).

DAY 133

Righteous Fruits

"Tell the righteous it will be well with them, for they will enjoy the fruit of their deeds" (Isaiah 3.12 NIV).

It is difficult to walk in obedience to the Holy Spirit and not see the fruit of our work right away. Many times, God allows us to plant seeds in what seems like an arid wilderness, because He knows that His rains of blessings will pour over our efforts in due time. Patience is one of the main testers of our faith. Do we trust God at His Word and continue planting for a harvest that seems impossible? Or do we give up and never realize the fountain of abundance that lay just beneath the surface of our dry circumstances? It's easier to sacrifice our time, energy and resources into areas where we receive tangible awards (paycheck, diploma, attention, acclaim, etc.), but it takes a great amount of faith and trust working a field for years on end that never seems to produce a crop. God uses this delay to reveal if our obedience is motivated by love or selfishness. Once our love stands the test of time, God will produce a bounty in our lives that will divinely overshadow our human efforts. And the world will know that God's promises stand true: "the righteous will enjoy the fruit of their deeds."

"Give, and you will receive. Your gift will return to you in full–pressed down, shaken together to make room for more, running over, and poured into your lap. The amount you give will determine the amount you get back" (Luke 6.38 NLT).

DAY 134

Great light

· — · — ·※· — · — · ·

"The people who walked in darkness have seen a great light; those who dwelt in a land of deep darkness, on them has light shone" (Isaiah 9.2 ESV).

There are many metaphors to describe Jesus in the New Testament: vine, shepherd, gate, cornerstone, bread, water, word, etc. However, one that Isaiah prophesies in the Old Testament by the inspiration of the Holy Spirit and that Jesus testifies to in the New Testament is "light." Our world is in darkness because the sins of humanity have separated us from a perfect God. We have been given free will to dwell in the light of Christ, which ushers us into the presence of God, or we can remain in the darkness of separation from our Creator. The world will continue to remain dark until the completion of God's plans on this earth, yet Christians have an eternal burning light that guides our way. The darker the path, the better because we won't be able to use our eyes and place faith in our own understanding. As the atmosphere around us gets darker and the corruption of this world peaks, Christians must let go of trust in temporal things and cling tightly to the only Light that truly saves, Jesus. And once others see our peace even in the darkness, they will be drawn to the Light as well.

"The fundamental principle of Christianity is to be what God is, and He is light." – John Hagee

DAY 135

Can't Save Yourself

"Surely God is my salvation; I will trust and not be afraid. The LORD, the LORD himself, is my strength and my defense; he has become my salvation" (Isaiah 12.2 NIV).

In our society today, much emphasis is placed on individual strength, ability, talent and determination. These are all great attributes, but they give us very little authority and meaning outside of our relationship with God. When we focus too much on this temporal life and worldly acclaim, we can forget that there's an eternity to which we belong. This world in which we now live is merely a shadow and a whisper of an eternal existence. The impact of anything done outside the will of God–no matter how brilliant and awe-inspiring–will not continue with God in heaven. Only actions done in obedience to God will make a lasting impact on eternity. In light of this truth, our strength is weak and our ability is lacking without the hand of God powering our actions. For this reason, we must always place our hope and trust in God's strength and salvation. We can do everything in our power to follow the Holy Spirit's leading, knowing that God is in complete control and He holds our victory. Only through Christ have we achieved the salvation of our sins, and He releases His saving work to every area of our lives–emotional, physical, intellectual, relational and spiritual.

"For God did not give us a spirit of timidity (of cowardice, of craven and cringing and fawning fear), but [He has given us a spirit] of power and of love and of calm *and* well-balanced mind *and* discipline *and* self-control" (2 Timothy 1.7 AMP).

DAY 136

The Watchman

"For thus the Lord said to me, 'Go, get a watchman; let him announce what he sees'" (Isaiah 21.6 ESV).

A watchman stood on the highest tower built onto the fortified wall surrounding the city. Day and night, he would stay attentive to his surroundings, looking for the coming presence of friend or foe. When he saw movement in the distance, he would report it to the city's authorities, warning the town of what was to come. Today, we call a spiritual watchman a prophet. A prophet is a woman or man who attentively waits at the foot of God's throne, looking and listening for the movement of God and proclaiming His words. Although everyone is gifted with prophecy in some capacity in their lives, God does anoint a portion of His people with the gift of prophecy. Like any spiritual gift (teaching, edifying, shepherding, helps, etc.), this gift can be used incorrectly and actually lead people away from God instead of toward Him. First, a prophet must only speak the words of God, so his/her words should never contradict the Bible (Jeremiah 23.30 & 2 Peter 1.21). Second, the prophet must use his/her gift for the edifying of the local and global church in love, which means the prophet needs to be under authority at a Christ-centered church (Romans 13.1 & 1 Corinthians 13.2). Third, the prophet usually does not translate the information into action for the people–he/she merely reports what has been heard from God. God uses other spiritually gifted people to use the information for decisive plans: Ezra, the prophet and Nehemiah, the leader, worked together building the wall. God gives each of us a portion of His divine revelation that works in relation to the portion given to others in the Body of Christ (1 Corinthians 12).

"Dear friends, do not believe every spirit, but test the spirits to see whether they are from God, because many false prophets have gone out into the world" (1 John 4.1 NIV).

DAY 137

Beyond the Former Things

"Forget the former things; do not dwell on the past. See, I am doing a new thing! Now it springs up; do you not perceive it? I am making a way in the desert and streams in the wasteland" (Isaiah 43.18-19 NIV).

God is both a God of order and a God of creativity. There are no limits to what He can do, but there also seems to be a system of how He operates in the lives of His beloved people. After walking this life with Jesus for a while, one might start to come to the conclusion that God's character is simultaneously familiar and surprising. So many times Christians want to categorize God's movements to one side of the spectrum: either very patterned or always new. But God is both and all, thus causing us always to rely daily on His Spirit. God does "make a way in the desert," but we have to actually travel through the wilderness with Him. God will do something "new" in our lives, but we have to willingly and joyful walk through the mundane and the normal. Many people will never get to the supernatural because they are not willing to wander the natural with Jesus. We must never forget that our Savior, Jesus Christ, was both flesh and spirit. He had to plod down the same ordinary paths that we find ourselves on today. God created power within the commonplace. We can anticipate God to create something "new" in our lives when we've obediently made our way through the "former things."

"No one can sum up all God is able to accomplish through one solitary life, wholly yielded, adjusted, and obedient to Him." – D. L. Moody

DAY 138

And God Came Down

✦ ─ • ─ ✦ ─ • ─ • ─ ✦

"Oh, that you would burst from the heavens and come down! How the mountains would quake in your presence!" (Isaiah 64.1 NLT).

The prophets only dreamed about the day and age that we live in today. If only God would "burst from the heavens and come down!" We are so blessed to be living in the New Testament age where we have the blood of Jesus Christ, atoning the entire world. All the striving God's Children did after the laws were set on Mount Sinai through the Prophet Moses is finally finished. We know from history and from our own lives that we can never live a life pleasing to a Holy God in our own strength. We need the sacrifice of the Pierced Lamb to not only forgive us, but to also make our efforts acceptable to God. God came down from heaven, allowed Himself to be born into the flesh of humanity. He lived the perfect life on earth and gave us all His righteousness through His Finished Work on the Cross! Jesus is God with us. He is God in the flesh. He is our Sabbath Rest from human striving. He is the New Wine Covenant, reconciling us back to our Creator God. We should rejoice today with the clap and applause of the mountains—God has come down to us!

"Look! The virgin will conceive a child! She will give birth to a son, and they will call him Immanuel, which means 'God is with us'" (Matthew 1.23 NLT).

DAY 139

Two Sins

"My people have committed two sins: They have forsaken me, the spring of living water, and have dug their own cisterns, broken cisterns that cannot hold water" (Jeremiah 2.13 NIV).

We sometimes condescend the Old Testament Chosen People for worshipping idols instead of the Living God; however, we do the same thing today. Instead of wood and metal idols, we worship our will as the ultimate voice of truth in our lives. Although we claim God's authority with our words, our actions declare that we are choosing to be our own mini Gods. We have forsaken God and placed ourselves on His throne. But a throne is a very sad place for any imperfect human to be. Little do we know that we have stopped drinking from the "spring of living water" and opted for "broken cisterns" of our own self-effort and personal dictatorship. We are so busy listening to our flesh that we have become desensitized to the powerful prompting of the Holy Spirit. When we die and come before the seat of judgment, we will finally see that our sweat and strength was wasted doing things outside the will of God. Yes, God loves us and will bless us, but we will be confronted with the reality that we could have accomplished so much for God's eternal kingdom if we would have drunk deeply from the spring of living water instead of forging our own useless wells. Understanding that we have such a short life to make an eternal impact should motivate us daily to rely on the Holy Spirit to lead us into His truth.

"When the Spirit of truth comes, he will guide you into all the truth, for he will not speak on his own authority, but whatever he hears he will speak, and he will declare to you the things that are to come" (John 16.13 ESV).

DAY 140

Truth Snack

· — · —❋— · — · —

"When I discovered your words, I devoured them. They are my joy and my heart's delight, for I bear your name, O Lord God of Heaven's Armies" (Jeremiah 15.16 NLT).

Eating Scripture can be paralleled to eating food, but instead of benefiting the body directly, consuming the Bible benefits the spirit, which in turn benefits every aspect of a person's life–mind, body, soul, relationships, work, ministry, etc. Not consuming God's Holy Word daily is literally like starving oneself spiritually. Christians must have God's Word in order to live a life of faith victoriously. God's Word can be found in many mediums: lyrics, novels, poetry, sermons, testimonies, etc., and Christians who surround themselves with several buffers of His Truth will stand strong. Consuming God's Word prepared by others is very helpful, especially when we are young Christians or when we are in a season of rest. However, eating verses straight from the Source packs a powerful punch of nutrition. Just like whole foods, "whole Scripture" may take time to digest raw, but spiritual goodness will destroy worldly toxins and boost faith energy in our lives. And once we consume a portion of the Holy Spirit's revelation for us personally, we can prepare what we learned as a "Truth Snack" for others to taste, eat and enjoy.

"Preach the word; be prepared in season and out of season; correct, rebuke and encourage–with great patience and careful instruction" (2 Timothy 4.2 NIV).

DAY 141

Desperately Sick

"The heart is deceitful above all things, and desperately sick; who can understand it?" (Jeremiah 17.9 ESV).

It seems like such a negative idea to call the heart "desperately sick." Before the Fall when humanity allowed sin to enter the world, God created our hearts in His image and they were good (Genesis 1.27 & 31). But sin is death, and it corrupts everything–both physically and spiritually (1 Cor. 15.21). Many people like the thought that we are born perfect into this world, and it is society that corrupts us. However, the Bible explains that we are all born sinners, separated from a Holy God (Romans 3.23). There is hope, though, through the work of Jesus Christ on the cross. Yes, we fall short of the glory of God, but Jesus died to give us His righteousness (Romans 3.22). He transforms our corrupted hearts into new hearts that love Him (Ez. 36.26). Without Jesus, our hearts will deceive others and even ourselves. And when we hide areas of sin from the revealing work of the Holy Spirit, the sickness and darkness will continue to poison our entire lives. We can allow God full access to our hearts–the beautiful and the ugly–knowing that He loves us no matter what and nothing surprises Him. Once the Holy Spirit has full reign of our hearts, He will begin the process of transforming us into the perfect image of Christ from glory to glory (2 Cor. 3.18).

"And he who searches our hearts knows the mind of the Spirit, because the Spirit intercedes for God's people in accordance with the will of God" (Romans 8.27 NIV).

DAY 142

A Voice for God

"This is what the LORD Almighty says: 'Do not listen to what the prophets are prophesying to you; they fill you with false hopes. They speak visions from their own minds, not from the mouth of the LORD'" (Jeremiah 23.16 NIV).

A prophet is someone who speaks the heart of God. God places a word into a prophet's mouth, and the prophet is now accountable to declare His words when the Holy Spirit wills it. Prophets who speak opinions that blatantly go against God's Word, the Bible, are obviously misguided and false prophets. However, the tricky distinction occurs when a false word is spoken that pronounces what we want to hear, not necessarily the true heart of God. Truth spoken in love is not always pleasant and doesn't always align with our plans. We may gravitate towards people who will agree with our wants and desires, and who will declare that our will is part of God's plan. But what if they are simply trying to please us? What if they really haven't heard a confirmation from the Lord about our situations? Christians must be very careful when they are encouraging people. We don't want to give them "false hopes" in the Lord. When we speak God's authority with our own mouths, we have now set ourselves up as prophets; and if we are not seeking the will of the Holy Spirit, our advice may be opposing the very heart of God. We can easily transform into false prophets when we don't daily commune with God. Love compels us to walk in truth. An encouraging word leads to heartache if it opposes the true heart of God. Fear of the Lord will ensure that we never presume to speak our minds, for we must only speak His heart.

"Most importantly, I want to remind you that in the last days scoffers will come, mocking the truth and following their own desires" (2 Peter 3.3 NLT).

DAY 143

Confined with God

"Ask me and I will tell you remarkable secrets you do not know about things to come" (Jeremiah 33.3 NLT).

We all know those people who always have something to say about what God is showing them. During every conversation we have with them, they describe how God has revealed certain insight to them. Their speech is full of words like "The Holy Spirit taught me this" or "God told me that." And we wonder how they get their ears so tuned into God. Jeremiah also heard a lot from God. The book named after him in the Bible contains a plethora of "This is what the Lord says" and "The Lord gave another message to Jeremiah" lines. In fact, the Lord told Jeremiah to ask, and He would share "remarkable secrets" with him. The answer to why Jeremiah heard so much from God is found in verse 1 of Jeremiah 33: "While Jeremiah was still confined in the courtyard of the guard…" Jeremiah was "confined," and with the isolation, all the world's distractions were gone, and he was able to focus on the Lord. It should come as no surprise that the people who hear most from the Lord are the people who take time to isolate themselves in order to listen and speak with Him. If we want a relationship with God where He tells us "remarkable secrets," we must take time out of our busy schedules to sit with Him.

"Very early in the morning, while it was still dark, Jesus got up, left the house and went off to a solitary place, where he prayed" (Mark 1.35 NIV).

DAY 144

A Harvest of Good

"She defiled herself with immorality and gave no thought to her future. Now she lies in the gutter with no one to lift her out. 'Lord, see my misery,' she cries. 'The enemy has triumphed'" (Lamentations 1.9 NLT).

Traditionally, Jeremiah is believed to have written the sorrowful, poetic book of *Lamentations*. It is suggested that *Lamentations* was written shortly after the fall of Jerusalem in 586 B.C. Along with the other prophets, Jeremiah had spent much of his young life warning God's Chosen People about their consistent disobedience to God's commands. Instead of heeding God's conviction through the prophets, God's people ignored them and continued to forsake God with no thought to their future repercussions. God's anger in this situation is perfectly in line with His love. Out of His love, He had to discipline a people who no longer listened to His warnings by allowing the full effect of their negative choices to cave in on them. God's People lost everything. God knows that as Christians we will always make mistakes, and because of His amazing grace, He forgives us. However, what ignites God's righteous anger is when He convicts us of our sin, and we do not heed the promptings of the Holy Spirit. We reap what we sow, and God desires that all His children reap a harvest of blessings. And He will warn us when our actions today are creating disasters for tomorrow.

"Do not be deceived: God cannot be mocked. A man reaps what he sows. Whoever sows to please their flesh, from the flesh will reap destruction; whoever sows to please the Spirit, from the Spirit will reap eternal life" (Galatians 6.7-8 NIV).

DAY 145

New Mercies

"The faithful love of the Lord never ends! His mercies never cease. Great is his faithfulness; his mercies begin afresh each morning" (Lamentations 3.22-23 NLT).

The worst thing that could happen had happened. Israel's Promised Land had been taken from them. Reading how God established His children in the Promised Land through the demonstration of His love and power in the Old Testament makes the destruction of the Chosen Nation that much more heart-wrenching. No wonder *Lamentations'* description of Israel's affliction is so passionate and outspoken. The people of Israel had forsaken their God, and the full force of their consequences devoured them almost to extinction. Yet, even in the midst of the turmoil and heartache, the writer of *Lamentations* declares that God's mercies are new every morning. No matter the circumstances we find ourselves in, God will pour out His mercy and compassion on us when we turn to Him. Our situation may not change right away, but we can have the greatest gift of all–reconciliation with God our Father through His mighty grace. And when we stay obedient to the Holy Spirit, God will transform us and our lives into a pleasing aroma to Him, changing our ashes into something beautiful for His glory (Isaiah 61.3).

"For we are to God the pleasing aroma of Christ among those who are being saved and those who are perishing" (2 Corinthians 2.15 NIV).

DAY 146

My Portion

"The LORD is my portion," says my soul, "therefore I will hope in him" (Lamentations 3.24 ESV).

As Christians, the Lord is our portion; and this is a truth that will change every person's life when he/she fully grasps the weight of it. Although we could never contain the vastness of God—He is the Creator and beyond our understanding—His grace does enable us to be filled with His presence through the Holy Spirit. Every day we have a mighty portion of the Lord, and He will shape our portion to fit our daily needs. Moreover, when we consider the character of God–full of mercy, grace, love, hope, provision, joy, peace, etc.–we realize that we are tapped into a supernatural River of Living Water that is not based on our temporal circumstances. Yes, it is nice when this world offers us happy situations, and I do think we are supposed to enjoy the mountaintop moments we experience during this life, but for certain we will also walk through the "valley of shadows." And during both our valley and mountaintop experiences, we can claim the portion of the Lord. He is our joy and hope. He is our peace and love. Through the Father, we have an abundance of grace and mercy, empowering us to make our lives a pleasing offering for His intended purpose and victory. We will never thirst, for our soul has learned to hope in the Lord.

"…but whoever drinks the water I give them will never thirst. Indeed, the water I give them will become in them a spring of water welling up to eternal life" (John 4.14 NIV).

DAY 147

Depravity of Walking Away

"The hands of compassionate women have boiled their own children; they became their food during the destruction of the daughter of my people" (Laminations 4.10 ESV).

No one would have thought that a mother would boil and eat her own children. The fact that the writer of Lamentations saw this as a first-hand account is shocking, especially when we take into account that the people committing this heinous act were not strangers to God; rather, they were God's Chosen People. What started as a slow forsaking of God's commands turned into one of the most terrible acts of depravity ever documented. It is obvious that God's Chosen people have walked away from God, and now they are consuming the very crop of disobedience that they planted. As we walk down our paths of faith, we may get enticed to choose a step that veers a little from God's chosen direction for us. The step is done in disobedience, but it seems innocent and trivial at first. However, one step leads to another and to another until we reach a point of utter depravity far from God's instruction and blessing. We must count the cost before we start down a road that leads outside of God's will. If we truly open ourselves up to the end result of our poor choices, we may quickly repent and run back to our Father. Better yet, we may skip the horrible diversion altogether and stay on the path of righteousness that only comes when our steps remain obedient to God.

"Do not turn to the right or the left; keep your foot from evil" (Proverbs 4.27 NIV).

DAY 148

Restore Us

"Restore us, O Lord, and bring us back to you again! Give us back the joys we once had!" (Lamentations 5.21 NLT).

Let's face it: Lamentations is a depressing book to read, which makes it an even harder book to write about. We get a bird's eye view of a once prosperous, God-centered kingdom falling into complete devastation because they walked away from their God. The only hope they had left was that God may restore them, but even that hope was more of a desperate plea. It's hard for us to find hope when we are completely devastated, but Jesus is our hope. He came into this world, knowing that we needed help. God understood that we couldn't make it through this life alone, so He sent His Son, Jesus, to die for our sins. Once Jesus swapped His righteousness for the world's sin, God's Spirit (the Holy Spirit) was unleashed onto the earth. Any person who finds forgiveness of sins through Jesus' Finished Work on the Cross receives the Holy Spirit in their lives. And no matter how dark and how desperate our circumstances and situations may be, the Holy Spirit will travel it with us! We are restored to holy God even in our imperfect state. We can have joy knowing that God is right here with us during the good times and the bad.

"And I will ask the Father, and he will give you another Advocate, who will never leave you" (John 14.16 NLT).

DAY 149

Eating God's Word

"And he said to me, 'Son of man, feed your belly with this scroll that I give you and fill your stomach with it.' Then I ate it, and it was in my mouth as sweet as honey" (Ezekiel 3.3 ESV).

God anointed Ezekiel a watchman over the people. He also gave Ezekiel His words and visions to share with others in order to warn and prepare them for things to come. Thousands of years later, Ezekiel's writings are still empowering God's people to live in His Truth. But before Ezekiel was chosen to fulfill this special purpose that God had entrusted to him, he needed to "eat" God's Scroll, His Holy Word contained in the Bible. God gave Ezekiel a vision of him literally consuming the Holy Scrolls, which parallels the time Ezekiel (as a priest) spent reading God's Word. As Christians, God has a special purpose designed specifically for us to fulfill; however, we must be spending time in His Word. The Bible gives us the spiritual fuel we need to accomplish our supernatural goals for God. When we understand how amazing and satisfying the Bible is to the entirety of our lives, the verses will literally taste "as sweet as honey" to us. God wants to take us to new levels of faith, but we must not starve spiritually on the way. We can gorge ourselves on His Word, knowing that our strength and endurance will have the sustenance they need so we can finish our race strong (2 Timothy 4.7).

"I am the living bread that came down from heaven. Whoever eats this bread will live forever. This bread is my flesh, which I will give for the life of the world" (John 6.51 NIV).

DAY 150

More Than They

"She has rebelled against My judgments by doing wickedness more than the nations, and against My statutes more than the countries that are all around her; for they have refused My judgments, and they have not walked in My statutes" (Ezekiel 5.6 NKJV).

It seems like just yesterday that Joshua was ushering the Children of God into their Promised Land. God was doing miracles left and right, and great walls of resistance tumbled down by faith, unleashing the fledgling nation of Israel into victorious independence. The people declared their allegiance to God. They would serve no other God, and they would obey His commands (Joshua 24.15-24). They rooted out the evil in their Promised Land and established themselves as a nation with only one King: Jehovah God! But it didn't take long for the people to forsake their God, and soon enough, the Bible says in Ezekiel that they were more wicked than the other nations around them–nations that did not know God! How could this be? How could a Chosen People in love with their God drift so far away from Him and His commands? It is devastating to watch a blessed nation fall from the very Source of their blessing. God is the maker of all that is good, and He even works out the evil created by free will into His eternal good for those who love Him (Romans 8.28). We need to be careful not to fall in love with the blessings more than the Blessing Maker. God is the gift! He is our blessing! Through Jesus Christ and His finished work on the Cross, we get to enjoy the Gift of God every day!

"O Lord, You are the portion of my inheritance and my cup; You maintain my lot" (Psalm 16.5 NKJV).

DAY 151

Bossy Pots

"Will you still say, 'I am a god,' in the presence of those who kill you, though you are but a man, and no god, in the hands of those who slay you?" (Ezekiel 28.9 ESV).

Ezekiel has several prophecies against the leaders of his day. The prophecy found in Ezekiel 28.9 is specifically to the King of Tyre who had set himself up as a god in his heart and kingdom. His wealth and power had gone to his head, and he forgot or never comprehended the truth that the God of the Universe is the creator and giver of everything in heaven and earth. Although today people don't usually declare themselves as a "god" to others, they do position themselves in a god-like role in their hearts. Any time we put our own needs, desires, decisions, thoughts, plans, etc. before God's, we automatically have set ourselves on His throne in our hearts and minds, and the repercussions of our selfish pride are devastating, only leading to darkness and death. The truth of the matter is that we are mortal and will all one day die. Only our Creator God is ageless, dwelling outside of time in the supernatural realm of eternity (Revelation 1.8). We are His creation, and we will never be able to comprehend the magnitude of His Kingdom of heaven and earth; however, we can remain obedient co-heirs of His plan through Jesus Christ (Romans 8.17). But the most amazing aspect of our Creator God is that He loved us so much that He willingly stepped inside our earth, wearing the decaying flesh of humanity and dying for the sins of the world. He died on this earth, piercing His hands and feet, so that even in our sinful state He can be the King of Kings and Lord of Lords of our lives.

"It is bad for the one who works against His Maker. He is just a clay pot among the other pots of earth. Will the clay say to the pot-maker, 'What are you doing?' or, your work say, 'He has no hands'?" (Isaiah 45.9 NLV).

DAY 152

Giving Up Control

"And when I bring you back, people will say, 'This former wasteland is now like the Garden of Eden! The abandoned and ruined cities now have strong walls and are filled with people!'" (Ezekiel 36.35 NLT).

Something truly stunning happens when we finally give God the mess of our lives: He turns our "wasteland" into a "Garden of Eden." But when we allow our pride and shame to prevent us from giving our lives fully to God, we stop God's amazing work of redemption from transforming us and our situations. The truth, however, is that if Jesus' work on the Cross was strong enough to cleanse all history of its sin, it is more than capable of cleansing us of our poor choices and circumstances. We just need to come to the conclusion that we obviously don't know what we are doing, and we need our awesome God to take over. We can rely on God's strength and wisdom when we realize that we don't have the answers and we don't know how to find "paths of righteousness" on our own (Psalm 23.3). God wants to shine His glory in our lives, so this unbelieving world can see His love and mercy in us. He wants to create something beautiful in our lives not because we deserve it, but because of His great love for us as our Heavenly Father. But God will not force us to follow His lead. He waits for us to freely give Him the reigns of our lives, so He can create something beautiful out of our ashes (Isaiah 61.3).

"He makes me lie down in green pastures. He leads me beside still waters. He restores my soul. He leads me in paths of righteousness for his name's sake" (Psalm 23.2-3 ESV).

DAY 153

Sons of Zadok

"They will teach My people the difference between what is holy and what is not. And they will teach them to know what is unclean and what is clean" (Ezekiel 44.23 NLV).

In Ezekiel chapter 44, God gives Ezekiel some amazing prophecies about a certain group of people called the Sons of Zadok. While the other religious leaders had neglected the Temple of God and/or worshipped false gods with their religious duties, the Sons of Zadok maintained a pure relationship of service to the Lord. Because of their faithfulness, they were the only ones allowed to minister before the Lord at His holy place near His table. This intimacy with the Lord opened their eyes and hearts to the difference between what is holy and what is not, so they could actually teach others how to live in holiness before the Lord. This faithfulness to the Lord stemmed from the original Zadok who didn't abandon King David, God's anointed king, when his sons clamored to dethrone him. In fact, Zadok helped carry the Ark of the Covenant as David once again found himself wandering the wilderness, wondering if God was going to allow his kingship to end (2 Samuel 15.24). As Christians, we must endeavor to be like the Sons of Zadok. When the entire world neglects the Temple and dwelling place of God (our bodies–cumulating to the Church–are now the temples of God because of Jesus' accomplished work on the cross), we can remain faithful to cultivating our relationship with God's Spirit in us personally and collectively as the Body of Christ. As we remain faithful to our relationship to the Lord, He will continue His best work in us. And one day He will set us apart from the crowd, allowing us to minister to Him personally, so we can teach others everything He shares with us during our time at His table.

"You cannot drink the cup of the Lord and the cup of demons too; you cannot have a part in both the Lord's Table and the table of demons" (1 Corinthians 10.21 NIV).

DAY 154

Reading Path

"…Train these young men in the language and literature of Babylon" (Daniel 1.4 NLT).

Some people are fearful about consuming literature that is not necessarily a designated part of the Christian genre. Indeed, the Scriptures are absolutely the most profound and important work for any of us to read. Jesus is the Word, and His thoughts towards us are found in the Bible (John 1.1). We must drink from His Living Water (the Bible) daily, so our spirits find the nourishment they need to flourish. However, when other "supplemental" writings that are rich in perspective are consumed by a reader and submitted under the authority of the Holy Spirit, a more dynamic and layered understanding is gained. Daniel in the Bible found himself taken from his home of Israel and placed in the courts of the Babylonians. He had to learn their language and read their literature. But instead of the foreign literature swaying him away from Truth found in Scriptures, he became more knowledgeable and better able to shine God's glory in new, larger capacities. To be sure, we must always base our reading time on the approval of the Holy Spirit, and there are definitely works of literature we should protect our hearts from (Proverbs 4.23). But when God gets a hold of us, we will find that the reading path He lays before us will only solidify His holiness and the perfection of His Word. God's wonder can be found in the resources all around us.

"We are perishing for lack of wonder, not for lack of wonders." – G.K. Chesterton

DAY 155

Eternal Kingdom

"In the time of those kings, the God of heaven will set up a kingdom that will never be destroyed, nor will it be left to another people. It will crush all those kingdoms and bring them to an end, but it will itself endure forever" (Daniel 2.44 NIV).

The New Testament goes into detail about the Kingdom of God or Kingdom of Heaven. Jesus successfully established His Eternal Kingdom in this life by dying for the sins of humanity and reconciling God's perfect plan on earth through a system of grace and faith (Ephesians 2.8). Two thousand years ago, John the Baptist was the voice crying out from the wilderness, preparing us for Jesus' ministry: "Repent, for the kingdom of heaven has come near" (Matthew 3.2). When the religious leaders during the time of Jesus asked Him when the Kingdom of Heaven would arrive, Jesus answered that this eternal kingdom was already with them (Luke 17.20-21). Daniel prophesied about this Kingdom hundreds of years before Jesus walked this earth. God's children wanted a savior to come in strength and power to force the world under his rule. However, Jesus came lowly and meek, living a perfect life and receiving all who would freely come to Him (Matthew 11.29 & Isaiah 53.2-3). This earth, this life is merely a shadow of an amazing Eternal Kingdom that God has created for His people, but our only chance in the door is Jesus Christ. He is the gate, the key, the way, the light (John 10.9). None of us can get to a Holy God without the righteousness of Jesus Christ. No matter how good enough we think we are, we will always fall short of the glory of God (Romans 3.23). God has created an eternal life with Him, but only when we accept the gift of salvation through Jesus Christ will we be able to be with God for eternity in heaven.

"Jesus answered, 'I am the way and the truth and the life. No one comes to the Father except through me'" (John 14.6 NIV).

DAY 156

The Power of Humility

- • ——— • ——— ☼ ——— • ——— • •

"Then he continued, 'Do not be afraid, Daniel. Since the first day that you set your mind to gain understanding and to humble yourself before your God, your words were heard, and I have come in response to them'" (Daniel 10.12 NIV).

Daniel's words to God were heard, and God responded to them. What did Daniel do to deserve God's attentive ear? Why was Daniel so esteemed by the Lord? The answer is not in Daniel's righteousness, for the Bible says that all have sinned and fallen short of God's holy perfection (Romans 3.23). God knows our human nature. Like any good Father, He knows that His children are flawed and that we make mistakes. He does not expect us to be perfect, which is why He sent His Son, Jesus, to die for our sins in order to give us His righteousness. What God desires is our humility and our earnest desire to grow in our understanding of His character and His kingdom. If we are honest about our weaknesses, we are better able to rely on God's strength. If we are honest about our lack, we are better able to rely on God's abundance. If we are honest about our sin, we are better able to rely on Jesus' holiness and His finished work on the Cross. When we are broken to ourselves, God is better able to fill us with Himself. Humility does not mean perfection and it does not mean weakness. Humility means we have an objective understanding of our design–weaknesses and strengths– and we know beyond a doubt that we are nothing without God. God created us, formed us in His image, gave us His Spirit and placed us on this earth at this particular time for a purpose. All we can offer Him for everything He has given us is our obedience, trust, faith, love and heart.

"The fear of the LORD is the instruction of wisdom; and before honor is humility" (Proverbs 15.33 KJV).

DAY 157

Persecution

"And some of the wise will fall victim to persecution. In this way, they will be refined and cleansed and made pure until the time of the end, for the appointed time is still to come" (Daniel 11.35 NLT).

There are many layers to Daniel's prophesies–some speak to actual events throughout time and others speak metaphorically to a Believer's personal life. Just like the Bible influences the world-view of all history, the Bible also dives deeply within each of us, applying truth to our inner and outer lives. Daniel has a vision of a time when God's Children will fall under great persecution. This vision can include the Israelites during the Maccabean Revolt, the New Testament Church during seasons of persecution, End Time persecution for all believers and/or the lives of God's followers personally. The gist of the verse is that God allows persecution into this world because He knows that it is the struggle that refines us. Just like we lift weights or run to work out our physical muscles, God uses the struggles of this life to strengthen and build our spiritual muscles. We obviously need to grow spiritually; otherwise, God would call us to heaven right when we receive Christ as our Lord and Savior. For this reason, we can't run away from difficulty or hide safely in our own little worlds. We must follow the Holy Spirit's leading, and many times He leads us into situations that seem scary and uncomfortable. But if God is calling us, we can always claim the final victory in Christ.

"Dear friends, don't be surprised at the fiery trials you are going through, as if something strange were happening to you. Instead, be very glad—for these trials make you partners with Christ in his suffering, so that you will have the wonderful joy of seeing his glory when it is revealed to all the world" (1 Peter 4.12-13 NLT).

DAY 158
The Book End

"At that time Michael, the archangel who stands guard over your nation, will arise. Then there will be a time of anguish greater than any since nations first came into existence. But at that time every one of your people whose name is written in the book will be rescued" (Daniel 12.1 NLT).

We don't need to know Bible Eschatology (study of end time events) to see what is already a prevalent theme in our culture. Movies, television shows, books, songs and art have all analyzed the topic of "What happens when the world ends?" Whether by ice, comets, aliens or atomic weapons, people have considered the possibility of this organic earth wasting away and/or dying in a cataclysmic event. Life as we know it is fading away. Our bodies die, generations die, civilizations die and this earth will eventually die. However, as Christians, we have hope in a New Heaven and New Earth (Revelation 21.1). We also have the promise of eternal bodies and rebirth in God's Eternal Kingdom (2 Corinthians 5.1-5, John 3.3 & Romans 6.4). However, in our sinful state, we are separated from the Father. Based on our own merit we cannot dwell in the presence of a Holy God in heaven with our decaying sin on board. We must be holy as God is holy. God knew we couldn't reach this right-standing (righteousness) alone, so He sent Himself into the world to take our sins and give us His righteousness (Romans 3.23 & John 3.16). Through Jesus Christ, God's love and law co-exist. Those who accept Jesus' finished work on the Cross and receive Him as Lord and Savior will have their names "written in the book" that will rescue them from an eternity void of God (hell).

"Lift up your eyes to the heavens, look at the earth beneath; the heavens will vanish like smoke, the earth will wear out like a garment and its inhabitants die like flies. But my salvation will last forever, my righteousness will never fail" (Isaiah 51.6 NIV).

DAY 159

Children of the Living God

"Yet the number of the children of Israel shall be like the sand of the sea, which cannot be measured or numbered. And in the place where it was said to them, 'You are not my people,' it shall be said to them, 'Children of the living God'" (Hosea 1.10 ESV).

Hosea is not a very uplifting book in the Bible. In fact, many harsh prophecies are declared against Israel because of their unfaithfulness to God. Just like an adulteress wife, the Children of God have been lusting after other gods, namely Baal. God who has been a faithful, doting husband to Israel will allow the rampant unfaithfulness of His people no longer. His hand of protection will be lifted, and the people of Israel will feel the full effects of their disobedience. However, in the midst of the devastating news, God vows redemption and reconciliation. God will fulfill the oath He made to Abraham that all nations will be blessed through his descendants and the promised Messiah. A voice crying out in the wilderness of time declares that all the people of earth can be counted as God's Children through faith in Jesus Christ and His finished work on the Cross (Matthew 3.9). This beautiful promise pierces the darkest moments of our lives today. As Christians, no matter what chaos, destructions or heartache we are experiencing, we can hold tightly to the Truth that we have salvation through Jesus Christ. Regardless of what this world throws at us, we can find peace and joy, knowing that we will someday dwell with God in Heaven where pain, suffering, sorrow and hopelessness will be no more.

"What's more, the Scriptures looked forward to this time when God would declare the Gentiles to be righteous because of their faith. God proclaimed this good news to Abraham long ago when he said, 'All nations will be blessed through you'" (Galatians 3.8 NLT).

DAY 160

Tenderness in the Wilderness

"But then I will win her back once again. I will lead her into the desert and speak tenderly to her there" (Hosea 2.14 NLT).

God offers each of His children personal promises and plants in us a deep desire to see them fulfilled. Yet, the promises never come right away. In fact, God deliberately leads us into the wilderness of our dreams, so He can do an internal work in us, preparing us for the burden and blessing of those promises. Those promises are a part of God's glory, yet He withholds them for a time, so we can learn to trust and love Him with no strings attached. In the book of Hosea, God is about to lead Israel into the wilderness yet again. He has "lavished on her silver and gold," but they took God's gifts and worshipped Baal (a false god) with them (Hosea 2.8). Because of their unfaithfulness, He will strip them of everything, so Israel can learn to love and trust Him again. As Christians, we can't run away from our time in the wilderness. Both Jesus and John the Baptist did their time, working out their faith in the wilderness (Matthew 4.1 & Matthew 3.1). The wilderness is a necessary part of entering our Promised Land. There is no side-stepping or walking around it unless we want to wander for years and years. However, God promises us that He is especially "tender" in the wilderness. While we wait, He establishes a beautiful vineyard in our lives that will bear much fruit, bringing hope to those around us (Hosea 2.15). Once we learn to put our complete trust in God in the wilderness, our fulfilled promises will not cause us to forsake our relationship with Him.

"Those who do not hope cannot wait; but if we hope for that we see not, then do we with patience wait for it." – Charles Spurgeon

DAY 161

The Lowest Place

"Don't point your finger at someone else and try to pass the blame! My complaint, you priests, is with you" (Hosea 4.4 NLT).

It seems that everyone wants to be a leader. People are vying to have a position of power and are compromising Jesus' standard of "taking the lowest place" (Luke 14.10). The sad part is that Christians have totally bought into the race to be counted first. We are purchasing apps to falsely boost our Twitter numbers, spending hours on social media to gather comments and researching the latest marketing fads in order to get our name known. And we forget that John the Baptist preached in the wilderness–without using a marketing plan–and still the crowds came to him. To be certain, there was a time when he preached and no one came, but God unleashed his platform at the appropriated time. Christians must be careful during their desperate leap to be first. God has continually demonstrated in the Scriptures that He will hold the leaders accountable. God gives us a realm of influence when He can trust us to lead people into a real relationship with Him. God will make sure that we are not under the yoke of self-righteousness or a religious spirit; rather, we are humbly chasing after His heart, relying not on our perfection but His faithfulness. If we are having to coerce an audience, demanding their attention, it might not be our appointed time or designated place of influence. Instead, we can serve others, choosing the lowest place, and God will honor us with a position of influence when the time is right.

"Humble yourselves, therefore, under God's mighty hand, that he may lift you up in due time" (1 Peter 5.6 NIV).

DAY 162
The Hand of Fellowship

—⟡—

"I will return again to my place, until they acknowledge their guilt and seek my face, and in their distress earnestly seek me" (Hosea 5.15 ESV).

Once we receive Jesus as our Lord and Savior, God will always hold onto us with His hand of salvation. There is a covenant that binds us eternally to God through the blood of Jesus Christ. That is why the blood is so important—it is the ink that signed on the dotted line to rescue us from an eternity without God who dwells in heaven. Because of Sin, we are separated from a Holy God, but Jesus becomes that bridge, restoring our relationship with the Creator God. However, God also offers us His hand of fellowship, and this hand He will not force on us. We have a free will choice to grasp His hand of fellowship, to let it go and/or to ignore it. Much like a married couple who live separate lives; we can be bonded with God in covenant and have a faithless marriage with Him. Yet, Hosea offers us a simple way we can take hold of God's hand of fellowship and continue to hang on tightly. We can humble ourselves (admitting our sin) and seek God, which is actually the solution to fellowship in all our relationships. Pride is an isolated sin that pushes others away. However, humility draws others to us, including our Holy God. And like any good relationship, when we consistently seek God's face, we will come to know Him more and more, and He will return to His rightful place in our hearts—Center Stage!

"If you know that God loves you, you should never question a directive from Him. It will always be right and best. When He gives you a directive, you are not just to observe it, discuss it, or debate it. You are to obey it." – Henry Blackaby

DAY 163

Take Up Your Words

"Take words with you and return to the LORD. Say to him: 'Forgive all our sins and receive us graciously, that we may offer the fruit of our lips'" (Hosea 14.2 NIV).

Christians will eventually come to a place when we realize that we can't live victoriously alone. Like the prodigal son, God allows us to waste away our own efforts, abilities, resources and resolve until we come to the conclusion that we have nothing and can do nothing without God. Our self-reliance will never accomplish the fullness of God's will for our lives, but our brokenness to the Lord will unleash His power and strength in us. It's easy to say that we rely solely on the Lord, but we must take up our words and move them into action. Total submission on the Lord means we sacrifice our dreams and desires at the altar of His sovereignty. We recognize our weakness, so God's abundance can permeate the areas of our lack. God loves to shine His glory in our imperfect vessels, and our brokenness allows His light to radiate through. However, our words mean nothing if our lives do not reflect this submission to the Lord. God loves a broken and contrite spirit because it gives Him full reign to pour forth His grace in our lives, accomplishing the beautiful things He has prepared for those who love Him (1 Corinthians 2.9). When we place our entire dependence on God's faithfulness, we will find ourselves completely affixed to God and freely able to move where He leads.

"The sacrifice you desire is a broken spirit. You will not reject a broken and repentant heart, O God" (Psalm 51.17 NLT).

DAY 164

Torn Hearts

"Don't tear your clothing in your grief, but tear your hearts instead. Return to the Lord your God, for he is merciful and compassionate, slow to get angry and filled with unfailing love. He is eager to relent and not punish" (Joel 2.13 NLT).

Tearing the clothes was symbolic of deep grief, mourning and repentance; however, like many symbolic traditions, the "rending of garments" had become a hollow action with no implication of true humility. When Caiaphas, the High Priest, tore his clothing, claiming Jesus (God in the flesh) to be blasphemy, he did so in an atmosphere of self-righteousness. Pride caused Caiaphas to miss the Truth standing right in front of him, and as he tore his clothes, he puffed up his own deceived heart. His actions did not reflect the true nature of his heart. The Bible declares that God is merciful and wants to forgive us. But our actions mean nothing if they are not stemmed from a repentant heart. We can't be deceived in thinking that our symbolic actions are enough to ignite the Lord's compassion. The Lord sees the heart, and He knows when we are covering up a hardened heart with a torn facade (1 Samuel 16.7). True repentance comes when our heart is broken before the Lord, and we are exposed and vulnerable to the power and mercy of an almighty God. When we return to the Lord with torn hearts, He is eager to rescue, redeem and restore us because of His unfailing love towards us.

"Come, let us return to the LORD. He has torn us to pieces but he will heal us; he has injured us but he will bind up our wounds" (Hosea 6.1 NIV).

DAY 165

Two Kisses

"Then the LORD became jealous for his land and had pity on his people" (Joel 2.18 ESV).

Several emotions get a bad rap but none more than jealousy. Like almost everything, there is a holy and unholy expression of it. Christians are so quick to label things as inherently good or bad without realizing that it is the intent filling it that makes it so. Judas gave Jesus a Kiss of Death, yet Paul exhorts Believers to give each other a Holy Kiss (Luke 22.48 & 2 Corn. 13.12). A kiss is not inherently good or bad, but how we use it is. One kiss expresses betrayal and deception and the other expresses loyalty and love. There is one unshakeable truth: God is ALWAYS holy. So if God is holy, there must be a holy expression of jealousy. Jealousy can be ignited by "envy" or "zeal." Since God is the Creator of everything, we know that God's jealousy means He is zealous for His people, not envious. In the Book of Joel, God's people are being crushed by those around them–a result of their unfaithfulness–but God will redeem them with the unstoppable zeal of a father, fighting for His lost children. As Christians, we can remember that God will allow people to persecute us, but we can stand on the promise that He will fight our battles for us if we will only trust Him. He loves us and is jealous for us, and He has already claimed the ultimate victory.

"Fight the good fight of faith, and God will give you spiritual mercies." – George Whitefield

DAY 166

Early and Latter Rains

———————✴———————

"Be glad, O children of Zion, and rejoice in the Lord your God, for he has given the early rain for your vindication; he has poured down for you abundant rain, the early and the latter rain, as before" (Joel 2.23 ESV).

The Bible has many themes on the Promised Land. God plants our promises across the wilderness at the foot of Zion, the place where He dwells. When we start our journey to our dreams, we usually start in a flesh-centered atmosphere (our strength, our resources, our abilities, our plans, etc.) but as we wander with God, we eventually learn to walk in a spirit-centered atmosphere (His strength, His resources, His abilities, His Ultimate Plan, etc.). Since all our promises from God are "yes" in the spiritual realm with Christ, we must learn to be controlled by the spirit, so the promises can be brought into the natural realm through our obedience (2 Corinthians 1.20). God gives us these promises because they draw us out of our selfishness and into a Christ-centered state, which is the only way we can accomplish God's glorious plans in our lives (Psalm 85.5-7). As we start our journey to achieving our God-given dreams, the Holy Spirit will pour out His Spirit with the "early rain." This rain breaks up the soil of our hearts and allows God's seeds of promise to germinate. We obediently plant the seeds, working first in our flesh then embracing the work in the Spirit. And as we wait for the fruit of our obedience to ripen, we know that the Holy Spirit will pour out the "latter rain." This rain ripens our small, bitter fruit with the sweetness and the fullness of the Lord. Without God's Spirit raining down on our lives, our efforts could never bless others with the supernatural power of God that manifests in both this world and eternity. A Promised Land without the Living Water of the Holy Spirit is a wasteland of constant thirst and emptiness.

"She said, 'Give me another gift. You have already given me land in the Negev; now please give me springs of water, too.' So Caleb gave her the upper and lower springs" (Joshua 15.19 NLT).

DAY 167

Never Wasted

"The Lord says, 'I will give you back what you lost to the swarming locusts, the hopping locusts, the stripping locusts, and the cutting locusts. It was I who sent this great destroying army against you'" (Joel 2.25 NLT).

The Lord sent devastation to God's chosen people because they had forsaken Him. They disobeyed His commands and took control of their own destinies–no more relying on an All-knowing God. Therefore, the consequences of their decisions were devastating. God had already warned them to choose blessings or curses (Deuteronomy 30.19). However, once God's people repented, He was quick to redeem and restore them. But according to Joel 2.25, not only did God restore them, He gave them back everything they lost during the wasted years that their disobedience devoured their abundance. This is good news for us today! All of us have seasons in our lives where we know that we disobeyed God, and many of our years in relationship with Him were wasted in our self-occupied pride. However, the Lord says that if we humble ourselves and repent, He will restore everything we squandered. This means that no matter how much we messed up, we can always finish well. We can still gain our full reward from God; it is never too late for us! God has an infinite imagination and the world's resources at His disposal, so He can ALWAYS write a new Plan-A for our lives that still includes our fullest reward in Christ. We must never conclude that our bad decisions can prevent God from having His will accomplished through us. When we repent and submit our lives to God, He is more than capable of restoring all that we have lost.

"Therefore do not throw away your confidence, which has a great reward. For you have need of endurance, so that when you have done the will of God you may receive what is promised" (Hebrews 10.35-36 ESV).

DAY 168

A Warrior Heart

"Beat your plowshares into swords, and your pruning hooks into spears; let the weak say, 'I am a warrior'" (Joel 3.10 ESV).

We find in the Book of Joel that God is fighting for the people whom He loves. God will fight for us too. Whatever arena to which we are called, God has special plans for us in His battle for good on this earth. He can transform the everyday resources at our disposal to win victories in His Kingdom. Many of God's People in the Old Testament worked the land, cultivating fields of crops and vineyards. God encouraged His people to transform their "plowshares into swords" and their "pruning hooks into spears." Both these tools were used agriculturally, but God called His people to take those same tools to establish their destiny as People of the Lord! We also have tools that we use daily to accomplish the natural tasks that God has assigned us; however, as we are faithful at implementing these tools in God's service, He will call us to use those same tools in a spiritual battle that reaches into eternity. Whatever tool we use on a daily basis–computer, stethoscope, classroom, business, pulpit, home, hands, voice, etc. God will call us to use it for His glory and heaven's ultimate victory. We may not see ourselves as warriors for His kingdom, but God does. God calls us to reach past our limitations and situations and declare that we have warriors' hearts that are obedient to Him!

"He who is faithful in a very little thing is faithful also in much; and he who is unrighteous in a very little thing is unrighteous also in much" (Luke 16.10 NASB).

DAY 169

Point of Humility

"The words of Amos, who was among the shepherds of Tekoa, which he saw concerning Israel in the days of Uzziah king of Judah and in the days of Jeroboam the son of Joash, king of Israel, two years before the earthquake" (Amos 1.1 ESV).

Amos was a shepherd from Tekoa, a small village close to Bethlehem. He lived in a time when the rich were exploiting the poor, never considering that they would be accountable for their actions. Amos would definitely not have been respected, and his words would not have been honored during this time. A lowly shepherd would have been scoffed at and the people would never believe that Amos could write something eloquent, let alone of value. But Amos surprised them all. Not only did he declare the words of God with accuracy, he also declared them with literary brilliance. The shepherd was a writer! Too many literary devices to list, Amos obviously had a special gift to communicate. Who would have thought that such a skilled writer would come from a man who cared for sheep all day? But God does love to confound the world, and He knows that those He uses for His great purposes must have a point of humility. So we must not fight God's effort to humble us. We can't get upset when we feel like our talents are wasting away as we continue to walk faithfully in obscurity. God will use us when the time is right, and we will boldly put our talents to work, giving all glory to God. While we wait, we can get to know the love of our Heavenly Father more and more each day, relying on His faithfulness and filling our lives with belief in His promises.

"Instead, God chose things the world considers foolish in order to shame those who think they are wise. And he chose things that are powerless to shame those who are powerful. God chose things despised by the world, things counted as nothing at all, and used them to bring to nothing what the world considers important. As a result, no one can ever boast in the presence of God" (1 Corinthians 1.27-29 NLT).

DAY 170

Masterpiece Made Known

"For the Lord God does nothing without revealing his secret to his servants the prophets" (Amos 3.7 ESV).

So many times we run desperately to God, exhausted from trying to guess what He is doing in our lives. We feel lost and confused, and we wonder why God is not being clearer about His plans for us. Yes, there is a point of trust and step of faith that all Christians must incorporate in their journey as Believers in Christ; however, God does not leave us empty-handed and clueless. He has supplied us with His Word, with His Spirit and with His prophets. God has laid a foundation of His nature found in His responses and interactions with His people. There are principles rising up in every book of the Bible through the lives of biblical figures that can be applied to our lives personally. God wants to reveal His will to us. He wants us to find secure footing in His plans for our lives. We may not know every detail, but we should be aware of His movement in our day-to-day actives. We can read His Word every day. We can wait in the presence of the Holy Spirit, listening for His instruction. And we can seek the prophets/teachers/preachers of the Gospel for inspiration and direction. We are not alone in our race of faith. There are people who have gone before us who can encourage us, and there are people just starting their faith journey who need to hear words of encouragement from us. We can trust that God is a revealer of destiny. He wants us to claim the good purposes He has planned for us before time began.

"If God was faithful to you yesterday, you have reason to trust Him for tomorrow."
– Woodrow Kroll

DAY 171

Seeded in Flesh

"'Present your bread made with yeast as an offering of thanksgiving. Then give your extra voluntary offerings so you can brag about it everywhere! This is the kind of thing you Israelites love to do,' says the Sovereign Lord" (Amos 4.5 NLT).

God's Chosen People were continuing with their religious ceremonies that God had called them to long ago; however, their obedience had lost the true nature of repentance and worship. Instead of offering out of pure hearts, their intentions were all wrong. First, they were giving with hollow hearts, merely as an act of religious norms. Second, they were giving so they could brag about their "righteous" deeds. Third, they were giving in order to manipulate God and gain His favor by human effort. But God saw right through their false intentions, and Amos uses sarcasm to describe their deceitful hearts. The sad truth is that two people can give the same sacrifice to the Lord, but they each can have contrasting motives. An outward fruit is always tied to either the flesh or to the spirit. Any sacrifice made for the Lord that is seeded in the flesh (our own efforts, our own interest, our own control) will be birthed in the natural, thrive in the natural and die in the natural world. But a sacrifice for the Lord that is seeded in the spirit in response to the prompting of the Holy Spirit will be birthed in the supernatural, thrive in both the supernatural and the natural world and continue into eternity. We must be very careful that we are listening to the Holy Spirit's call to obedience and not to our own tactics of self-reliance. Our efforts may look pretty to the human eye, but God sees to the core of each of us. Any effort done outside of the will of God–no matter how good it looks–will have no lasting effect on eternity.

"Our greatest fear should not be of failure but of success at things in life that don't really matter." – Fancis Chan

DAY 172

A Harvest of Choices

"Hear this, you who trample on the needy and bring the poor of the land to an end, saying, 'When will the new moon be over, that we may sell grain? And the Sabbath, that we may offer wheat for sale, that we may make the ephah small and the shekel great and deal deceitfully with false balances'" (Amos 8. 4-5 ESV).

Amos lived in a society where his own countrymen were prospering at the expense of the poor and destitute. Israel and Judah were amassing wealth and times looked good for them; however, they were not in obedience to the Lord. The rich and the affluent were abusing their power, gaining wealth and living in sin for a brief moment. But little did they know that only a few years later they would lose everything, including their own name as an independent country. Christians may walk in their self-directed path for a time, and they may get away with their disobedience for a little while; but God's Word always stands firm. We reap what we sow. If we are sowing disobedience to God's commands, we will eventually reap the absence of His blessings. If we are sewing obedience to God's commands (found in Scripture and related to us daily by the Holy Spirit), we will eventually reap the fullness of God's blessings. There can be a delay before the full effects of our actions manifest in the natural because our seeds take time to ripen and mature. But to be certain, our seeds will come to term and we will eat from the harvest we have created. God's grace always forgives us but the principle of the harvest stands firm–the fruits of our labor whether for good or evil will manifest for all to see (Luke 12.3).

"Your potential is the sum of all the possibilities God has for your life." – Charles Stanley

DAY 173

New Wine

"Behold, the days are coming," says the Lord, "When the plowman shall overtake the reaper, And the treader of grapes him who sows seed; The mountains shall drip with sweet wine, And all the hills shall flow with it" (Amos 9.13 NKJV).

The writer of Amos prophesies that a New Wine would soon drip from the mountains and flow through all the hills of the earth. This wine represents redemption and salvation from the sins and efforts of humankind. The land will be so full of abundance that the people harvesting will gather the fruit just before a new crop is being planted! The Children of God have tried and tried to be good enough to meet God's holy standard only to fail time and time again. That Law was given to Moses on Mount Sinai to show God's people that they will always fall short of the glory of God (Romans 3.23). However, the New Wine of Jesus is about to fill the earth with a fresh covenant of salvation! Jesus calls His body, the bread, and His blood, the wine. In order to get to the New Wine, Jesus would have to take on the flesh of humankind, allowing His body to be broken, so His blood could pour forth into the earth! During the Last Supper, Jesus broke the bread and poured the wine for His disciples. He was symbolically showing them what they would witness first hand in just a few days on Passover. Jesus would become the new Passover Lamb, forgiving the sins of all the people of the world once and for all. The Sour Wine of bitterness was about to be transformed into the New Wine of Salvation, allowing the Living Water to penetrate this earth and bear fruit in all the lives connected to the Great Vine!

"And as they were eating, Jesus took bread, blessed and broke it, and gave it to the disciples and said, 'Take, eat; this is My body.' Then He took the cup, and gave thanks, and gave it to them, saying, 'Drink from it, all of you. For this is My blood of the new covenant, which is shed for many for the remission of sins'" (Matthew 26.26-28 NKJV).

DAY 174

Two Eagles

"Though you soar aloft like the eagle, though your nest is set among the stars, from there I will bring you down, declares the Lord" (Obadiah 1.4 ESV).

The eagle is a beautiful image of individuality and preeminence. Eagles are distinct from other birds because of the great heights of solo flight that they are able to soar. Because of their elevation in the sky, they surpass all other birds. This image can be applicable to Christians in two opposing ways. When we separate ourselves from the will of God and listen to our own hearts versus the heart of God, we begin to establish ourselves in our strength for our own glory. Since God is the King of the Universe and rightful receiver of all glory and praise, any person who tries to contain God's glory for him/herself will be brought down. However, if we stay obedient to God's will and seek to establish His glory in our lives, we become like eagles that always gain "new strength." We will continue our flight for God and never grow tired or weary because He will establish our great heights in Him. We won't have to concern ourselves with being brought down, since we are resting in the strength and power of the Lord. All we will have to do is hold on tight and get ready for an amazing ride.

"Yet those who wait for the LORD Will gain new strength; they will mount up with wings like eagles, They will run and not get tired, They will walk and not become weary" (Isaiah 40.31 NASB).

DAY 175

The Edomites

"Because of the violence done to our brother Jacob, shame shall cover you, and you shall be cut off forever" (Obadiah 1.10 ESV).

The Bible teaches us to forgive others. Once we forgive the people who have hurt us, we are released from the negative and ugly influences they have on our lives. God will turn our ashes into a crown of beauty once we let go of bitterness, shame and unforgiveness (Isaiah 61.3). We don't have to worry about justice being served because God also says that people reap what they sow (Galatians 6.7). The full effects of someone's hateful choices will eventually catch up. God's forgiveness is always available to all of us, but we are still accountable to the repercussions of our actions. The Edomites persecuted Israel during a time of humbling in their nation. God finished His correction of Israel, but once the nation was brought into submission to the Lord, God turned His attention to the Edomites. The prophecy for Edom was not a good one. In fact, they were "cut off forever." As Christians, we don't want to rejoice over the misery of others, but we can rejoice in both the mercy and justice of God. We can love and forgive others even when they hurt us, releasing ourselves from their spiral of bad decisions against God's commands. God will avenge us in His way and His timing with both His mercy and justice. We can let go of avenging ourselves, knowing that our Heavenly Father cares passionately for us.

"Mercy, detached from justice, grows unmerciful.'' – C.S. Lewis

DAY 176

The Day of the Lord

"For the day of the Lord is near upon all the nations. As you have done, it shall be done to you; your deeds shall return on your own head" (Obadiah 1.15 ESV).

"The day of the Lord" is seen as declaration of the coming Messiah in both His first coming (which happened over 2000 years ago) and His final coming (which will happen in the final days). Jesus is our Messiah. When He first entered our world, He broke His body, spilling out His atoning blood onto the earth. Because of the Finished Work of Jesus Christ on the Cross, we are reconciled back to God. When Jesus comes the second time, He will judge the earth. Therefore, the fullness of God's love will be poured out, which encompasses both His grace and mercy and His law and judgment. Jesus died on the cross not only to save us from our sins, but also so we can accomplish His will on this earth. We squander the life we have been blessed with when we are not about our Father's business. This doesn't mean we all need to be in fulltime ministry at a church or on the mission field. We can be in fulltime ministry with the Lord in the big and small areas of life to which He calls us. Ministry means to serve, and serving God every day in our natural daily tasks honors Jesus' sacrifice for us. So when Jesus does come back in His shining-greatness, He'll look upon our lives and tell us, "Well done, good and faithful servant!" (Matthew 25.23 NIV).

"If God is your partner, make your plans BIG!" – D.L. Moody

DAY 177

Running from God

"Then the men were exceedingly afraid and said to him, 'What is this that you have done!' For the men knew that he was fleeing from the presence of the Lord, because he had told them" (Jonah 1.10 ESV).

Out of God's great love for us, He will pursue us when we are living in disobedience, but we must be willing to admit it. Jonah knew and confessed to others that he was not obeying the Lord's commands. Jonah didn't try to twist God's commands to fit his personal agenda and he didn't try to deny his selfish actions. He confessed his wrong even if it meant he would be thrown out into the storm. When we truly love the Lord, we will know when we are not pleasing Him because every fiber in our bodies will feel the weight of our disobedience. In fact, just like Jonah, we will come to the point where we would rather be "thrown" into the storms of life rather than live in our disobedience one more day. When our flesh struggles against our spirit, the first step we must take is to confess our sins to a faithful person we respect. Pride will try to keep us miserable in our sin, but humility will lead us back into the loving arms of our Heavenly Father.

"Therefore confess your sins to each other and pray for each other so that you may be healed. The prayer of a righteous person is powerful and effective" (James 5.16 NIV).

DAY 178

Victory and Failure

"Then the men feared the Lord exceedingly, and they offered a sacrifice to the Lord and made vows" (Jonah 1.16 ESV).

Jonah had sinned against the Lord by trying to run away to Tarshish when God had called him to prophesy to Nineveh. While he was on the boat to Tarshish, God caused a great storm to threaten the boat and risk the lives of the workers on board. When the workers finally threw Jonah overboard, the storm quieted. Even though Jonah was living in sin, God was able to use the situation to further His glory and make believers out of the boat workers. God can use both our stories of triumph and our stories of defeat to establish His presence on this earth. When we admit our wrongs, God is able to build us back up again using His power and strength. Our testimonies of failure become showcases of God's love and faithfulness. Our stories of victory in Christ will shine God's glory, but our stories of defeat can be just as effective at showing His mercy and grace. Jonah's story is about a struggle of faith, which includes a message of disobedience and obedience. We can be honest about our victories and failures, knowing that God can use them both for His glory.

"All of this is for your benefit. And as God's grace reaches more and more people, there will be great thanksgiving, and God will receive more and more glory" (2 Corinthians 4.15 NLT).

DAY 179

A Declaration of Thanksgiving

"But I with the voice of Thanksgiving will sacrifice to you; what I have vowed I will pay. Salvation belongs to the Lord!" (Jonah 2.9 ESV).

Jonah's life was literally in the pit of despair. He found himself in the belly of a whale for three days. He would have been knee-deep in organic, decaying material surrounded by soggy darkness with no hope in sight. The hardest sacrifice to offer God is our thanksgiving when we find ourselves in our own personal pit of despair. When there is no hope and we are knee-deep in a desperate situation, thanksgiving feels like the last thing we can give God. We'll give Him our complaints, our prayers, our petitions…but not our thanksgiving. But very little can shine our faith in God more than when we offer God our praises even though everything seems lost. Thanking God when our situation is bleak shows that we place more belief in Him than we do in our natural circumstances. God wants to intervene on our behalf. He wants to bring His glory into our lives. But He'll allow the darkness to swallow us for a time, so we can learn to claim His light by faith. The most powerful declaration we can make during hard times is a thanksgiving of God's faithfulness. Make a choice to praise and thank God without ceasing, and His salvation will be a beacon in your life to all the world.

"The salvation of the righteous comes from the LORD; he is their stronghold in time of trouble" (Psalm 37.39 NIV).

DAY 180
A Second Chance

"Then the word of the Lord came to Jonah the second time...." (Jonah 3.1 ESV).

After Jonah was thrown into a storm and swallowed by a whale, God gave him a second chance to do what He had commanded Jonah to do. This time Jonah obeyed the Lord. If Jonah would have obeyed immediately, he would have spared himself all the additional trouble, but God stayed with him during every inch of the journey. God was in the mighty sea storm and God was in the pit of the sea monster with Jonah. God never left his side because Jonah did not deny the fact that he was running from God. Sometimes, it takes a few times for us to get it right and obey God's commands. But as long as we are willing to admit our struggle and embrace the fact that we are having trouble obeying God's command, He will continue to stay with us until we finally give up control and obey. God loves us and He knows that we are flawed mortals trying to follow a holy God. He is patient with us, and He will give us time to work through our issues until we finally come to the end of ourselves and take that scary step of faith He is asking of us.

"The Lord is good to everyone. He showers compassion on all his creation" (Psalm 145.9 NLT).

DAY 181

Do You do Well to be Angry?

"And the Lord said, 'Do you do well to be angry?'" (Jonah 4.4 ESV).

Jonah was angry with God. Jonah finally submitted to go to Nineveh and give the people a prophecy of doom and gloom because of their sinful living. But instead of the city hardening their hearts against God and His warning, they repented. And God relented from His anger and gave Nineveh a second chance—the very same second chance Jonah was given. Jonah was not happy about the second chance because the prophecy he had struggled so hard to give did not come true. Jonah's expectations of his steps of obedience were not realized, and he was disappointed. Many times we take steps of obedience for God only to be heartbroken by the results. However, God may not promise a certain result. Many times our own imagination envisions a glamorous finale to our faithful actions, and when the end does not turn out like we had hoped, we become upset with God. God rightly asks us during those times of disappointment, "Do you do well to be angry?" We are accountable for our actions, and God is accountable for the fruition of His plan on earth. We can't be angry at the results because we don't see the big picture of what God is accomplishing for His Kingdom. Some day in heaven we may have a clearer vision of things on earth, but right now we simply need to obey and trust God with the results.

"For the word of the Lord holds true, and we can trust everything he does" (Psalm 33.4 NLT).

DAY 182

Incurable Wounds

"For her wound is incurable, and it has come to Judah; it has reached to the gate of my people, to Jerusalem" (Micah 1.9 ESV).

Micah lived during a time in which Judah had not yet been annihilated by Babylon. But there was a sickness of sin in Judah that had festered so long that it finally made its way to the heart of Judah, which was Jerusalem where God's Holy Temple was located. God wanted to heal Judah of its sin, but the people denied their sickness for so long that the wound they carried became incurable. The sickness spread to the point where God finally needed to cut the sin right out of the people, but it was so widespread that the entire nation of Israel was destroyed besides a small remnant. God wants to heal us of our sickness of sin, but if we keep pushing His hand away, the sin continues to corrupt us and make us sicker. If we ignore God's spiritual work in our lives, we will get to the point that our situation becomes incurable. We will have hit rock bottom, so God can cut away the corrupted areas of our lives. Let us not harden our hearts to the healing work of the Holy Spirit. Let us not get to that point in our walks of faith that decaying areas of our lives have to be completely cut off. God wants to heal us, but we have to let Him do His mighty work in our lives.

"Blessed is the one whom God corrects; so do not despise the discipline of the Almighty. For he wounds, but he also binds up; he injures, but his hands also heal" (Job 5.17-18 NIV).

DAY 183

Mind Games

"Woe to those who devise wickedness and work evil on their beds! When the morning dawns, they perform it, because it is in the power of their hand" (Micah 2.1 ESV).

Sometimes we think that our thoughts aren't hurting anyone. We commit dozens of sins in our minds (lusting, coveting, revenge, etc.), but since we are not taking action, we believe that our thoughts are okay. The only problem is that when we have the power in our hands to actually commit the sin and the circumstances all line up to where we can get away with it, we may slip easily into a trap of action. We have rehearsed the sin so many times in our minds that our bodies easily enact our mediations. The term for this is visual training, and people in sports know how powerful it is to imagine a play over and over again in order to perform it. When we imagine something, all we are left with is the memory of it. That memory can become like a past reality to us—a recollection mixed in the box of memories in our minds. Just like riding a bike, we can pluck the mediation that we have performed in our minds and follow through with or bodies. Therefore, it is important to stop the meditation of sin right when it enters our thoughts. We must recognize that Jesus said to sin in our minds is equal to actually performing it.

"We demolish arguments and every pretension that sets itself up against the knowledge of God, and we take captive every thought to make it obedient to Christ" (2 Corinthians 10.5 NIV).

DAY 184

Prophecy of Truth

"Thus says the Lord concerning the prophets who lead my people astray, who cry 'Peace' when they have something to eat, but declare war against him who put nothing into their mouths" (Micah 3.5 ESV).

Nothing can cause crankiness more than when we are hungry. Food is one of our most basic human needs. Hunger definitely affects people's moods, which alters their perception of reality, skewing their understanding of truth. A prophet is someone who claims that he or she has a word from God. This word doesn't necessarily have to be a vision of the future; rather, it merely needs to state the heart of God. In this verse, Micah is showing how the prophets changed their "word" from God based on their hunger. They allowed their current state of fullness (their hunger was satisfied) to cause them to joyfully say that everything was at peace. Yet, they allowed their prophecy to claim destruction to those who would not feed them. They were dictated by their bellies and not by God's Truth. When giving advice, Christians need to be certain that our mood is not altering our words, especially when we are trying to speak the heart of God. We must root our feelings in the spirit and not the flesh. If we stand as a mouthpiece of God, we are taking a big risk if our words are skewed by personal feelings. It is better to admit that we don't have the answer than to declare an answer that doesn't align with God's heart. When we are emotionally compromised in a situation, it's better to keep our mouths shut.

"He (the devil) always sends errors into the world in pairs–pairs of opposites…He relies on your extra dislike of one to draw you gradually into the opposite one. But do not let us be fooled. We have to keep our eyes on the goal and go straight through between both errors. We have no other concern than that with either of them." – C.S. Lewis

DAY 185
Cast-Offs

"I will make the lame my remnant, those driven away a strong nation. The Lord will rule over them in Mount Zion from that day and forever" (Micah 4.7 NIV).

A cast-off is someone who has been thrown away, devalued or seen as useless. All Christian have or will experience being a cast-off in the world's eyes (even in Christian circles) as they walk the path to their destiny. God loves the underdog, and He loves seeing His children circumvent the world's system to greatness. When God honors us outside of the world's carefully structured expectations, it shines His glory, not ours. When we choose to walk the humble road with Jesus, God is able to use our faith in Him to propel us further than we could ever think or imagine. The Holy Spirit will lead each of us in a direction that is counter-culture and doesn't make sense to a human perspective. However, our obedience shows that we rely on God more than we rely on the world, and it gives God complete control to work in our lives in ways beyond our comprehension. We simply need to realize that being a cast-off is part of God's plan to achieve His eternal greatness in our lives! So when we feel like we are overlooked and undervalued, we can realize that God is doing a work in us that no one sees. But when the time is right, He will establish us as faithful children of God!

"And the God of all grace, who called you to his eternal glory in Christ, after you have suffered a little while, will himself restore you and make you strong, firm and steadfast" (1 Peter 5.10 NIV).

DAY 186

Perfect Morality

"O my people, what have I done to you? How have I wearied you? Answer me!" (Micah 6.3 ESV).

God has perfect morality. His morality is eternal, and it is complete. God's own morality mandates that He cannot commit sin—nothing tainted with the ugly stains of evil can come from God. The only exception is when Jesus took our sins, losing His morality on our behalf. He chose to lay down His life for us, but because He is God, He was able to take His life up again. With God's perfect morality in mind, we must conclude that our hardships in this life do not come from God. But since God is the Creator of the Universe, where does the evil come from? The answer is free will. God created a perfect world, but He gave us free will to choose to obey our perfect God or disobey Him. When we disobey God, the ugly stains of evil spill onto the world. We live in a corrupted world, but someday we will be with God in heaven. We will experience hardships during this life, and one of the easiest things to do is to blame God since He is the Creator. God does not cause evil, but when people continue to persist in their disobedience, they use their free will to hurt people, including themselves. But God sees the beauty in humanity, and He allows the pain for a time until His Kingdom plan comes to fruition and He can bring all of His beloved children home.

"He will wipe every tear from their eyes, and there will be no more death or sorrow or crying or pain. All these things are gone forever" (Revelation 21.4 NLT).

DAY 187

look to the lord

"But as for me, I will look to the Lord; I will wait for the God of my salvation; my God will hear me" (Micah 7.7 ESV).

There is nothing wrong with receiving and giving help to others. God made people to be social beings that need one another. However, the help from others is directly stemmed from God. He is the Maker of everything, and He can move the hearts of people to intervene in the lives of others. So when we seek help, we must always go to the Lord first and foremost. And when we receive help, we can thank those who have helped us, but we must remember that the help ultimately came from God. When we keep this in mind, it reminds us to not put any human on a pedestal. God is the only One who deserves our highest praise and adoration. We waste time and energy trying to beg people to support us. If God has not opened a door in our life, we must continue to wait patiently for Him to move. And while we wait, we can continue praying prayers filled with faith and belief! Many times as we wait an interesting thing occurs—God doesn't use someone else to open that door for us; instead, He uses us! The entire time we were expecting God to send someone to do something that He had ordained us to do! So wait on the Lord, and you will find out just how resourceful you can be.

"My help comes from the Lord, Who made heaven and earth" (Psalm 121. 2 AMP).

DAY 188

Delayed Destruction

"The Lord is slow to anger and great in power, and the Lord will by no means clear the guilty. His way is in the whirlwind and storm, and the clouds are the dust at his feet" (Nahum 1.3 ESV).

The book of Nahum is much like the sequel to the book of Jonah. Both Jonah and Nahum prophesy warnings of God's judgment against the city of Nineveh, the capital of Assyria. After Jonah gave his prophecy, the city turns from their sin, but the season of repentance did not last. At least 150 years after Jonah confronted Nineveh with God's Word, Nahum also confronts them, but this time the sins of the city would end in their complete destruction. God is always slow to anger, but His righteous judgment will have the final say. The minor repentance of people may buy them some time, but unless they are completely surrendered to the Holy Spirit, their sin will continue to create chaos in their lives. A second chance should not be taken lightly. We cannot take for granted the slow anger of our Heavenly Father. Eventually, if we do not submit to His authority, the devastating actions of our disobedience will lead us into certain destruction, especially after we've been given a second chance.

"God will judge us for everything we do, including every secret thing, whether good or bad" (Ecclesiastes 12.14 NLT).

DAY 189

Publishing Deeds

———————————————————

"Behold, upon the mountains, the feet of him who brings good news, who publishes peace…" (Nahum 1.15 ESV).

There is a peace manufactured by the world and a peace established by God. One peace is fleeting and the other peace is eternal. One peace brings good news that changes lives and the other brings news that only distracts and entertains us. When we as Christians consider publishing works that bring good news and peace to others, we need to carefully consider our motive. Is our motive to honor God and establish His glory on earth or is our motive ruled by other forces? There is nothing wrong with the entertainment value of any news. God Himself conveys His glory in beautiful and awe-inspiring ways through many types of mediums. However, our core motive should always be to lift the name of Jesus and help spread His salvation onto the earth. Once that motive is aligned with the heart of God, everything else is just icing on the cake.

"For I am not ashamed of this Good News about Christ. It is the power of God at work, saving everyone who believes—the Jew first and also the Gentile" (Romans 1.16 NLT).

DAY 190

Deadly Harvest

"Behold, I am against you, declares the Lord of hosts, and will lift up your skirts over your face; and I will make nations look at your nakedness and kingdoms at your shame" (Nahum 3.5 ESV).

People can single out verses like Nahum 3.5 from the Bible and declare that God is a mean God. But before we make judgments, we must examine the verse in the context of the entire Bible. In actuality, the Bible states that God is slow to anger and merciful (Psalm 145.8). But how can this be? God has a holy standard, and there is a system of sowing and reaping that He has set in place in both the natural and supernatural worlds (Galatians 6.7). This concept makes total sense to us in the natural—if we plant an orange seed, we will get oranges. But we have a double standard when it comes to our supernatural harvest. We want to disobey God and do our own thing according to our own standard, yet we expect our harvest to have the goodness, beauty and blessing of God. But how can this be? Nineveh is about to be destroyed. But it is not God who has chosen it for them. They have chosen it for themselves by their evil actions. The people of Nineveh have planted so much wickedness in the world that they are experiencing the results of their own disobedience to God. God loves all His children, and He desires all of us to live according to His holy standard (Micah 6.8), but we have the free choice to choose blessings or curses (Deuteronomy 30.19). Those who truly have an intimate relationship with God through the finished work of Jesus on the cross know that God is what He says He is. He is truth, love, life and hope.

"God showed how much he loved us by sending his one and only Son into the world so that we might have eternal life through him. This is real love—not that we loved God, but that he loved us and sent his Son as a sacrifice to take away our sins" (1 John 4.9-10 NLT).

DAY 191

Rhetorical Question

"There is no healing for your wound; your injury is fatal. All who hear of your destruction will clap their hands for joy. Where can anyone be found who has not suffered from your continual cruelty?" (Nahum 3.19 NLT).

Nahum ends his book with a rhetorical question (a question that is asked without expecting an answer). It is interesting to note that the only other writer in the Bible who ends his book with a rhetorical question is Jonah—the writer of the prequel to this story of Nineveh. In the book of Jonah, God showed mercy to Nineveh because they repented even though their morality was still questionable, but now the fruition of their evilness has touched everyone on the earth, which is demonstrated by the final question: "Where can anyone be found who has not suffered from your continual cruelty?" Their cruelty as a kingdom was well known to all, not just to the decimated nation of Israel. Thankfully, we live in the New Testament age where we have forgiveness for sin; however, we are still accountable for our actions. When we disobey God and His will, we will experience the results of that disobedience. God is merciful though and slow to anger, and He willingly gives us second chances to live obediently to Him. He can always turn our mistakes into something beautiful when we confess (admitting our wrongs) and repent (turning from our wrongs). God will never let go of His hand of salvation when we accept Jesus as our Lord and Savior, but the hand of fellowship is up to us. And the benefits of holding His hand of fellowship are always for our good.

"Many a humble soul will be amazed to find that the seed it sowed in weakness, in the dust of daily life, has blossomed into immortal flowers under the eye of the Lord." – Harriet Beecher Stowe

DAY 192

Silent Tears

"How long, Lord, must I call for help, but you do not listen? Or cry out to you, 'Violence!' but you do not save?" (Habakkuk 1.2 NIV).

Sometimes God is quiet during hard times, but it's not because He has left us. Once we receive Jesus Christ as our Lord and Savior, the Bible says that we have the Great Counselor, the Holy Spirit, with us always. So why is it that God seems to be missing in action when we need Him most? The point of our time on earth is to become the people we will be for eternity. Every weight of difficulty thrown against us during our lives on earth is simply a means of getting us stronger in Christ. God is like our Master Trainer, helping us to get into the best shape before we begin our eternal lives. He allows us to carry the weight, so we grow in Him. But like any good trainer, He is always ready when the weight becomes too heavy and we buckle under the pressure. He reaches into our lives and carries just enough weight, so we have the power to continue without giving up.

"But you will receive power when the Holy Spirit has come upon you, and you will be my witnesses in Jerusalem and in all Judea and Samaria, and to the end of the earth" (Acts 1.8 ESV).

DAY 193

Tolerance of Evil

- - - ❋ - - -

"Your eyes are too pure to look on evil; you cannot tolerate wrongdoing. Why then do you tolerate the treacherous? Why are you silent while the wicked swallow up those more righteous than themselves?" (Habakkuk 1.13 NIV).

A holy God who allows evil to exist is a difficult truth to grasps. God did not create evil, but out of His great love, He created life to share in His love. From the Bible, we know that God is a Creator God—He created angels, humans, animals, plants, etc. In His love, He gives us free will. Anything that exists has its absence, so we have the free will to choose a path in God (a holy standard) or a path in the absence of God (a sin standard). From what we know of the Bible, both angels and humans have fallen from God's holy standard. But should the fact that we sin and make mistakes negate the beauty we also create for God's glory? Should God have avoided making humanity altogether knowing that sin would dwell on the earth for a time? God is not surprised by sin—that's why He created a redemption plan from the start through the sacrifice of Jesus Christ. However, God does not waste the difficulty that sin produces in our lives. He tolerates sin because He knows that hardships grow our character and mold us into the image of Christ. To prove that one could live in a sin-filled world and remain sinless, He sent His Son, Jesus Christ, to be our example. Most importantly, Jesus absorbed all of the world's sin for us, so we could live in the freedom of grace. The victory has already been won—sin will not be tolerated for long. But until God establishes us in His eternal kingdom, we must trust that God will work everything out for His glory and good.

"Yet God freely and graciously declares that we are righteous. He did this through Christ Jesus when he freed us from the penalty for our sins" (Romans 3.24 NLT).

DAY 194

Live by Faithfulness

"Look at the proud! They trust in themselves, and their lives are crooked. But the righteous will live by their faithfulness to God" (Habakkuk 2.4 NLT).

Faithfulness is a rare virtue these days. Faithfulness to marriages, jobs, churches, goals and God's commands many times goes to the wayside as selfish desires come to the forefront. Jesus says that anyone who wants to save his/her life must lose it. We must not base our actions on our whimsical, ever-changing emotions. Faithfulness overrides emotions and roots us to the purpose for which God created each of us. Whenever we face a fork in the road, we must always ask ourselves which choice leads to faithfulness and which choice leads to selfishness. This simple question will save us so much grief from relying on the changing weather of our mood. In the Bible there are two kinds of people: the wicked and the righteous. Today we live in a time of grace, so our sins are forgiven, yet we will have nothing to show for our lives on earth if we are not faithful to the things of God. "The righteous will live by their faithfulness," not their feelings, desires, emotions or circumstances. We can trust that God has already instilled in us the passions of His heart, so when we align our lives with Him, we will find complete satisfaction in our calling. Faithfulness won't always feel and look good, but it should always be our default answer in every situation.

"For whoever wants to save their life will lose it, but whoever loses their life for me will save it" (Luke 9.24 NIV).

DAY 195

Desperate Praise

"Though the fig tree does not bud and there are no grapes on the vines, though the olive crop fails and the fields produce no food, though there are no sheep in the pen and no cattle in the stalls, yet I will rejoice in the Lord, I will be joyful in God my Savior" (Habakkuk 3.17-18 NIV).

Habakkuk lives in a time in which the world's wealth is built on agriculture. So when the prophet lists the shortage of figs, grapes, olives, crops, sheep and cattle, he is declaring a state of complete poverty and lack. However, Habakkuk announces something amazing in this desperation situation: "I will rejoice in the Lord, I will be joyful in God." Praising God when we are completely blessed and have need of nothing is easy, but praising God when we are desperate and hurt takes faith. Praising God in our abundance is natural. Praising God in our lack is supernatural because it doesn't make sense in the natural. We may not feel like praising God, and we may even feel hypocritical praising Him when our emotions are not in it. But praise is not simply a feeling—it is a choice. We can choose to praise God in all situations, knowing that rejoicing resonates when it comes from an aching heart.

"Be thankful in all circumstances, for this is God's will for you who belong to Christ Jesus" (1 Thessalonians 5.18 NLT).

DAY 196

All-Consuming Fire

"For they go up to their roofs and bow down to the sun, moon, and stars. They claim to follow the Lord, but then they worship Molech, too" (Zephaniah 1.5 NLT).

Tearing down idols can be a continual process. Every day we must choose to put God first in our lives. We have to make a conscious effort to step out of our selfish will and walk in submission to the Holy Spirit. But it is the struggle that reveals that we are truly trying to make God the center of our world. In a marriage, we must work daily to ensure that our union with our spouse is protected from outside forces that scheme to break the sanctity of our relationship. The same is true for our union with God through the Finished Work of Jesus Christ on the Cross. The enemy wants to bust through the doors of our relationship with God, tempting us to worship anything other than God. When people say that they worship God by the blood of Jesus Christ, but then go off and worship other manmade deities, they are committing spiritual adultery. And although they profess to love God, their feelings are fleeting and not established in a greater love, which includes submission, obedience, monogamy and faithfulness. When God is fully alive in our lives, there is no room for counterfeits. We can't control God and shape Him into our comfortable, self-willed expectations. He is an all-consuming fire, and our worship belongs to Him alone.

"For the LORD your God is a consuming fire, a jealous God" (Deuteronomy 4.24 ESV).

DAY 197

Stagnant Complacency

―・―――・―※―・―――・―

"At that time I will search Jerusalem with lamps, and I will punish the men who are complacent, those who say in their hearts, 'The Lord will not do good, nor will he do ill'" (Zephaniah 1.12 ESV).

God is not a stagnant God. When He created the earth, He established the system of sowing and reaping. Whatever we plant—whether good or evil—is what we harvest in our lives. Yes, as Christians, we have forgiveness of sins through Jesus Christ and we have the counsel of the Holy Spirit. Our salvation is always secure in Christ, yet we can push away the Holy Spirit's authority by asserting our own will. And to think that we will experience no consequences if we disobey God's commands and rebuke the leading of the Holy Spirit is foolish. Complacency is a sin that is readily overlooked. We can't squander the life that God has given us and think that it doesn't matter. We can't bury our talents in the ground and act like they mean nothing. Complacency mocks our God who died to give us free will, so we could exert our creative authority on earth for His glory. God has given each of us a purpose. Our actions can make a difference for God's Kingdom Agenda. We were specifically designed for a reason, and we must make it our life's goal to fulfill the plans that God has for us.

"God's will is simply for Heaven's reality to become earth's reality." – Bill Johnson

DAY 198

Seeking Paths

"Seek the Lord, all you humble of the land, who do his just commands; seek righteousness; seek humility; perhaps you may be hidden on the day of the anger of the Lord" (Zephaniah 2.3 ESV).

The Prophet Zephaniah's name means, "God has hidden, protected and treasured." Zephaniah is prophesying after the Northern Tribes of Israel were destroyed by Assyria and before the smaller tribe of Judah was taken by Babylon. Zephaniah lived during King Josiah's quest to reestablish God's commands and tear down the idols that had been allowed by previous kings. Even during this time of great revival from the leading authority of the day, many of God's Children were still seeped in sin and disobedience. Zephaniah warned the people of God's coming judgment. Zephaniah does give hope to the few people wanting to be "hidden," "protected" and "treasured" during the dark aftermath of consequences. All the people had to do was seek God, seek righteousness and seek humility. These three things are not impossible to ascertain because they are inner qualities that can be easily called upon once we learn to sacrifice our pride and submit our will to the Lord. Seeking God is always the first step. When we passionately and unabashedly seek after God, He will guide us in all other paths of righteousness and humility.

"He restores my soul; He leads me in the paths of righteousness for His name's sake" (Psalm 23.3 NKJV).

DAY 199

Healing Correction

"She listens to no voice; she accepts no correction. She does not trust in the Lord; she does not draw near to her God" (Zephaniah 3.2 ESV).

The Holy Spirit is very good at correcting us when something in our lives is not pleasing to Him. He doesn't correct us to shame us; rather, He corrects us to help us avoid danger and to stay on His path of blessings. Many times our pride prevents us from hearing correction from the Lord. His voice is loving, yet stern; and if our hearts are not humble and our ears not open, we will miss His words of life to us. When we accept correction from the Lord, we are showing Him that we trust Him. We trust Him with our hearts and lives, and we know that He will not do anything to destroy us. Instead, as we draw near to Him, we feel Him building us up and making us stronger. Correction may feel like it is tearing us down, but in actuality, it is molding us into the perfect image of Christ. Correction stings at first, but God always lathers our rawness with healing peace, as we give our pride to Him.

"We often learn more of God under the rod that strikes us than under the staff that comforts us." – Stephen Charnock

DAY 200

The Beauty of Breaking

"On that day it shall be said to Jerusalem: 'Fear not, O Zion; let not your hands grow weak'" (Zephaniah 3.16 ESV).

All of us will go through a time of "tearing down." This is nothing new. When bodybuilding, people must actually tear their muscles in order for them to grow back bigger and stronger. God must tear us down, so we can grow bigger and stronger in Him. But it is hard not to be discouraged. It is difficult not to look around and feel defeated and weak. But God says loudly to each of us, "Let not your hands grow weak!" Yes, we are tired. Yes, we have been through a breaking season, but our stories will not end there. God will restore us when we rest in Him. He will rebuild us if we let Him. God is about to bless what He has broken and serve His presence to the world through our lives. God wants to multiply His glory in and through His People. He can only do this when we see our absolute need for Him, and we allow Him to shine through our brokenness.

"God blesses those who are poor and realize their need for him, for the Kingdom of Heaven is theirs" (Matthew 5.3 NLT).

DAY 201

Effort of People

"You have sown much, and harvested little. You eat, but you never have enough; you drink, but you never have your fill. You clothe yourselves, but no one is warm. And he who earns wages does so to put them into a bag with holes" (Haggai 1.6 ESV).

God's Chosen People have neglected to rebuild God's house, the Temple. Since they have taken their eyes off the things of God and placed them on the things of people, they find themselves never having enough. It's frustrating when we put so much effort into something, and we see very little in return. One very valid reason for this is that God is saving our efforts for when He will supernaturally bless them. If our work is being done in obedience to God, and we are not seeing the fruit manifest yet in the natural world, we must believe by faith that the fruit is so big that it is still maturing. However, if we are working in the flesh, committing to efforts—no matter how spiritual and good they may seem—that are not done in obedience to God, we will never manifest the results that we seek. Our strength does not measure up to much without the powerful strength of the Lord on our side. We spin our wheels in vain when we are not rooted in the Vine of Christ. We must put God's agenda first, knowing that His agenda is always for our benefit and good. His ways may not make sense at first, but we must trust that God loves us and He wants to supernaturally bless us with His abundance.

"But seek ye first his kingdom, and his righteousness; and all these things shall be added unto you" (Matthew 6.33 ASV).

DAY 202

I Am with You

"Then Haggai, the messenger of the Lord, spoke to the people with the Lord's message, 'I am with you, declares the Lord'" (Haggai 1.13 ESV).

If God says He is with us, there is nothing too impossible for us to achieve with His nod of approval. We can't wait until the world says we are good enough, or until we have the right credentials or until we have the needed resources—we must walk boldly on the word of the Lord alone. If God says He is with us, we can move with childlike faith and not reason our way out of obedience. God is with us! That's all we need to know. What could be more powerful than the creative, life-giving and perfect voice of the Lord, saying that He is with us? God created the heavens and the earth with His words, so His word is all we need to move mountains! We must not fear, doubt or hesitate. The moment we wait before throwing ourselves into wholehearted obedience, we allow Satan to whisper lies and deceit into our minds. If God says He is with us, there is nothing more on which to base our confidence. His promises are as good as done, so it's time to move on His powerful word!

"…Be strong, all you people of the land, declares the Lord. Work, for I am with you, declares the Lord of hosts" (Haggai 2.4 ESV).

DAY 203

Presence of the Lord

"This is what I covenanted with you when you came out of Egypt. And my Spirit remains among you. Do not fear" (Haggai 2.5 NIV).

We worry about so many external things when working for the Lord—money, connections, time, talents, presentation, numbers, etc.—yet, our primary focus should always be the presence of the Lord. If the presence of the Lord is not the central theme of all we do, we waste what little resources we do have. Yes, it does take many necessary external things to achieve the will of God on earth, but who is the Creator and Owner of every single thing in existence? The Lord! All the silver and the gold on earth belong ultimately to God. We get anxious when we get caught up in the numbers. We can be aware of our need and of what is going on around us, but our eyes must be steadfastly fixed on the Lord. If we have asked God to come into our situation, we don't have to fear. When the presence of the Lord is with us, we have everything we need to make our efforts pleasing and profitable to Him.

"Always, everywhere God is present, and always He seeks to discover Himself to each one." – A.W. Tozer

DAY 204

Nothing but Blessed

* * *

"Is the seed yet in the barn? Indeed, the vine, the fig tree, the pomegranate, and the olive tree have yielded nothing. But from this day on I will bless you" (Haggai 2.19 ESV).

When we allow God to move in our lives, He will strip us to nothing. Though we don't live in an agricultural society like God's people did when the Prophet Haggai spoke this declaration, there is much in our lives that God will need to remove in order for us to learn complete reliance on Him. He will strip of us anything in which we find our worth, value and significance. This process is not fun, but it is necessary. God can't bless us with His supernatural abundance if the weight of the blessing will break us. Every blessing comes with a burden, and we will never be strong enough to carry the load alone. This is why we must learn to be totally dependent and reliant on the Lord and not the things of this world. Once we realize that God is our Supreme Provider, He will be able to bless us with the desires and plans He has appointed for us because He will know that the blessings will not break us or draw us away from Him.

"Every good and perfect gift is from above, coming down from the Father of the heavenly lights, who does not change like shifting shadows" (James 1.17 NIV).

DAY 205

Return to Me

"Therefore say to them, Thus declares the Lord of hosts: Return to me, says the Lord of hosts, and I will return to you, says the Lord of hosts" (Zechariah 1.3 ESV).

What a beautiful promise God gives us. He will return to us when we return to Him! He never says we have to be perfect. He doesn't say that our lives need to be in order. He simply says, "Return to me." Isaiah 53.6 explains that the Messiah will take the iniquities of all of us, and the main source of our iniquities is important to note. The sole culprit of all of our sin is "turning our own way." Turning our own way—or taking the place as God in our lives—leads to devastation and sorrow. When we take the reins from God's hands and run our lives according to our needs and our limited understanding, we will not receive the blessings that only He can lead us to. However, if we "turn away" from our self-directed lives, and allow God to lead us, He will fill our lives with His glory, beauty and purpose. This turning away is not just a single decision that occurs once in our lives. Rather, it is a decision we must make every day, laying down our self-directed will and submitting to the holy will of the Father. We can rate and categorize sin, but really that is fruitless. Trying to dictate our own lives is the number one sin that creates havoc in our lives. But at any moment we can stop the madness. All we have to do is turn back to God, and He will turn to us!

"We all, like sheep, have gone astray, each of us has turned to our own way; and the LORD has laid on him the iniquity of us all" (Isaiah 53.6 NIV).

DAY 206

Hope Blossoms

"So he said to me, 'This is the word of the Lord to Zerubbabel: Not by might nor by power, but by my Spirit,' says the Lord Almighty" (Zechariah 4.6 NIV).

The Prophet Zechariah is speaking to Zerubbabel, the governor of Israel after the people returned to their homeland from Babylon. The foundation of the Second Temple had already been laid, but the construction of the temple had been delayed over and over again by the many obstacles impeding it. It seemed like the entire world was against the rebuilding of the temple. The tiny nation of Israel had so many enemies trying to stop every effort they made to obey God's command to rebuild. It became easy to get discouraged and the temptation to give up was enticing. However, God gives Zerubbabel an amazing promise that is spoken to everyone who is trying to accomplish a great task of God. God says, "Not by might nor by power, but by my Spirit." God knows that we can't accomplish His will alone. In fact, He allows all the obstacles to come in the way of our dreams to force us to rely on Him, so all glory will go to Him and not to our own "might" and "power." The dreams God gives us will never come easy. Just the opposite, they will seem impossible. But when we continue forward even during the bleakest situations, we show our trust in an all-powerful God. No matter the situation, if God has given us the command to go forward, we must believe that His Spirit will make a way when there is no way.

"Where hope grows, miracles blossom." – Elna Rae

DAY 207

Broken Favor

———————— ✦ ————————

"Then I took my staff called Favor and broke it, revoking the covenant I had made with all the nations" (Zechariah 11.10 NIV).

God says in Deuteronomy 11:27 that He places before us blessings and curses. If we obey His commands, we shall be blessed. God wants to bless us. He wants to shine His favor on our lives. He wants to be good to us. He knows we will never be perfect, but because of Jesus, God will bless us even in our imperfect state. However, God will not continue to bless us if we insist on walking away from His commandments. He will give us many chances to obey His will, but once we've admitted we've done wrong, we need to turn away from our sin and follow after Him. If we continue making the same mistakes over and over again, even though we know we are disobeying God, God will eventually break his staff of favor in our lives. He will give us up to our own devices, allowing us to feel the full repercussions of our disobedience. This doesn't mean we will lose our salvation—our salvation has been signed by the blood of Jesus and is unbreakable—but He will take His hand of blessing away from us. God will not bless disobedience. He will not bless sin. He can only bless that which is under His authority to bless. It is for our own good that we seek the Lord's will and obey His commands. We have the free will to build the staff of favor or to break it.

"Jesus replied, 'All who love me will do what I say. My Father will love them, and we will come and make our home with each of them'" (John 14.23 NLT).

DAY 208

Fleeting Life

"On that day living water will flow out from Jerusalem, half of it east to the Dead Sea and half of it west to the Mediterranean Sea, in summer and in winter" (Zechariah 14.8 ESV).

The Old Testament prophets could only dream about the New Testament promises that the Messiah would bring. Not only would this Messiah restore Israel, He would also restore the entire world and its people. Because of Jesus' death on the cross, our sin has been redeemed and we have been reconciled to our perfect Creator. Jesus is the carrier of the Living Water. He was made flesh and broken, so that Living Water could be poured onto the physical earth from a spiritual heaven. Much like a grape, Jesus is Living Water wrapped in flesh, squeezed out on the earth in the form of the New Wine of Grace, replacing the Old Wine of Law. In this era of New Wine, we as Believers have many promises granted to us. We can have a relationship with God. We can have God's favor even in our imperfect state. We are Children of God and coheirs with Christ. We have the Holy Spirit as our guide. We have a purpose and our lives have meaning. We are loved by our Creator. We can live forever with God in heaven. And the list goes on. No matter the heartache our day brings, we can have joy in the fact that God is a lover of our souls, and He has given us a way to be with Him forever. Living Water literally flows into our lives from the east and west, and we no longer have to thirst for meaning in this fleeting life.

"Give me the love that leads the way, the faith that nothing can dismay, the hope no disappointments tire, the passion that will burn like fire; Let me not sink to be a clod: Make me Thy fuel, Flame of God." – Amy Carmichael

DAY 209

A Father's Honor

"A son honors his father, and a servant his master. If I am a father, where is my honor? And if I am a master, where is my fear? says the Lord of hosts to you, O priests, who despise my name…" (Malachi 1.6 ESV).

It's easy to say we love someone, but to actually show it takes our best efforts. God is speaking through the Prophet Malachi to the priests—people who profess with their mouths that God is their Master, yet do not honor Him with their actions. Specifically, these priests were offering blemished sacrifices to the Lord, which is symbolic of not giving God their best. In fact, they were offering God their worst. God confronted the priests, and asked them if they were to give those same sacrifices to people they honored, would they expect to find favor in their eyes? Probably not. People don't show favor to others for their worst efforts. We can't judge the priests because we too have a tendency to treat God with contempt if we are not following Him with all of our heart. We can give everything in our life 100% of our time, energy and resources, leaving God with the leftovers. God is a forgiving God, and He is slow to anger. But there will come a time when we will stand at the crossroads of life, and God will ask us for all or nothing. We will either serve Him with our whole heart, or we will go our own way. Lip service of devotion to God will only last so long. Eventually, we will have to live up to the words we speak or else our life will not demonstrate His divine favor. If God is our Master, and we see Him as our Father, we will want to give Him the best of everything we have to give. We will want to please Him above all else.

"And the one who sent me is with me—he has not deserted me. For I always do what pleases him" (John 8.29 NLT).

DAY 210

Marriage Covenant

"Did he not make them one, with a portion of the Spirit in their union?" (Malachi 2.15 ESV).

A marriage is more than simply a contract; it is a covenant that stands not only before our government but also before God. It is beyond our understanding what happens when a man and a woman say the words, "I do," but we do know that God now considers the two unique individuals as one entity. Each person—male and female—are now bonded in a supernatural metamorphosis that unites them into one flesh. God's Spirit testifies to their union, being the bonding agent that joins them together. The significance of being one flesh can be mind-boggling when considering our treatment of our spouse. We literally hurt ourselves and damage our lives when we dishonor, abuse and loathe our spouse. And if we don't keep the eyes of our marriage on God, we can twist and turn our marriage out of His grip. But nothing is ever hopeless. Because of Christ, we can have the resurrection power of Jesus in our relationships, restoring even the sickest areas of our marriage. But we must remember that we are in a covenant marriage with the Spirit of God binding us. When we feel like our marriage is being torn apart, we can turn our hearts back to God. Only He can resurrect what seems dead and find what feels lost.

"That is why a man leaves his father and mother and is united to his wife, and they become one flesh" (Genesis 2.24 NIV).

DAY 211

The Tithe

"Bring the whole tithe into the storehouse, that there may be food in my house. Test me in this," says the Lord Almighty, "and see if I will not throw open the floodgates of heaven and pour out so much blessing that there will not be room enough to store it" (Malachi 3.10 NIV).

Tithing is one of the most difficult acts of obedience we can make, especially if we allow jealousy, envy and covetousness to exist in our life. With social media and our culture's obsession with knowing everything about everyone, it is easy to think that others have it better than we do. We may want to cling onto our money, so we can buy more and bigger homes, cars, vacations, gadgets, etc. But true joy and peace do not come from materialism; they come from the Lord. Everything else is just icing on the cake. If we are having trouble obeying God's commandment to tithe to the local church, we will have to take a moment to ask ourselves why. We have to trust God at His Word. He says that if we tithe, He will be able to bless us with "so much blessing that there will not be room enough to store it." We can stop analyzing what everyone else owns and put our focus on what God wants to give us through our obedience. He wants to bless us, but we must realize that God's ways are higher than our ways. The system of give-and-receive may not make sense in the natural, so we have to take a risk and put our faith in the supernatural. God even asks us to test Him and His system of tithing that He has established. So let us test Him and see if He does not "open the floodgates of heaven" for us.

"As the heavens are higher than the earth, so are my ways higher than your ways and my thoughts than your thoughts" (Isaiah 55.9 NIV).

NEW TESTAMENT

Part 2 of a 366-Day Devotional

DAY 212
Ready or Not

"The book of genealogy of Jesus Christ, the Son of David, the Son of Abraham" (Matthew 1.1 NKJV).

Satan had 42 generations from the time Abraham was given the promise to be the father of many nations to the time Jesus Christ was born to cloud Jesus' kingly lineage. By the time Jesus was born, the promise of a Messiah was no longer anticipated by God's people. In fact, three wise men from other nations were the only ones mentioned who actually did their research and were prepared for the coming of the King. God's promises for our lives do seem to tarry sometimes, but the worst thing we can do is lose hope and get sidetracked. The promise is not late. In fact, it will be right on time, but we need to be ready when it arrives or we will miss the divine intervention of God in our lives. Satan will try to get us off course, but God is always rooting for us. He wants to display His glory in our lives. He wants to stand up in the middle of our longing and say, "It's time!" We must cling onto belief even when the way is clouded and time seems to be running out. God will provide in His abundance if we wait on Him.

"God gave the promises to Abraham and his child. And notice that the Scripture doesn't say 'to his children,' as if it meant many descendants. Rather, it says 'to his child' –and that, of course, means Christ" (Galatians 3.16 NLT).

DAY 213
The Trinity

—————— ❀ ——————

"As soon as Jesus was baptized, he went up out of the water. At that moment heaven was opened, and he saw the Spirit of God descending like a dove and alighting on him. And a voice from heaven said, "This is my Son, whom I love; with him I am well pleased" (Matthew 3.16-17 NIV).

In these two verses found in Matthew, we find a beautiful image of God the Son, God the Holy Spirit and God the Creator – the Trinity. Like a man who can be a father, son and counselor through his normal day, God interacts with His Children in these three special ways. God is our Creator, our Savior and our Counselor. Many times we may want to use the three Persons of God interchangeably, but as we mature in our faith, we will find that each Head of the Trinity responds to us uniquely. God is our Creator. He designed us each with a purpose. He has a special plan for our lives, and we can come to Him with our questions, desires and troubles. Jesus is our Savior. He is the Godhead that chose to wear flesh and walk this earth with us. He took our sins, so He knows our struggles, and He prays for us continually before our Holy God. The Holy Spirit is able to dwell on this earth and in our lives because Jesus died for our sins and gave us His righteousness. The Holy Spirit is God's Spirit among us, guiding us, encouraging us and showing us the way. God desires so much to be a part of our lives that He chose to create three embodiments of His Person, so no matter where we turn, He is there with us. He is Emmanuel, God with us and all around us.

"If there be one God subsisting in three persons, then let us give equal reverence to all the persons in the Trinity. There is not more or less in the Trinity; the Father is not more God than the Son and Holy Ghost. There is an order in the Godhead, but no degrees; one person has not a majority or super eminence above another, therefore we must give equal worship to all the persons." – Thomas Watson

DAY 214

Obedient Difficulty

"Then Jesus was led up by the Spirit into the wilderness to be tempted by the devil" (Matthew 4.1 NKJV).

We have many hardships during our life on this earth. Some hardships are out of our control. Life hits us with difficulties because we live in an imperfect world with imperfect people. Other difficulties are repercussions of bad choices we've made in the past. Although we are forgiven and our slate is wiped clean, we still have to deal with the consequences of our mistakes. Yet other hardships are ordained by God, and we walk straight into them out of obedience. After Jesus was baptized by John the Baptist, God led Him into the wilderness to be tempted by the Devil. This temptation solidified Jesus' ability to conquer Satan and achieve victory over death. As Christians, God will allow "wilderness" seasons to occur in our life, and we have the ability to obediently walk the wilderness or run away from difficulty. The people who allow themselves to be led into the wilderness with the Lord, will come out stronger. The people who avoid obedient hardships at all cost will stay immature in their faith. Every difficulty that God brings our way is an opportunity for us to grow stronger in Christ, becoming more like Him. When we hide from hardships, we show a lack of trust in God and our spiritual muscles stay weak and small. Instead, we can be like Jesus Who willingly walked into the wilderness and overcame every obstacle Satan threw His way. When Jesus' wilderness experience was done, He went forth and saved the world.

"When we long for life without difficulties, remind us that oaks grow strong in contrary winds and diamonds are made under pressure." – Peter Marshall

DAY 215
Our Need

———————❖———————

"And again I say to you, it is easier for a camel to go through the eye of a needle than for a rich man to enter the kingdom of God" (Matthew 19.24 NKJV).

When we prosper with worldly abundance—money, health, fame, intelligence, accolades—it may be difficult to see past our worldly sufficiency to see our need for Christ. We want everything on this earth to be perfect, creating our own Garden of Eden, but we forget that without Jesus we are separated from God for eternity. One day we will die and leave behind the castles we have built on this earth. If we don't see our need for Christ in this life, we won't get the chance in the next. But how do we see our need for Him if we have comfortable lives that lack nothing? Jesus Himself said that it is easier for a camel to fit through a tiny hole than it is for a wealthy person to enter the Kingdom of God, but He also adds that God makes all things possible (Matthew 19.26). God allows hardships in our lives to help us understand our need for Him. He tolerates sin for a brief moment on earth to expose our self-made Garden of Eden, so we will reach out for Him and grasp a life with true meaning. It is the storms of life that cause us to see our need. Once we experience our need, we will cling onto Jesus as the Source of all Life that He is. And no matter the worldly possessions thrown our way, we will continue to understand that without Jesus we truly have nothing. We can rejoice in our trials because we know that they make a way for the rich man to enter into the kingdom of God—they make a way for us to seek and find Jesus.

"But store up for yourselves treasures in heaven, where moths and vermin do not destroy, and where thieves do not break in and steal" (Matthew 6.20 NIV).

DAY 216
Fearing the Mob

"Did John's authority to baptize come from heaven, or was it merely human?" They talked it over among themselves. "If we say it was from heaven, he will ask us why we didn't believe John. But if we say it was merely human, we'll be mobbed because the people believe John was a prophet" (Matthew 21.25-26 NLT).

The religious leaders of Jesus' time were always trying to trap Jesus in His choice of words. When Jesus was teaching in the Temple, they asked Him who gave Him the authority to teach (Matthew 21.23). Jesus can read the hearts of people, and He knew they weren't asking the question because they really wanted to know—they were looking for any excuse to accuse Him. Instead of falling into their scheme, He decided to ask them a question: Was John's authority to baptize from God or merely human inclination? Instead of trying to base their answer on God's Truth, they based their answer on what others thought. They allowed the opinions and actions of others to dictate their quest for understanding and their declaration of what they believed. Because they feared the people around them, they stated that they didn't have the answer. As Christians, we can't allow the people around us to regulate our understanding of Truth. Truth is found in God's Word and is the same yesterday, today, tomorrow and forever. It doesn't move, change or shift with the cultural feelings, opinions and beliefs. It is better to be isolated and standing on Truth than surrounded and standing on shifting sand. When asked a question about our faith, our first thought shouldn't be about what others think; rather, it should be about what God says.

"When darkness veils His lovely face,
I rest on His unchanging grace;
In every high and stormy gale
My anchor holds within the veil.
On Christ, the solid Rock, I stand;
All other ground is sinking sand
My Hope is Built on Nothing Less."
                    - Edward Mote

DAY 217
Abundant Servant

———◦———◦⊰❋⊱◦———◦———

"The greatest among you will be your servant" (Matthew 23.11NIV).

God's Kingdom seems upside down, but in actuality, it makes sense when we apply it to real life. Jesus says the greatest will be the one who serves. This doesn't make sense to us, but when we apply His words to parenthood, we will come to understand. When a baby is born to her mother and father, she is completely helpless. She is unable to feed, clothe or shelter herself. The one who is able to help is the one who has the resources and ability to provide. The one who feeds is the one with the food. The one who clothes is the one with the wardrobe. The one who shelters is the one with a home. However, the one who receives takes out of her lack. Therefore, the mom and dad serve their baby girl from their abundance because she still has need. That is why Jesus came to the earth. He has ownership of the boundless wealth of God our Father because He is God's Son. He chose to leave His spiritual throne, wrapping on physical flesh, so He could bring that abundance—God's wealth—to His Beloved Children, to us! For this reason, Jesus is the supreme example of a servant, and He wants to bless us with His resources and abilities, so we can in turn serve others. There is nothing wrong with having a blessed life when those blessings feed the hungry, clothe the poor and shelter the homeless—including the children in our own homes. When we love Jesus above all else, we will change into His likeness—we will transform into servants bringing God's abundance to our families and the world.

"We think sometimes that poverty is only being hungry, naked and homeless. The poverty of being unwanted, unloved and uncared for is the greatest poverty. We must start in our own homes to remedy this kind of poverty." – Mother Teresa

DAY 218

Fame

"And immediately His fame spread throughout all the regions around Galilee" (Mark 1.28 NKJV).

Many people want to be famous, but they may not count the cost of fame. Before Jesus began to speak and work with authority, He fasted 40 days in the wilderness and allowed Himself to be tempted by the Devil. Satan tempted Jesus to work in human selfishness—rather than in accordance with the Holy Spirit—three times. Although these temptations looked different on the outside, the main culprit of each one was disobedience to God and obedience to self. Satan tried to coerce Jesus into defying God, but Jesus would not budge from His complete surrender to His Father. God did not allow Jesus' fame to spread until after He had proven Himself to be rooted in His will. The other price that we may not consider is that fame invites the exaltation and abhorrence of others based on a very shallow understanding. The fame that God allows into our lives is not our own—it is actually His glory that shines upon us. Just like people both hated and loved Jesus—people will both hate and love us when they see the life of Jesus in us. Until we are completely rooted in the will of the Father and our security is fixed in Him, the love and hate of others will move us like the shaky waves of the sea on a windy day. We will bounce from high to low, depending on the positive and negative opinions of those around us. We must be so secure in who we are in Christ that the fleeting views of the world don't uproot us. Only then will we be wholly surrendered to the Father that we do His will no matter what the world thinks or says about it.

"God has allowed us to be trusted with the Good News. Because of this, we preach it to please God, not man. God tests and proves our hearts" (1 Thessalonians 2.4 NLV).

DAY 219
Lord Over the Sabbath

———— ❈ ————

"Then Jesus said to them, 'The Sabbath was made to meet the needs of people, and not people to meet the requirements of the Sabbath'" (Mark 2.27 NLT).

The first mention of Sabbath comes after God frees the Israelites from slavery. God requires the Israelites to rest on the seventh day of every week (Exodus 16.23). That Sabbath given in the Old Testament offers us an amazing foreshadowing of the Finished Work of Jesus on the Cross in the New Testament. Sabbath comes from the Hebrew word, *Shabbath*, which means *Day of Atonement*. When something is atoned, it is absolved from all wrong and the penalty of sin is paid in full. So when God tells His Children to rest on the seventh day, He is giving them a picture of Jesus, Who is Lord over Sabbath. Finally, Jesus would absolve each of us of our wrong and pay the penalty for our sin through His sacrifice. We don't have to prove ourselves to God anymore because God sees us through the blood of His Son. We are perfect and holy in God's eyes, and now we can have the Holy Spirit living in and among us. The religious leaders of Jesus' time had twisted the Sabbath, making it a burden to God's people. They didn't realize there was a spiritual meaning to the Sabbath along with the physical rest. Sabbath is not just a day; it is a reality that Christians can enjoy every moment. We can rest from our constant human striving, knowing that Jesus' Blood atones for our imperfect efforts making our work pleasing to a holy God. The Sabbath meets our most dire need: We are reconciled back to our Holy God, and even in our imperfect state we can have a personal relationship with Him!

"For the Son of Man is Lord of the Sabbath" (Matthew 12.8 NIV).

DAY 220
A House Divided

"And if a house is divided against itself, that house cannot stand" (Mark 3.25 NKJV).

If peace is God's plan for the Body of Christ, division is Satan's main agenda. He does not want God's people to be united, because only through the hum of harmony can the Church be a light to a dark world. Satan wants to divide not only the Church—he wants to divide peoples, nations, cities, families and marriages. Satan doesn't care what he uses to pull us a part. He will divide God's people, throwing any arrow he can get his wryly hands on to create cuts of division. When we feel like a division is occurring in our lives—whether it be in our church, in our family, in our marriage or in our nation—we must stop and focus on what is really causing the discord. Most likely the division is a tactic of Satan. We have to be able to look at the situation through God's eyes and see what is really going on. Many times it's not just about hurt feelings and irreconcilable difference—there is a spiritual battle being waged against us, and we let Satan win when we fall into self-preservation mode. God will fight for us. He will ensure that our situation is redeemed, but our main focus should be preventing what's been divinely united from being torn to pieces. We all have differences, but the bond that holds us all together is Jesus and His sacrifice for us because we have all fallen short of the glory of God (Romans 3.23). Until we stop allowing ourselves to be divided, we will never stand securely as a beacon of hope to a lost world.

"You are the light of the world. A town built on a hill cannot be hidden" (Matthew 5.14 NIV).

DAY 221
Public and Private

"And Jesus, immediately knowing in Himself that power had gone out of Him, turned around in the crowd and said, 'Who touched My clothes?'" (Mark 5.30 NKJV).

Jesus was asked by Jarius, one of the rulers of the local synagogue, to heal his twelve-year-old daughter. On the way to heal the little girl, a woman "who had a flow of blood for twelve years" also received healing by Jesus. She touched Jesus' garment and by faith her blood flow stopped. In the middle of the multitude, Jesus demanded that the healed woman show herself. This woman who had been relegated to the outskirts of society for twelve long years (because a woman during her menstrual cycle was considered unclean) was now the center of attention. However, when Jesus went to Jarius's house and healed his little girl, he demanded that they keep silent about the miracle. So in one day Jesus healed a woman suffering for twelve years and a twelve-year-old girl, yet He dealt with each miracle differently. The first miracle He pronounced to the crowd, but the second miracle He kept a secret. What He did with each miracle was in accordance with the Father's will because Jesus always obeyed God (John 4.34). God will do many miracles in our lives if we believe, perceive and receive them. Some miracles He'll give us an audience and other miracles He'll keep secret. It's difficult to understand why God will do something miraculous and not share His goodness to others, but He has a plan for everything He does. If God has not given us a platform for what He has done, we shouldn't question Him. We can share our joy with our small inner circle and continue living in the victory that God has given us.

"He gave strict orders not to let anyone know about this, and told them to give her something to eat" (Mark 5.43 NIV).

DAY 222
A Little Child

"Assuredly, I say to you, whoever does not receive the kingdom of God as a little child will by no means enter it" (Mark 10.15 NKJV).

Parents were bringing their young children to Jesus, and the disciples rebuked the parents. Undoubtedly, if the parents were bringing Jesus gold, food or accolades, the disciples would have ushered them in. The children were not a welcomed sight and seen as a nuisance rather than a blessing. They needed to be cared for and taught, and they were at a place in life where they had nothing of great value to offer—intelligence, resources or stature. In fact, the parents wanted Jesus to touch their children—to impart something beautiful to them. The only virtue the children did have was the willingness to receive, so Jesus "took them up in His arms, laid His hands on them, and blessed them" (Mark 10.16). Jesus told His disciples that the only way to get into the Kingdom of God was to be as one of those helpless children. And that is the truth about receiving Jesus as our Lord and Savior today. There is absolutely nothing we can give God in order to earn His blessings. What can a mere human offer an almighty God to find His favor? There is nothing we can do to receive the salvation Jesus died to give us except to receive it. We can't buy it, earn it and we will never deserve it. Just like the little children, we can go to Jesus with our empty hands, ignoring all the people who say we are not good enough, and freely receive what He died to give us—salvation through the cross and reconciliation back to our Father.

"A simple, childlike faith in a Divine Friend solves all the problems that come to us by land or sea." – Helen Keller

DAY 223

Forsaken

"And at the ninth hour Jesus cried with a loud voice, saying, Eloi, Eloi, lama sabachthani? which is, being interpreted, My God, my God, why hast thou forsaken me?" (Mark 15.34 KJV).

The physical pain of the cross was tremendous. And the fact that Jesus took our sin is incomprehensible. However, the most excruciating aspect of the cross was the fact that Jesus would be forsaken by God. God is holy and can have no part of sin, and because Jesus took the sin of the world, God had to forsake Jesus until Jesus fought for victory over death. When Jesus cried out on the cross, the only thing that caused Him to despair was that the Father had forsaken Him. Forsaken means literally to leave something. Why would God leave Jesus for a time? He left Jesus so He could embrace us, His imperfect children. Jesus took our "forsakenness," so that we would no longer be separated from God. Because of the Finished Work of Jesus on the Cross, we now have been reconciled back to God forever—in this life and the next. God knew that Jesus would not be forsaken for long. The Bible says that Jesus was able to give His life and to take it back up again (John 10.18). So now through the death and resurrection of Christ all of creation is restored back to God, and Jesus is back on His rightful throne in heaven. One day soon, Jesus will swoop down from His throne a second time, but this time He will come to claim what He died to save!

"Look, I am coming soon, bringing my reward with me to repay all people according to their deeds. I am the Alpha and the Omega, the First and the Last, the Beginning and the End" (Revelation 22.12-13 NLT).

DAY 224

Unique Perspective

"Dear Theophilus, I have looked with care into these things from the beginning. I have decided it would be good to write them to you one after the other the way they happened" (Luke 1.3 NLV).

Most scholars believe that the Gospel of Luke was written by Luke, a physician and the only gentile (non-Jewish person) to write in the New Testament. He is writing his Gospel, which happens to be one of the most detailed, to a man named Theophilus. Luke is also known for writing the Book of Acts, which details the Apostle Paul's ministry. Before Luke begins to describe Jesus' life from his perspective, he admits that people before him have written such accounts. We have the Gospels of Matthew and Mark—both which were probably written before Luke sat down to write his point of view. No one knows why Luke decided to write his Gospel, but the world has been greatly blessed by his words. Luke could have decided against writing his account because there were already three accounts available, but God gave him an audience in Theophilus. Whether this figure was an actual man or symbolic of an audience, it was all Luke needed to take the time to write down everything He remembered of Jesus and His ministry. Sometimes we may feel God calling us to do something, but we don't want to obey because it's already been done before. We may feel like we have nothing special to add or that our time may be wasted. But we cannot see what God's sees. We don't know how our words and actions may reach people that others can't reach. We must trust that we have a special perspective that God wants to use. God made us each uniquely, and He doesn't want to waste what we have to offer. He knows that there is an audience out there just waiting to hear and see specifically what we have to say and show them.

"God has given each of you a gift from his great variety of spiritual gifts. Use them well to serve one another" (1 Peter 4.10 NLT).

DAY 225
Adopted

———◦———⋙❋⋘———◦———

"A light to bring revelation to the Gentiles, and the glory of Your people Israel" (Luke 2.32 NKJV).

When Mary and Joseph bring Jesus into the Temple after His birth to dedicate Him to God, two people filled with the Holy Spirit were waiting for Him: Simeon and Anna. Anna spoke of Jesus bringing redemption to Jerusalem, but Simeon's words were more specific. In his short prophecy, he united a segregated world—divided by Jew and Gentile. The Old Testament chronicled a people beginning with the Hebrew Abraham all the way through his lineage to David and then to the destruction of Israel. Although gentiles were a part of this story, the focus was always centered on the Jewish people. Now with one sentence, Simeon has combined Jew and Gentile into the purpose of God through Jesus Christ. Jesus would save not only the Jewish people, but everyone else too. Jesus would be a "light" to the Gentiles and the "glory" of the Jewish people. Jesus has come to save not just one group of people, but He has come to save everyone—the entire world (John 3.16). Like an adopted child, we can learn from God's interactions with Israel in the Old Testament, because Jesus will give us revelation that applies to our lives today. God adopts every person who professes Jesus is Lord, and no matter our background, race or nationality, we are called children of the Most High. We are daughters and sons of the King and royalty in His Kingdom.

"He gave the right and the power to become children of God to those who received Him. He gave this to those who put their trust in His name. These children of God were not born of blood and of flesh and of man's desires, but they were born of God" (John 1.12-13 NLV).

DAY 226
Confound the Wise

"And all spoke well of him and marveled at the gracious words that were coming from his mouth. And they said, 'Is not this Joseph's son?'" (Luke 4.22 ESV).

Jesus went to his hometown of Nazareth and spoke at the synagogue. Although the people marveled at what He said, they still couldn't see past His normalcy to comprehend His divine. The people relegated Jesus to being simply a carpenter's Son, and in their own minds they diminished the power of God in His life. God loves to take what seems average and make it amazing because it shows His glory even more. These people who knew Jesus growing up completely missed what God was doing through Jesus. They didn't get as many miracles and they didn't receive much of His revelation. In fact, instead of receiving Him, they tried to push the Son of God off a cliff (Luke 4.28-29). Their own limited viewpoints halted God's movement in their town and in their lives. When we limit people, we limit ourselves. God can use anyone to do His will, especially those we know well and tend to take for granted. The closer we are to people, the easier it is to focus on their flaws instead of their virtues. And the best virtue someone can have is the willingness to be used by God. God has so much glory that all He needs is a willing vessel to carry it. God is not looking for talent, good looks, charisma, intelligence or even sacrifice—He is looking for someone who loves Him, obeys Him and is eager to receive Him.

"Instead, God chose things the world considers foolish in order to shame those who think they are wise. And he chose things that are powerless to shame those who are powerful" (1 Corinthians 1.27 NLT).

DAY 227
The Faith Fight

—•———❧ ✳ ☙———•—

"And John, calling two of his disciples to him, sent them to Jesus, saying, 'Are You the Coming One, or do we look for another?'" (Luke 7.19 NKJV).

John the Baptist was the Voice in the Wilderness, preparing the way for Jesus. Very quickly when John was still only about 30 years old, his earth-shaking ministry was over. He was sent to prison, and midway through Jesus' 3-year ministry, he was beheaded by King Herod. He fulfilled his purpose of being the "voice" for Jesus, but his ministry of faith was still being tested. While in prison, John the Baptist sent two of his disciples to question Jesus. He wanted to know if Jesus truly was the Messiah. Jesus would not declare his Godhood. Instead, Jesus said for John to look at the signs: people were being healed, raised to life and set free by the Gospel. Jesus would not answer the question because He didn't want to usurp the ministry of faith, which John would live out until his death. John the Baptist will forever be known as the greatest prophet because he held onto faith and paved the way for the world to receive their King (Luke 7.28). Many times, we question the promises that God has given us. We wonder if we were simply hearing things. All circumstances declare that our promises are dead, and the enemy plants seeds of doubt in our soul. It is at this moment we beg God to split the heavens, send an angel or write His promises on the wall, so we can have proof that His promises are real. But how does that take faith? We must have faith in His promises and His Truth found in His Word. Jesus would not rob John the Baptist's claim to faith, and He won't do that to us today. He wants us to cling onto faith. So instead of waiting for supernatural intervention, we can reflect on all the "signs" that God has given us along the way. We must never let go of our ministry of faith because that is the "good fight" in which we claim victory.

"Fight the good fight of the faith. Take hold of the eternal life to which you were called when you made your good confession in the presence of many witnesses" (1 Timothy 6.12 NIV).

DAY 228
A Hard Man

"Then another servant came and said, 'Sir, here is your mina; I have kept it laid away in a piece of cloth. I was afraid of you, because you are a hard man. You take out what you did not put in and reap what you did not sow'" (Luke 19.20-21 NIV).

Jesus loved using parables when He spoke to the people. Parables are a form of fiction that relay a spiritual truth in a relevant way. God's Truths are holy and spiritual and we humans may have difficulty understanding them, which is why Jesus spoke these Truths in metaphors that we can appreciate. One such parable is "The Parable of the Minas" found in Luke. A nobleman, representing God, is leaving His country for a time, so He gives one mina (a form of money) to ten of His servants, telling them to "do business" until He comes back. One servant earns ten minas with the one he was given. Another servant earns five minas with the one he was given. The third, though, earns nothing—instead he kept his mina hidden in a handkerchief. How did he excuse his inactivity? He blamed it on the nobleman, declaring that the nobleman was hard and dishonest. But this servant's excuse did not hold. If the servant believed that the nobleman was hard, he would have at least put the mina in the bank to gain interest. The main culprit of this servant's inactivity is laziness. He did not want to do the business that his Master asked of him. Many people want to blame God for their inactivity, declaring that God is mean and hard. But how can this be? God is the embodiment of love. God is good to His children. God gave His Son, Jesus, so He could have a relationship with us and never have to forsake us even in our sinful state. The people who declare God as wicked truly have no clue of the character of God. They speak out their ignorance believing that it will excuse their laziness, but it will not. They will be judged by their own words.

"God is love. Therefore love. Without distinction, without calculation, without procrastination, love." – Henry Drummond

DAY 229
Busy Hands

───────※───────

"But on the first day of the week, at early dawn, they went to the tomb, taking the spices they had prepared" (Luke 24.1 ESV).

The women who followed Jesus were heart-broken. Their Savior, Lord and Friend had been crucified and His body placed in a tomb without its proper burial spices. The women obediently waited until after the Sabbath was over, and then they went straight to where Jesus' body lay. They would not let their feelings of sadness and devastation stop them from fulfilling the duties required of them. As they went to the tomb to complete the burial obligations of Jesus, a miracle was revealed to them: Jesus had risen! While the other disciples hid and halted their daily life, the women who continued with their work experienced the Resurrection first. Many times life throws terrible and damaging wounds our way, and God will give us a "Sabbath" to rest in our sorrow. However, when the Sabbath is over, we must pick ourselves up and continue our work. It is in the work of our everyday life that God will shine His greatest miracles. We have to trust that God can intervene even in the middle of our daily obligations. Life doesn't have to stop. In fact, when we keep our hands busy and our minds focused on the task, God can weave our efforts into His redemption plan. So instead of hiding and wallowing, let us renew our strength in the hope that the Resurrection Power of the Cross will penetrate even the darkest of moments.

"For his anger lasts only a moment, but his favor lasts a lifetime! Weeping may last through the night, but joy comes with the morning" (Psalm 30.5 NLT).

DAY 230
Jesus the Word

"In the beginning was the Word, and the Word was with God, and the Word was God" (John 1.1 NIV).

A "word" is a supernatural thought that is made into existence by the one who professes it. John declares that Jesus is the Word. He is the supernatural thought of God manifested into our earthly reality. And before God spoke our world into existence, He made sure that Jesus would be His Mouthpiece. Jesus, the Word, was with God, and He is the part of God who ushered our Creator God's thoughts into existence. Only through Jesus would the redemption plan of all creation be fulfilled. God made us in His image and gave us free will to create using our words and the actions that promote them. Our actions will always be in direct relation with our thoughts—the original seed of our words. What words are we thinking today? What thoughts are we going to usher into our own life? We have the ability with our free will to choose good thoughts of hope or evil thoughts of despair. The choice is ours. No matter our circumstance or the actions of others, we can funnel every word that we think, speak and enact through the Mouthpiece of God, which is Jesus Christ.

"A man's life will be of the character of his thought. His outward life will be as the inner impulse is." – John G. Lake

DAY 231
Best for Last

"And he said to him, 'Every man at the beginning sets out the good wine, and when the guests have well drunk, then the inferior. You have kept the good wine until now'" (John 2.10 NKJV).

Jesus' first miracle was at the wedding at Cana where Jesus turned water into wine. There were 6 large stone water pots filled with 20 to 30 gallons of water each, equaling to anywhere from 120 to 180 gallons of new wine. Jesus told the servants to bring the wine to the Master of Ceremony (a guest of honor who oversaw the festivities), and he declared to the bridegroom, "You have kept the good wine until now." This declaration is symbolic of Jesus being the New Wine poured out, offering grace to the entire world. But there is another meaning behind this statement: God loves to save the best for last, but the best only comes after Jesus has masterminded it. Sometimes in our life, God seems to tarry with His promises, but we forget that Jesus is overseeing every single promise that God has made in our life. The world will try to tempt us with cheaper versions of God's "wine," but these instant gratifications will not have the transforming power of Jesus in them. We must wait in the process that Jesus is conducting in our lives, gathering as many stone pots as possible. So when Jesus does finally come through for us, we will have gallons of water ready for His best. The wait is part of the process, and it will be worth it once we taste the sweetness of what Jesus can accomplish when we rely and wait on Him.

"Now all glory to God, who is able, through his mighty power at work within us, to accomplish infinitely more than we might ask or think" (Ephesians 3.20 NLT).

DAY 232
Believe or Gossip

———————————————

"Then many of the Jews who had come to Mary, and had seen the things Jesus did, believed in Him. But some of them went away to the Pharisees and told them the things Jesus did" (John 11.45-46 NKJV).

Mary, the sister of Lazarus, and everyone around her just experienced one of Jesus' greatest miracles: He raised a man to life who had been dead and buried for four days. Many people who witnessed the entire miracle unfold believed in Jesus. Observing Jesus' love and power being established on earth irrevocably changed the people's lives and souls. Jesus waited four days, knowing that although Lazarus would die, "This sickness will not end in death. No, it is for God's glory so that God's Son may be glorified through it" (John 11.4 NIV). God's glory was greatly demonstrated and because of it many people believed Jesus was the Son of God. However, there were other people who also saw first-hand the death and resurrection of Lazarus, but instead of believing, they ran to the worldly powers that be (the Pharisees) and gossiped. These people valued the opinion and esteem of humankind more than the presence of the world's Lord and Savior. God's glory is all around us. It doesn't take much to perceive His hand moving on His earth and in the lives of His people. But many times we are so focused on what the world thinks and what the world is doing that we miss what God thinks and what God is doing. Sometimes we just have to cut out the noise and take in the beauty and the goodness of the Lord. If we are too busy absorbed in popular gossip, our deepening belief in Jesus will be stunted. It is better to be people with hearts that believe versus mouths that gossip.

"For the earth will be filled with the knowledge of the glory of the Lord, as the waters cover the sea" (Habakkuk 2.14 NKJV).

DAY 233
Out of the Vine

"Yes, I am the vine; you are the branches. Those who remain in me, and I in them, will produce much fruit. For apart from me you can do nothing" (John 15.5 NLT).

Jesus uses a metaphor, comparing Himself to the Vine. It is no coincidence that His first documented miracle was turning water into wine at the Wedding of Cana. Wine is symbolic of Living Water mixed with earth and God mixed with Flesh, which represents Jesus. Jesus is the Living Water and He clad Himself in flesh in order to break His body like bread and pour out His blood like New Wine onto the earth. The New Wine is the New Covenant of Grace extended to a people who are incapable of keeping the Law (Old Wine). When we are connected to Jesus, we bear fruits on this earth that are ripe with Living Water. Our fruit will share the love and grace of Jesus to a world that thirsts for Him. If we are not connected to the Vine and we commit to actions that do not stem from Him, our fruit may seem plump and juicy, but they will only be filled with the dirty water of human effort. This fruit is counterfeit and will leave people thirsty for Living Water. This fruit may appear to offer sustenance, but really they have no eternal value. Jesus explains that anything apart from Him will be "nothing"—no matter how good and righteous it looks. For this reason, we must always make sure that everything we do is connected to the Vine of Christ or else we will waste time and leave a legacy of thirst.

"However strong the branch becomes, however far away it reaches round the home, out of sight of the vine, all its beauty and all its fruitfulness ever depend upon that one point of contact where it grows out of the vine. So be it with us too." – Andrew Murray

DAY 234

The Vine

"I have glorified You on the earth. I have finished the work which You have given Me to do" (John 17.4 NKJV).

Jesus being the perfect Son of God accomplished everything that God had planned for Him. He glorified God and completed His assignment. Even though He hadn't been crucified yet, Jesus had already confirmed inside Himself to do the Father's will (John 6.38). He would be obedient even to death on a cross (Philippians 2.8). Although we are not perfect, and we will never be able to accomplish the complete and perfect will of God in our lives, we can definitely finish our race well. We can't ignore our assignment just because we know we will stumble. We have to believe that the grace of Jesus is continually resurrecting our efforts into His perfection and righteousness. If our efforts are secure in Christ, we can trust that they will be pleasing to the Father. And if we are obedient, we don't have to wonder if our efforts are glorifying God. God will ensure that our steps of faith will magnify His glory on this earth and in heaven. So instead of giving up on our dreams, we can continue forward with the faith that Jesus is filling in the gaps of our mistakes. He will complete the work that He has started in us.

"Small deeds done are better than great deeds planned." – Peter Marshall

DAY 235
Sour Wine

"Now a vessel full of sour wine was sitting there; and they filled a sponge with sour wine, put it on hyssop, and put it to his mouth. So when Jesus had received the sour wine, He said, 'It is finished!' And bowing His head, He gave up His spirit" (John 19.29-30 NKJV).

Many people become confused by these verses in the Gospel of John. Jesus drank sour wine or old wine before giving up His spirit to God. We are baffled because in the Book of Matthew, Jesus tells His disciples, "I will not drink wine again until the day I drink it new with you in my Father's Kingdom" (Matthew 26.29 NLT). Also, Jesus refused to drink a wine that was mixed with gall that the soldiers offered Him before nailing Him to the Cross (Matthew 27.34). What we find is that Jesus is purposefully making a beautiful allusion to the reason for His sacrifice. The sour wine is a symbol of the Old Wine of the Law, the Covenant that God made with His Chosen People through Moses. The people stated emphatically that they could achieve God's holy standard (Exodus 19.8), so they had to experience failure to realize how much they needed a savior. By the time Jesus was born, the people have proven themselves unable to keep God's holy standard. A New Wine was needed—a Covenant of Grace between God and His People. Before Jesus died on the Cross, He drank from the Old Wine to illustrate He was consuming the Old Wine and bringing forth the Blood of the New Wine that would save the entire world—Not by Law but by Grace, not by our goodness but by His. Jesus would not drink the sour wine mixed with gall because "gall" is a symbol of bitterness. Jesus was not bitter when He drank the Old Wine of the Law that we were unable to fulfill. Rather, Jesus was so in love with us, His Creation, that He consumed it freely. He knew that next time He would be drinking the New Wine of Grace with all of us in heaven for eternity. Today we live in the New Covenant of Grace because of what Jesus did on the Cross and the blood that flowed from His broken body. We don't need to feel ashamed when we fall short of God's glory. Instead, we find undeserved salvation in Jesus.

"One of the soldiers, however, pierced his side with a spear, and immediately blood and water flowed out" (John 19.34 NLT).

DAY 236
Too Busy

———⟡———

"Then he said, 'Throw out your net on the right-hand side of the boat, and you'll get some!' So they did, and they couldn't haul in the net because there were so many fish in it" (John 21.6 NLT).

After Jesus died, many of His closest disciples went back to the familiarity of life before ministry. They experienced the death of their beloved Messiah and tried in vain to reestablish their purpose in fishing for fish instead of fishing for men. They fished all night without any yield from their vigorous labor. However, one command from their resurrected Savior the next morning caused a single cast of their nets to bring forth a bounty. Many times God tests our faithfulness to Him. He becomes silent for a moment, and we are left with the choice to busy ourselves with our own fruitless efforts or to wait quietly for His next command. Instead of working exhaustingly in their own strength, the disciples could have gotten a good night's sleep, hopped into their boat at daybreak and received Jesus' blessing of abundance just before they threw out their first cast. God's timing is never late and it's never early. His divine door opens right in the nick of time, right when we need it to. So instead of spinning our wheels until we finally hear Jesus give us our next step of faith, we should wait patiently at His feet and rest with an unshakeable trust that He will certainly come through for us.

"Waiting for a vision that 'tarries' is the true test of our faithfulness to God. It is at the risk of our own soul's welfare that we get caught up in the practical busy-work, only to miss the fulfillment of the vision." – Oswald Chambers

DAY 237
Staring at the Sky

"'Men of Galilee,' they said, 'why are you standing here staring into heaven? Jesus has been taken from you into heaven, but someday he will return from heaven in the same way you saw him go!'" (Acts 1.11 NLT).

After Jesus was resurrected back to life, He showed Himself before many people, including His apostles. He explained that He had to be taken up, so God would send them the Holy Spirit. Jesus told the apostles to wait for the power of the Holy Spirit, but that didn't mean they could all stand around staring where Jesus disappeared. Once Jesus vanished into thin air, two angels confronted the men who were gaping at the sky. They said that Jesus would come back the same way He left, and there was no sense in just waiting for Him. The apostles had work to do. They were to use the power of the Holy Spirit that God would unleash onto them to be witnesses in the world—witnesses of Jesus' saving grace and salvation. The Holy Spirit has authority and power He wants to impart on each of us, but we can't wait around for it. We need to continue to obediently work in the calling God has given us, believing that He will ignite us with His power as we learn to trust and follow Him. It's not about earning the Holy Spirit's power; rather, it's about having the character to use it with integrity and obedience. God wants to anoint us with His authority, but we can't just sit around staring off into space waiting for it to fall on us. We must be about the Father's business, working in our weakness so God can pour out His strength.

"If the Holy Spirit can take over the subconscious with our consent and cooperation, then we have almighty Power working at the basis of our lives, then we can do anything we ought to do, go anywhere we ought to go, and be anything we ought to be." – E. Stanley Jones

DAY 238
Bear Witness

"Then Peter stepped forward with the eleven other apostles and shouted to the crowd, 'Listen carefully, all of you, fellow Jews and residents of Jerusalem! Make no mistake about this'" (Acts 2.14 NLT).

Jesus finished His ministry, died on the cross, showed Himself resurrected to the multitude and ascended to the right hand of the Father. Now it was time for the apostles to take over the work that Jesus began on earth. Peter, Jesus' passionate yet imperfect friend and disciple, began the great work of building the Body of Christ, the Church. Once the Holy Spirit was imparted to a reconciled world, Peter stood up boldly, opened His mouth and gave testimony to all the information his heart and mind had gathered over the years. He needed to bear witness to everything Jesus meant to Him and relate his understanding to the audience that God had given him. This too is our mission. There is a lot about faith and Christianity that may seem confusing or difficult, but the main focus of our days is to give testimony to what Jesus means to us and what He has done in our lives. Some people will be loud like Peter. Others will be quiet like the Apostle John, but they all bear witness to Jesus in their own personal way. The power of God through the blood of Jesus Christ will also bear witness on our behalf when we take that step of faith and use our words and actions to proclaim the saving grace of Jesus Christ.

"They triumphed over him by the blood of the Lamb and by the word of their testimony; they did not love their lives so much as to shrink from death" (Revelation 12.11 NIV).

DAY 239
Repent and Refresh

———✦———

"Now repent of your sins and turn to God, so that your sins may be wiped away. Then times of refreshment will come from the presence of the Lord, and he will again send you Jesus, your appointed Messiah" (Acts 3.19-20 NLT).

Peter and John are preaching everywhere in Jerusalem. On their way to the Temple, they saw a man who had been lame since his birth. Peter not only demanded in Jesus' name this crippled man get up, but he also pulled him to his feet. The man suddenly could walk! Now Peter had everyone's attention. After explaining Jesus's sacrifice for the world's sins, Peter insisted that the people needed to repent and turn to God. This is a two-part command. The people could not turn to God if they had not yet repented from their sins. This is true for us today. To truly turn toward God, we must repent of any sin that the Holy Spirit is highlighting in our lives. This repentance and turning does not happen all at once. We each have layers of sin that God must pull away sheet by sheet. Just like an animal molting, we shed our flesh in repentance and become more like Christ over time. As we turn toward God, letting go of sin, we delve into a deeper relationship with Him. The life of faith is a process. Once we receive Jesus as our Lord and Savior, we begin to allow that seed of salvation—a gift to us through grace and received by us through faith—to permeate our entire being. And each time we struggle to repent and turn toward God, we receive supernatural refreshment from the Lord, a sweet reward on our difficult walk of faith.

"I will refresh the weary and satisfy the faint" (Jeremiah 31.25 NIV).

DAY 240

Ordinary

———·———⊰❈⊱———·———

"The members of the council were amazed when they saw the boldness of Peter and John, for they could see that they were ordinary men with no special training in the Scriptures. They also recognized them as men who had been with Jesus" (Acts 4.13 NLT).

Bold. Ordinary. Jesus. Here are three words that can confound the world. Peter and John were untrained, yet they had wonderful insights of Scripture. They had no degrees, no acclaim, no recognition—yet they spoke with boldness. Peter and John proclaimed the name of Jesus Christ and amazed the people around them. God uses the ordinary to confound the wise. There is nothing wrong with earning a theology degree if God wills it, but a theology degree will not move mountains. Only the Holy Spirit working in our lives will cause people to stand in amazement of the goodness and power of God. We don't need a university to learn about Jesus. The Holy Spirit is our personal teacher, eager to teach us daily if we would only give Him the time. Being homeschooled by the Holy Spirit might not get us a degree or a certificate, but it will change our lives with more power than any manmade honor can offer. We must never give up on learning from the Lord. We have to get out of the "public school" mentality and realize that we have a personal tutor with endless guidance, wisdom and understanding to reveal. The only thing it will cost us is our time and energy, but our tiny bit of resources devoted to enrolling into God's school will pale in comparison to the wealth of God's resources He will impart to us.

"The wise men shall be put to shame; they shall be dismayed and taken; behold, they have rejected the word of the Lord, so what wisdom is in them?" (Jeremiah 8.9 ESV).

DAY 241
Kick Against the Goads

"Then he fell to the ground, and heard a voice saying to him, 'Saul, Saul, why are you persecuting Me?' And he said, 'Who are You, Lord?' Then the Lord said, 'I am Jesus, whom you are persecuting. It *is* hard for you to kick against the goads'" (Acts 9.4-5 NKJV).

"To kick against the goads" was a rural expression during Jesus' time. Farmers would use "goads," sharp, pointed sticks, to encourage the ox to continue its course on the field. Sometimes the ox would resist moving and stubbornly kick against the goads, not wanting to work with the farmer to move in the desired direction. The resistant kicking of the ox would usually cause bodily damage because the goads would penetrate its flesh. Obviously, Saul (later named Paul who wrote half the New Testament) was kicking against the goads that the Lord was using to move him in the right direction. Finally, the Lord had to supernaturally intervene and cause Saul to lose his sight. Because Saul ignored the Lord's promptings, God needed to completely stop Saul's life in order to gain his attention. Many times, God puts "goads" in our lives. But instead of allowing those painful situations to move us in the right direction, we kick harder making our situation even worse. We fight and fight against the Lord, hurting ourselves and the people around us. Finally, the Lord has to supernaturally intervene to stop our downward spiral of disobedience and unresponsiveness. It would be better to have paid attention to the "goads" than to have our own stubborn way of fruitless and damaging kicking. We must always be aware of how we are doing in our walk of faith. Are we kicking and fighting the Lord's will or are we submitted to His greater plan? If we just take a moment to look at ourselves and our surroundings, we might recognize some goads that we had been ignoring.

"Teach me to do your will, for you are my God. May your gracious Spirit lead me forward on a firm footing" (Psalm 143.10 NLT).

DAY 242
Grace is Higher than Law

"And after the meeting of the synagogue broke up, many Jews and devout converts to Judaism followed Paul and Barnabas, who, as they spoke with them, urged them to continue in the grace of God" (Acts 13.43 ESV).

God has made two covenants throughout time with His people: The Old Testament Covenant of Law and the New Testament Covenant of Grace. Both covenants fulfill the redemption plan of God that He put in place when He gave us free will. Two trees were in the Garden of Eden. The Tree of Knowledge of Good and Evil represents free will. The Tree of Life represents Jesus Christ. Together both trees fulfill the amazing plan of God for His people. The Covenant of the Law is a set of rules that God designed that were humanity's only shot to achieve holiness on their own. However, even with the many rules of holiness, a system of sacrifice and redemption through the blood of animals was created because God knew His children would fall short. Once humans exhausted all effort to achieve holiness on their own, the time of Grace became ripe. Grace is higher than Law. Grace is not an excuse to do whatever we want. Grace is the ability to achieve God's perfect standard even in our sinful state. The blood of Jesus continually washes over our best efforts, making them holy and pleasing to God. Grace sets the highest standard, knowing that Jesus has achieved it on our behalf.

"And he gives grace generously. As the Scriptures say, 'God opposes the proud but gives grace to the humble'" (James 4.6 NLT).

DAY 243
Tent-Making

"Paul lived and worked with them, for they were tentmakers just as he was. Each Sabbath found Paul at the synagogue, trying to convince the Jews and Greeks alike" (Acts 18.3-4 NLT).

During his ministry in Corinth, Paul supported himself with tent-making. He would work during the week and on Sabbath he could be found in the synagogue, preaching about the name of Jesus. Paul may be one of the greatest New Testament evangelists who ever lived, and here he is doing manual labor. Many people mistakenly believe that once we follow the call of ministry (whatever shape that ministry takes) that we don't have to spend any of our own money getting that ministry running or work another job to support ourselves. We think that since the ministry is the Lord's that He should miraculously pay for everything with money to spare for our own wages. Although this may be eventually true for some people, the rest of us need to see our "tent-making" ministry as an integral part of our ministry in the "synagogue." Walking in accordance to God's plan for our lives will cost us everything we have, including our money. We will have to sweat, commit to menial tasks and humble ourselves to whatever manual labor God demands. The manual labor looks different for each person, but we all must engage in tasks that seem to have nothing to do with ministry. But our labor is not wasted. When we look from God's point-of-view, we will realize that God uses all our hard work for His glory and for our refinement.

"The Savior of the world a carpenter! The greatest preacher of the gospel a tent-maker!" – Philip Schaff

DAY 244
Jesus At Your Side

———•———⤜❋⤛———•———

"The following night the Lord stood by him and said, 'Take courage, for as you have testified to the facts about me in Jerusalem, so you must testify also in Rome'" (Acts 23.11 ESV).

Paul was in deep trouble. All his enemies surrounded him, and death seemed to be just around the corner. In fact, when Jesus came to his side and told him to take courage, more than 40 Jewish leaders were taking an oath not to eat or drink until Paul was dead. Paul was bringing the Good News of Grace to everyone who would listen, and the power-hungry religious leaders were irate. They didn't want to lose their position of prestige that they held onto so tightly. In the middle of the storm with the possibility of death on the heels of each morning, Jesus told Paul to "Take courage." Jesus was right next to Paul when the crushing weight of circumstances was at its peak. Today, we can trust that Jesus' presence will intensify as the hardships of our situation increase. When we find ourselves in an overwhelming situation, the Lord comes alongside us to encourage us and to guide us through the murky waters of oppression and despair. God will match our heartache with His grace, and He will come to the rescue with His love, comfort and peace when life seems to be falling apart.

"We must accept finite disappointment, but we must never lose infinite hope." – Martin Luther King

DAY 245
Disbelieving Truth

———•———❖———•———

"For this people's heart has grown dull, and with their ears they can barely hear, and their eyes they have closed; lest they should see with their eyes and hear with their ears and understand with their heart and turn, and I would heal them" (Acts 28.27 ESV).

After many trials, Paul finally makes it to Rome. He is still under arrest, but the authorities allow him to discuss the Good News of Jesus to the local Jewish leaders. Some of the people believed the Gospel, but others would not believe the Truth. As these unbelievers left, Paul quoted a verse from Isaiah about the hardened hearts and clogged ears of the people. God wanted to bring healing to His people, but they would not receive it from Him. The time of grace was at hand, but the leaders had twisted the laws to fit their agenda, and they didn't want to let go of their authority. They've allowed their hearts to become dull and have chosen to take their ears and eyes off of eternity, busying themselves with worldly understanding, prestige and opinion. The Truth of Jesus Christ is the Truth no matter if we want to perceive it or not. People do not want to turn from their selfish ways and desires, so they make a choice to ignore God or they try to control His presence in their lives. Either way, they will not receive the fullness of His grace and blessings. It is our choice. God will not force His goodness on us. We must receive it. The only way for our eyes and ears to be open is to be completely surrendered to God and submitted to His Truth.

"Harden the hearts of these people. Plug their ears and shut their eyes. That way, they will not see with their eyes, nor hear with their ears, nor understand with their hearts and turn to me for healing" (Isaiah 6.10 NLT).

DAY 246

In Jesus' Name

"First, I thank my God through Jesus Christ for all of you, because your faith is being reported all over the world" (Romans 1.8 NIV).

Paul wrote the Book of Romans as a letter to the church in Rome. He documented many amazing themes in this book, but one of the first practices he illustrates is "through Jesus Christ." Paul realized as Job did so long ago that we need a mediator to approach a holy God (Job 9.33). There is absolutely no way in our own efforts, holiness or birthright that we have access to a perfect God. We can't even give thanks to Him without a righteous intercessor. We are imperfect creatures, riddled with sin because of our own choices. But because of Jesus' sacrifice on the cross, we have been reconciled back to God through Christ. We are in Jesus and Jesus is in the Father; therefore, we are now in the Father through Christ and our sins and imperfections have been wiped clean. Our entire relationship with God is built on the Rock of Jesus Christ. We are lost, hopeless and separated without Jesus' intervention. For this reason, "through Jesus Christ," is one of the most important themes we will ever understand. Everything is possible through the awesome name of Jesus and nothing eternal is possible without it. All our actions, thoughts and words must be filtered through a profound awe of what Jesus Christ has done to save us and to bring us into relationship with the Father.

"Outside of Christ, I am only a sinner, but in Christ, I am saved. Outside of Christ, I am empty; in Christ, I am full. Outside of Christ, I am weak; in Christ, I am strong. Outside of Christ, I cannot; in Christ, I am more than able. Outside of Christ, I have been defeated; in Christ, I am already victorious. How meaningful are the words, 'in Christ.'" – Watchman Nee

DAY 247
Law to Grace

"Therefore no one will be declared righteous in God's sight by the works of the law; rather, through the law we become conscious of our sin. But now apart from the law the righteousness of God has been made known, to which the Law and the Prophets testify" (Romans 3.20-21 NIV).

God has a design for everything. From the brief moments of our individual lives to the stretches of generations throughout time, God has a plan that is coming to completion. The focus of this plan is His Son, Jesus Christ. Jesus binds all of history in His hands and holds us close to the Father's heart. He is our midwife, bringing the birth of God's completed creation to fruition. Part of knowing and receiving Jesus Christ is acknowledging our sin. The Law of God in the Old Testament was a precursor to the Law of Grace. It makes us aware of our sin and helps us realize that we cannot achieve God's holy standard alone. Law came first, so we would openly receive grace next. The same historical precedence of acknowledging sin to receive grace happens every day in our own lives. As we become aware of sin each day, we repent and receive more grace. During the process of recognizing, repenting and receiving, we become more and more like Christ. The more we perceive our sin, the more we lean into grace. Slowly we work the salvation of Jesus we receive by grace into every nook and cranny of our being. We become lovers of God, obeying out of the freedom of God's Grace; rather than merely subjects of God, obeying out of the fear of the Law.

"Grace means undeserved kindness. It is the gift of God to man the moment he sees he is unworthy of God's favor." – D. L. Moody

DAY 248
A Greater Death

"Now if we have died with Christ, we believe that we will also live with him. We know that Christ, being raised from the dead, will never die again; death no longer has dominion over him" (Romans 6.8-9 ESV).

If death is no longer master over Jesus, it is no longer master over us. Since we have died in Christ and have been raised to life again through Him, then the sting of death won't bite us. But here we are talking about a death greater than the death of our mortal bodies. We are talking about the death that is separation from God—this kind of death will never touch those of us who have died in Christ. We are saved from eternal separation from God, which we call hell. Once we receive Jesus as our Lord and Savior, He becomes our mediator, binding us eternally to a perfect God. We have been spiritually born into the Kingdom of Heaven on earth, and when our mortal bodies die, we will live forever in the presence of God. Physical death is a scary proposition if we don't know where we will live the rest of eternity. The weight of physical death should never overshadow the weight of our spiritual death. There is nothing wrong with taking care of the physical needs of others, but their spiritual well-being should always be our prime focus. It is a sad thing when we feed, clothe and shelter the ones we love, but we never offer them eternal life through Jesus Christ. Physical death loses much of its sting when we know that we will be spending eternity with God in heaven.

"Then I heard a voice from heaven, saying, 'Write these words: "From now on those who are dead who died belonging to the Lord will be happy."' 'Yes,' says the Spirit, 'they will have rest from all their work. All the good things they have done will follow them'" (Revelation 14.13 NLV).

DAY 249
It Depends on God

"So then it depends not on human will or exertion, but on God, who has mercy" (Romans 9.16 ESV).

Paul had such a deep understanding of faith that he could share the Gospel with almost anyone and make a case for Jesus that was hard to dismiss. Although he is many times called the Apostle to the Gentiles, he was also excellent with presenting the Gospel to the Jewish people and to people who understood Jewish law. Paul himself was of the strict sect of the Pharisees, so he understood how their thought systems worked. One of the main difficulties the Jewish people had with accepting a Savior was turning from trying to achieve their own righteousness (which none of them could ever accomplish) to freely receiving righteousness by faith through Jesus Christ. The other difficulty they had was realizing that they weren't children of God just because they were descendants of Abraham. Both of these paths to God were based on human effort, and Paul wanted them to see that our righteousness (right standing with God) was now based solely on God's effort via the death and resurrection of Jesus Christ. As humans, we could never earn or achieve our way to heaven. It doesn't matter what family we were born to or how good we think we are. We cannot gain right standing with God on our own. God knew this, so He implemented a plan to bring us to the end of ourselves historically as a people and individually as a child of God, so we would see our need for a Savior. Only when we see our need, will we reach outside of our human efforts and admit that we need a Savior.

"For all have sinned, and come short of the glory of God" (Romans 3.23 KJV).

DAY 250
A Shaming Heart

"One person believes he may eat anything, while the weak person eats only vegetables. Let not the one who eats despise the one who abstains, and let not the one who abstains pass judgment on the one who eats, for God has welcomed him" (Romans 14.2-3 ESV).

The heart is very good at shaming us. When we don't have a full understanding of our righteousness through Christ, it is easy to fall into a pattern of shame, guilt and failure. Soon a horrible cycle of sin and shame creates a cyclone of human effort and failure, leading us further away from our freedom in grace. We begin to feel guilty about everything—what we eat, what we watch, what we say and what we do. We try to add more parameters into our life, trying to safeguard every single one of our steps, but we find we aren't strong enough—we always let ourselves down. But God is not disappointed by our failures. That is why He sent Jesus to give us His righteousness. Because of His great love, God wants to have a relationship with us, and He is not surprised by our sin. In fact, He saved us while we were still sinners (Romans 5.8). When we fully embrace that we are the righteousness of God through Jesus Christ—not because we are strong but because of God's great mercy—we will no longer allow the sin of shame to control us. God corrects and convicts us, but He does not shame. As Christians, we are in Christ, and God has no desire to shame His perfect Son. Jesus died to overcome our shame, so we are now free from it! Let us fully embrace our status as co-heirs with Christ and a holy people unto God (Romans 8.17). We will never be perfect, and we are a work in progress, but shame no longer has dominion over us. Now instead of feeling shame, we can receive the great love that God has for us, which is the only thing that will destroy the cycle of shame, guilt and failure.

"But because of his great love for us, God, who is rich in mercy, made us alive with Christ even when we were dead in transgressions—it is by grace you have been saved" (Ephesians 2.4-5 NIV).

DAY 251
Good Boasting

"So I have reason to be enthusiastic about all Christ Jesus has done through me in my service to God. Yet I dare not boast about anything except what Christ has done through me, bringing the Gentiles to God by my message and by the way I worked among them" (Romans 15.17-18 NLT).

There is one thing for which we can boast: What Jesus Christ has done in and through us. It doesn't matter how big or small. If we felt a call from God and worked with the Holy Spirit to accomplish His will, we can boast! Whether it be raising our kids in a Christ-centered home, building a business that honors God, working in ministry to help those in need, restoring a marriage from divorce or even cleaning our neighbor's gutters—we can praise the Lord for our accomplishments. We can feel satisfaction for furthering God's Kingdom Plan. We can give testimony to how great and mighty are God's movements. Paul worked diligently to bring the Gospel to those who didn't know Him, so Paul could be honest and excited about his efforts. He wasn't showing off his work to gain approval from people; he was thrilled about all that God was accomplishing in him. Paul was bringing the salvation of Jesus to many people, and he was excited about the fruits of his labor. There is boasting that is self-centered and boasting that is God-centered. When our boasting glorifies the Lord and His will, we have nothing to feel guilty about. We are simply sharing God's goodness to the world!

"Therefore, as it is written: 'Let the one who boasts boast in the Lord'" (1 Corinthians 1.31 NIV).

DAY 252
Shouting the Foolish

"For the word of the cross is folly to those who are perishing, but to us who are being saved it is the power of God" (1 Corinthians 1.18 ESV).

A few good synonyms for the word for "folly," are the words "foolish," "stupid," and "crazy." These are pretty strong words, which would cause average Believers to sweep the Good News of the Cross under the rug, letting the world around them perish into eternal separation from God. But Paul replaced these negative words with the Truth: The cross is the power of God. The cross not only reconciles us (brings us back) to God, it gives us His power on this earth. The Cross of Jesus Christ is the single most important utterance that all of us will ever say. The cross is what gives us access to our Creator God, it is what makes our efforts pleasing to Him and it is what gives us rest from all of our human striving. The cross should not only be spoken by Believers in their homes, schools and workplaces, but it should also be shouted from every mountaintop (literally and metaphorically) that exist today. Yes, the world may think the cross is foolish, stupid and crazy; but those who understand its significance have the power of God at their fingertips. We must not let the world's ignorance of the cross cause us to muffle our words concerning it. In fact, their ignorance should cause us to speak more loudly, so the people who are perishing can claim it.

"Men have said that the cross of Christ was not a heroic thing, but I want to tell you that the cross of Jesus Christ has put more heroism in the souls of men than any other event in human history." – John G. Lake

DAY 253
Spiritual Stomach

———— ❖ ————

"My teaching was as if I were giving you milk to drink. I could not give you meat because you were not ready for it. Even yet you are not able to have anything but milk" (1 Corinthians 3.2 NLV).

We have in essence two stomachs: our spiritual stomach and our carnal stomach. Our spiritual stomach feeds the part of us that is controlled by God and our carnal stomach feeds the part of us that is controlled by self. Both stomachs ache with hunger, but when we refuse to feed one, the growling subsides, digestion slows and hunger finally diminishes. Many people no longer feel the hunger pains of their spiritual stomach. They've concentrated all their energy feeding their carnal desires, putting the spiritual stomach's needs on the back burner. The ache and longing of the spiritual stomach fades until by chance or circumstance, it is fed a tiny morsel of food—a sermon, a book, a chat, a devotional or a friend drops in spiritual nutrients that causes the stomach to feel again. Suddenly, the spiritual stomach roars with hunger, willing the person to either feed it or ignore it once more. Feeding the spiritual stomach takes obedience and a listening heart. When we put our desires on the back burner and wait intently on God's voice, we are now feeding our spiritual stomach. Every time we seek His will, press into His character and dive into His Word, we pour substance into our spiritual life. We become spiritually strong and our carnal desires become less emphatic when our spiritual stomach is fed. As we continue to feed our spiritual stomach, it is able to take greater and richer nutrients, digesting spiritual truths with ease--moving from milk to meat.

"Blessed are those who hunger and thirst for righteousness, for they will be filled" (Matthew 5.6 NIV).

DAY 254
Talk or Power

"For the kingdom of God does not consist in talk but in power" (1 Corinthians 4.20 ESV).

Words are very important. The Bible says that the words we speak have the power of life or death (Proverbs 18.21). However, there must be a belief that powers those words. What is the motive? What is the root of those words? Are they spoken in falsehood and insecurity or are they spoken with the resounding vibrations of belief within them? Paul says that God's Kingdom is not merely built on words; it is built on the power behind those words. When we confess God's promises, we must believe that they will be fulfilled according to God's plan and timing. If we doubt, we must ask God for the belief that we need. There is no use of confessing words that are powerless. Believing is not a feeling. It is a choice. And when we make the choice to believe God, every step we make each day moves us closer to our belief coming true. If our feet are not moving and our mouth is not confessing belief, then our words mean nothing. Words alone will not usher in God's Kingdom Plan in our lives. The power of God resides in our belief and our actions that overflow from that belief, and our words will build God's Kingdom only when they are filled with the power of belief.

"If you declare with your mouth, 'Jesus is Lord,' and believe in your heart that God raised him from the dead, you will be saved" (Romans 10.9 NIV).

DAY 255
Keeping Company

"But now I have written to you not to keep company with anyone named a brother, who is sexually immoral, or covetous, or an idolater, or a reviler, or a drunkard, or an extortioner—not even to eat with such a person" (1 Corinthians 5.11 NKJV).

There are times when we are ministering to others and times when we are simply enjoying the company of others. Paul is explaining that when we are around non-Christians, we should always be in a position of ministry (serving). People who do not know Jesus are on the "outside" and people who know Jesus are on the "inside" of our circle (1 Corinthians 5.12). So when we are around people on the "outside," we should make ourselves available to them with the Good News of Jesus, but we should always keep our guard up in truth and love. However, Paul gives a further dividing line. He explains that even though a person may be on the "inside" and called "brother," we may have to be careful about keeping company with them. If the Christians are living in blatant sin or rebellion against the Lord, we must treat them as "outsiders" and love and minister to them, but not let our guard down. We are all sinners, but people who are resisting the Lord are currently not being led by the Holy Spirit. And they can be moved by the enemy to hurt us, our ministry and our family. We can love them, but parameters must be erected until God is able to get a hold of them and turn them back to Him. We may find that there are only a few people we can really get comfortable keeping company with, but at least when we do find those special few, we can find comfort in the inner circle that God has provided for us.

"The righteous choose their friends carefully, but the way of the wicked leads them astray" (Proverbs 12.26 NIV).

DAY 256
Beating the Air

"Therefore I run thus: not with uncertainty. Thus I fight: not as one who beats the air" (1 Corinthians 9.26 NKJV).

When a fighter "beats the air," she or he is merely warming up, practicing, working out and/or preparing for a fight. Anyone who has been in the ring before knows that shadowboxing is a lot different than engaging in an actual bout. There is no fear of being hurt, there is no fear of losing and there is no fear of humiliating oneself when simply beating the air. Shadowboxing alone has benefits, but it will never prepare a fighter for his or her fight if there isn't an opponent. Fighters must have an adversary in the ring to learn, grow and win. As Christians, we are merely shadowboxing when we practice our Christian faith in the confines of our own home without ever moving outside of our comfort zones. In fact, if we don't take our faith out into the world where we will receive blows, get knocked down and sometimes even knocked out, we will never grow as Christians. We might have great "spiritual form," but we may be "spiritual wimps," unable to withstand even the weakest of enemies. We have to get into the ring of faith and take a stand for the Good News of Jesus Christ. Yes, we will get hurt. Yes, we may fall. But we will not stay down for long. Every bout we have along our spiritual walk makes us stronger and more victorious.

"I have fought the good fight, I have finished the race, I have kept the faith" (2 Timothy 4.7 NIV).

DAY 257
Finishing Well

———❖———

"Then last of all He was seen by me also, as by one born out of due time" (1 Corinthians 15.8 NKJV).

Paul had already admitted that he was resistant to receive Christ, which is why God called him as a stubborn ox in Acts 9.4-5. In fact, it took an awesome supernatural demonstration and physical blindness to finally get Paul's attention. Because of God's extended grace, Paul ultimately put his faith in Jesus Christ, but he kicked and fought the entire way to salvation. Paul was the first apostle that followed Christ after He had already been crucified, resurrected and ascended into heaven. Paul's ministry encapsulates the expression, "Better late than never." He was the least of these in the beginning, but he wound up shaking the world for Christ. His influence has penetrated the very fiber of our faith today. His "spiritual birth" may have been forced and premature, but he grew into a powerhouse of faith that changed the world. The importance is not on how we begin our race, but how we finish it. This is great encouragement for us today. We may have messed up in the past. God may have extended us a ton of grace to get us where we are today. But our past does not dictate our future. We still have the ability to achieve a powerful finish!

"The end of a matter is better than its beginning, and patience is better than pride" (Ecclesiastes 7.8 NIV).

DAY 258
With Love

❖

"Let all that you do be done with love" (1 Corinthians 16.14 NKJV).

Many people don't realize that "love" is not just a feeling. It is a choice. Jesus commands us to love (Matthew 22.39), and He could not command love if it were only an emotion. Free will ensures that no one is capable of commanding feelings to magically appear in people. However, choices can be commanded—whether we feel like doing them or not—and love is a choice. When Paul writes that we should do everything "with love," he is not talking about the lovely, nice feeling at the beginning of a romance. He's talking about the choice to love others and care about their well-being no matter what it costs and how much it hurts. God so loved the world that He allowed His Son to be beaten, crucified and die for the salvation of sinners. This is not a very pleasant picture of love, but it is the strongest form of love. Jesus didn't feel like dying on the cross, but He chose to do it because the Father commanded it. Jesus made a choice to obey *with love* and God sacrificed His Son *with love*. When we do everything "with love" each day, we will have to make tough decisions that aren't always warm and fuzzy. In fact, it means we will have to discipline with love, confront with love and sometimes walk away with love. God's love is always true and pure, so whenever we are confused about how to handle a situation *with love*, we can just go to Him and He will lead us *with love*.

"For God so loved the world that he gave his one and only Son, that whoever believes in him shall not perish but have eternal life" (John 3.16 NIV).

DAY 259

Spreading Aroma

"But thanks be to God, who always leads us as captives in Christ's triumphal procession and uses us to spread the aroma of the knowledge of him everywhere" (2 Corinthians 2.14 NIV).

Many people can spread their theological knowledge, but if their lives don't "spread the aroma of the knowledge" of Jesus, then their words will not change lives. Even Satan has a cursory knowledge of Scriptures that he used to tempt Jesus in the wilderness (Matthew 4.1-11). Yet, even with this knowledge, Satan could never spread the aroma of Christ; he can only spread the aroma of evil. An aroma sticks with people. It enters their senses and lodges itself into their internal person. As Christians, we can't just throw around our memorized Bible verses and expect lives to be transformed. Our thoughts, words and actions must have the aroma of Christ. The only way we can achieve such a sweet, supernatural scent is if we are spending time with Christ, face to face in His presence. Not only will we begin to smell like Him, we will begin to act and look like Him. Now when we share the Good News of Jesus Christ with others, our words will be wrapped up in the perfume of Christ. People won't be able to shake the Truth because the aroma will have penetrated their spirits with the flavor of Jesus and all the beauty that dwells in Him. The sweetness will either cause people to be drawn to God or to be repulsed by the unfamiliar smell. Either way, God will be pleased by our scent that emulates Jesus.

"Our lives are a Christ-like fragrance rising up to God. But this fragrance is perceived differently by those who are being saved and by those who are perishing" (2 Corinthians 2.15 NLT).

DAY 260
Face of God

———— ✦ ————

"For it is the God who commanded light to shine out of darkness, who has shone in our hearts to give the light of the knowledge of the glory of God in the face of Jesus Christ" (2 Corinthians 4.6 NKJV).

We see the glory of God in the face of Jesus Christ. God is our Creator, and many times He seems so perfect and distant that we can't reach Him. In fact, we in our imperfect state cannot even come close to God. He is holy, and we are not. Our sin separates us from our Creator, but God's plan didn't end at our sin. Our sin merely ignited the rest of God's plan on earth and heaven. God rested in the 7th day of creation, knowing that Jesus reconciled each Believer back into His loving arms. From His place on High, God shines His glory onto the earth, revealing the face of Jesus in the darkest parts of our hearts. We no longer have to grope for a tangible God. He is here in each of us, guiding us, molding us and growing us into His glorious image. God in the flesh has come to walk with us on every step of our earth-journey. We don't have to be afraid or confused; we simply need to keep our focus on the light shining in the darkness—a light that has destroyed eternal separation from our Heavenly Father.

"The people dwelling in darkness have seen a great light, and for those dwelling in the region and shadow of death, on them a light has dawned" (Matthew 4.16 ESV).

DAY 261
Open Heart

———— ❈ ————

"O Corinthians! We have spoken openly to you, our heart is wide open. You are not restricted by us, but you are restricted by your *own* affections. Now in return for the same (I speak as to children), you also be open" (2 Corinthians 6.11-13 NKJV).

Paul is admonishing and encouraging the church in Corinth in his letter. He is acting very much like a father to these people, correcting and guiding them. Paul is being honest about his own difficulty, and he's demonstrating a great love for the people of Corinth, which includes offering both discipline and mercy. It would be easy for someone to get offended by Paul's letter. Pride (including arrogance and insecurity) can keep people from receiving Paul's words, but Paul has invested greatly in this church, and his words match up with his actions. He implores the people to not get offended but to "be open," as he is open to them. It is very difficult to receive correction from people, but we must pull away from the finite moment and examine if the correction is coming from someone who has demonstrated his/her love to us in words and actions. Usually, admonishing someone is not fun. It's honestly easier just to look the other way. However, if the person really cares, he/she will take the time to offer guidance. We can swallow our pride and keep our hearts open if the guidance is coming from someone who has a history of investing in our lives. Rather than building a wall in our hearts, we can receive the correction openly and allow God to take our pain and fill us with His peace.

"Being open to correction means making ourselves vulnerable, and many people are not willing to do that." – Dr. Myles Munroe

DAY 262
Rich

"For you know the grace of our Lord Jesus Christ, that though he was rich, yet for your sake he became poor, so that you through his poverty might become rich" (2 Corinthians 8.9 NIV).

Humanity began its life in the perfect world of the Garden of Eden, but because we allowed sin into our heavenly home, we were separated from God. In an instant, we lost everything. Our world became corrupted by sin, and we began to feel pain, heartache, disease, need and death. We cry out to God, wondering why He allows our lives to be so hard, but we fail to realize that the struggle is what forces us to reach outside of ourselves for something more. Our pain and heartache move us to grasp onto faith. It is only when we see our poverty that we accept the richness that the Lord died to give us. We may try to build our own version of the "Garden of Eden" in our lives, but no matter how rich we are in this world, we will be poor eternally without Jesus. Once we understand that lasting wealth only comes from the Lord, no money, resources, connections, position or fame can diminish the richness of the Holy Spirit inside of us. We live our lives with purpose, knowing that one day we will be united with our God in our perfect heavenly home once more.

"You say, 'I am rich; I have acquired wealth and do not need a thing.' But you do not realize that you are wretched, pitiful, poor, blind and naked" (Revelation 3.17 NIV).

DAY 263
Sow Bountifully

"Now this I say, he who sows sparingly shall also reap sparingly; and he who sows bountifully shall also reap bountifully" (2 Corinthians 9.6 NASB).

God has given us each unmerited favor. We all have been given grace and mercy and blessings that we don't deserve when we accept Jesus as our Lord and Savior. Namely, we have been given right-standing with God, so we can dwell with Him for eternity in heaven. However, God makes it obvious in His Word that His system of reaping and sowing on earth is not a socialistic structure. The amount of seeds we invest in God's Kingdom will decide the amount of fruit that we get to enjoy and share with others. There is a disconnect if we think we can enjoy God's fullness if we invest no resource, no effort and no time. From this we can understand two things. First, our efforts must be rooted in the Vine of Jesus Christ. From the start if we are not sowing our seeds in obedience to the Holy Spirit, the fruit we grow will not be eternal and they will not continue with us into eternity. Second, once we are submitted to the Holy Spirit's will, we can sow bountifully. Sowing may sound like a pretty word in our culture today, but in actuality it takes work and sacrifice and there is little return for your time until the rains finally come in. We can be reassured, though. When the rains are withheld and our efforts seem to not be making a difference, we can trust that God stands by His Word. We will reap what we have sown.

"God does not give us everything we want, but He does fulfill His promises, leading us along the best and straightest paths to Himself." – Dietrich Bonhoeffer

DAY 264
Secure Reliance

"To keep me from becoming conceited because of these surpassingly great revelations there was given me a thorn in my flesh, a messenger of Satan, to torment me" (2 Corinthians 12.7 NIV).

Besides Jesus, no one in this world will ever be perfect. In fact, every strength God has given someone is directly tied to a weakness that God has also sanctioned. Paul had amazing revelations from God, but he also had a thorn that kept him humble. When we look at someone who excels in an area, we can also assume that there is an area in which they struggle. God uses the works of Satan to keep us dependent on His mighty hand. It would be far too easy to fall into the trap of self-reliance if our weaknesses were never exposed. So instead of letting us wander into our own inadequate abilities, God permits a thorn to be placed in our flesh. This thorn twinges our nerves whenever we get too reliant on our own strength, willing us to stay close to the Lord. When we admit our weaknesses and give them to the Lord, God is able to pour out His strength into our raw areas. However, if we hide these weaknesses and pretend that they don't exist, we circumvent God's power in our life. It is much better to admit that we have a thorn, knowing that everyone—even the Apostle Paul who led much of the world to Jesus—has a thorn that forges a secure reliance on God.

"Fear not, for I am with you; be not dismayed, for I am your God; I will strengthen you, I will help you, I will uphold you with my righteous right hand" (Isaiah 41.10 ESV).

DAY 265
Getting into Faith

———— ❖ ————

"Examine yourselves to see whether you are in the faith; test yourselves. Do you not realize that Christ Jesus is in you—unless, of course, you fail the test?" (2 Corinthians 13.5 NIV).

Once we receive Jesus Christ as our Lord and Savior by faith, we are saved from our emptiness and reconciled back to God. We now have a relationship with a perfect God, not on our own merit but by the unmerited favor of Jesus. Death becomes a door to eternity and the relationship we have with God continues into heaven. However, if we don't have that relationship on earth, the absence of our relationship with God will continue into hell. Jesus is now in us, so we must continue living by faith. Sometimes we take our eyes off of Jesus and put them on the waves of circumstances around us. This will only make us sink into despair. It is easy to allow the hardships around us to drown us in a spiral of fear, anxiety and sorrow. That is why Paul says to "examine yourselves to see whether you are in faith." Choosing to walk by faith and not by sight is a daily decision. Every morning we must decide to place our thoughts and actions into our faith. If we are standing firmly on the Rock of Jesus in faith, nothing the world throws at us can knock us away from Him. We may lose our breath for a moment, we may stumble or slip, we may even find ourselves holding on for dear life; but our steady faith in God will keep us from sinking and floating away into the whirlwind of the world. It is our firm faith during troubling times that shows a broken world that we have found true hope in Jesus Christ.

"What good is it, dear brothers and sisters, if you say you have faith but don't show it by your actions? Can that kind of faith save anyone?" (James 2.14 NLT).

DAY 266

Appointed

"This letter is from Paul, an apostle. I was not appointed by any group of people or any human authority, but by Jesus Christ himself and by God the Father, who raised Jesus from the dead" (Galatians 1.1 NLT).

So many times we wait for a person, a church, a business or an audience to appoint us. We desire the creditability of a title or a position for our hard work. We don't want to sacrifice or put forth the effort if there aren't people watching, handing out credit, accolades or money. The King of the Universe has appointed us, but because there is no validation from people, we disobey a direct call of God. Paul knew what it meant to be appointed by God alone. God had declared him an apostle to the gentiles, and he didn't need a church leader or public figure to declare him so. Paul stated over and over again his position as an apostle. He knew in his heart that God had appointed him, and he didn't need verification from anyone else. He boldly walked in his calling, changing the entire world for Christ and freeing nations from the bondage of sin with the Good News of Jesus. Yes, it is nice to be recognized by others, but they can't see the full picture of what God is doing. People may not recognize that God is bringing forth something new in your life. We must learn to walk in the confidence of God's appointment for our purpose, not allowing the titles of this world to throw us off. If God says it is so, it is so. If God says you can, you can. If God says you will, you will. Never let the thoughts, words and actions of others derail the call of God on your life. Place His appointment above the accolades of the world, and you will fulfill your destiny in power and grace!

"This letter is from Paul, a slave of Christ Jesus, chosen by God to be an apostle and sent out to preach his Good News" (Romans 1.1 NLT).

DAY 267
The True High Priest

"For am I now seeking the favor of men, or of God? Or am I striving to please men? If I were still trying to please men, I would not be a bond servant of Christ" (Galatians 1.10 NASB).

Paul committed the first half of his life to pleasing people. He had done such an excellent job keeping the stout rules of the Jewish law and learning from the best Jewish religious leaders (Acts 22.3) that he had been given authority directly from the high priest to persecute Christians. Since the Jewish people no longer had their own king, the high priest was the highest-ranking position at the time. Paul was well on his way to having the fear and esteem of all his peers and predecessors. However, there was another High Priest that would shake Paul's world, "converting" him to his true position and giving him authority from God. Paul was not called to destroy the Gospel of Jesus Christ; he was called to nourish it. Paul committed the second half of his life to pleasing God. His Jewish position died, but his position as apostle to the gentiles was born. As Christians, our "position" in the world dies, and we are born again with a new "position" in Christ. Through the years, we may be tempted to please people and seek favor in their eyes over pleasing God and seeking His favor. To avoid this, we must always come back to our point of conversion. People did not die for our sins, Jesus did. Jesus has our best position prepared for us, so we need to please Him above all else. We can have many jobs and titles in this life, but our utmost calling is Child of God through Jesus Christ (Galatians 3.26-27).

"So then, since we have a great High Priest who has entered heaven, Jesus the Son of God, let us hold firmly to what we believe" (Hebrews 4.14 NLT).

DAY 268

Justified

"Yet we know that a person is made right with God by faith in Jesus Christ, not by obeying the law. And we have believed in Christ Jesus, so that we might be made right with God because of our faith in Christ, not because we have obeyed the law. For no one will ever be made right with God by obeying the law" (Galatians 2.16 NLT).

Some of the Christian leaders in Galatia wanted the gentile Christians to circumcise themselves according to Jewish law. In effect, they were trying to blend their Jewish heritage with their Christian faith. Although Christianity was birthed out of Judaism, they are each their own distinct creation. Jesus warned His disciples that new wine could not be put in old wineskins (Luke 5.37). Jesus is the New Wine, and only He could justify the sins of mankind. Circumcision in itself is not wrong, but it cannot justify the sins of men. Although the Christian leaders were justified by their faith in Jesus Christ, they still wanted to try to control and achieve their holiness in the eyes of people. Circumcision was a major demonstration of obeying the Law. Today we have other demonstrations of being holy or justified in our Christian culture. Obedience to them does not make us holy. Only faith in Jesus Christ will ever make us holy. Once we wrap our minds and hearts around this truth, Jesus will grow bigger in our eyes, becoming our only lifeline to God. When Jesus is all we see, we will begin to obey Him for the right reasons. We obey Jesus' commands out of love—not to justify ourselves. We are justified by faith in Him alone.

"Jesus replied, 'Anyone who loves me will obey my teaching. My Father will love them, and we will come to them and make our home with them'" (John 14.23 NIV).

DAY 269
The Guardian

"Let me put it another way. The law was our guardian until Christ came; it protected us until we could be made right with God through faith" (Galatians 3.24 NLT).

Why did God put us under the law before allowing Jesus to put us under His grace? The law not only reveals our need for grace, but it also guards us until we are willing and ready to receive grace through the Finished Work of Jesus Christ on the Cross. The law is a lesser, human-centered form of holiness that couldn't even scratch the surface of God's holiness. Yet, it gave us at the very least a standard for which to aim. However, after hundreds of years guarded by the law, people could only project a holiness that was based on deceit, fear and power. Once our human manufactured holiness was at its peak, Jesus entered the scene and accomplished it. He came to the world offering a standard of His own righteous holiness that is perfect in every way. This holiness is not human-centered; rather, it is Christ-centered. It is based on the work of Jesus, not human effort. It is the highest standard of holiness rooted in grace and based on faith, love and mercy. Through the law we look at ourselves for perfection. We may try to project a false holiness for a time, but we will eventually find ourselves looking for perfection in Jesus Christ, for He is the only standard that is pleasing and acceptable to God. The law guards us on our journey for holiness until we reach the throne of God via the cross. When we project Jesus to the world, they will see the holiness of God on earth and in our lives.

"And by that will, we have been made holy through the sacrifice of the body of Jesus Christ once for all" (Hebrews 10.10 NIV).

DAY 270
Filled Vessels

"So I say, walk by the Spirit, and you will not gratify the desires of the flesh" (Galatians 5.16 NIV).

Walking by the Spirit may sound ultra-religious, but it really is not. It is actually ultra-relational. Humans are considered vessels in the Bible, and vessels are like containers with the sole purpose of being filled up. There are only two things that we can be filled with: the flesh (which is led by the enemy) or the Spirit (which is led by God). There are no other alternatives. We are vessels, and we cannot by our very nature stay empty—something or someone will influence us. That's why walking by the Spirit is relational—we are making a choice to walk with God's Spirit every day. God's Holy Spirit is able to fill our imperfect lives because of the Work of Jesus Christ on the Cross. We are now holy because Jesus died for our sins, giving us His perfection. Having the Holy Spirit interacting with us in such a personal way is nothing short of a miracle, but by faith we have this amazing relationship with a holy God. Walking by faith is much like a marriage: it is simply a decision to fill our lives with God, leaning on Him and letting Him guide our every step throughout our day.

"But we have this treasure in earthen vessels, that the excellence of the power may be of God and not of us" (2 Corinthians 4.7 NKJV).

DAY 271
Never Give Up

"Let us not become weary in doing good, for at the proper time we will reap a harvest if we do not give up" (Galatians 6.9 NIV).

God's timing is not our own, and His ways are not our ways. This becomes apparent as we work in accordance to the Holy Spirit. We may work diligently for the Lord and not reap a harvest at the time we expect it to come. Our earthly minds don't match up with God's divine mind. In fact, a lot of God's ways make no sense in the natural. Many times we have to pour out our faith and trust in situations that seem to be dry and dead. But the truth is that God will never lead us into the wilderness without providing for us supernaturally while we are there. God purposefully draws us into the desert, so we can learn to rely on Him as He fills us with His understanding, wisdom and provision. Having faith in a harvest when the land is barren takes great faith, and a Christian who can wield such faith in God's promises when all circumstances are hopeless is making a choice to grow in the Lord. The influences of the world become faint when we look through the eyes of faith and hold onto hope without becoming dismayed or bitter. We don't have to lose our hope because we can trust that "we will reap a harvest if we do not give up." God will come through for us and He will finish the good work He started in us!

"Whenever God calls us to a task, He will equip us and enable us to complete the task." – Michael Youssef

DAY 272
Predestined

"For he chose us in him before the creation of the world to be holy and blameless in his sight. In love he predestined us for adoption to sonship through Jesus Christ, in accordance with his pleasure and will—" (Ephesians 1.4-5 NIV).

Predestination seems to create quite the debate, but in actuality it is quite simple. God is good and He has predetermined that all people should become His children, but we have the free will to accept or deny this invitation. Predestination is an appointment, not a requirement. It cannot overstep the bounds of our free will—we have to make a choice to consent to this appointment. Although God created each of us, He gives us the choice to call Him Father or not. And the only way we can call Him father is if we accept His Son, Jesus. We all have this gift of "sonship" set before us—co-heir with Christ, Child of God, a Holy Priesthood—but we must open this gift in order to activate it. Some people may never open their gift, but it doesn't mean that God didn't predestine them to have it. He loves all of His children, and He longs for each of us to be adopted into His family through Jesus Christ. But He does not want robots; He wants sons and daughters who choose to embrace His love and His will. The predestination of "sonship" shot across space and time when Jesus rose from the grave, and it is up to us to receive it.

"For whom He foreknew, He also predestined *to be* conformed to the image of His Son, that He might be the firstborn among many brethren" (Romans 8.29 NKJV).

DAY 273

Masterpiece

"For we are God's masterpiece. He has created us anew in Christ Jesus, so we can do the good things he planned for us long ago" (Ephesians 2.10 NLT).

God has a plan. We don't live on an accidental earth with no purpose. We have meaning, which is probably one of the best ways to attract unbelievers to God. Living a life void of purpose is hopeless. No matter how hard we work, our efforts will perish when we do. We may be able to influence the next generation, but eventually they too will perish. Without God and His Kingdom being established on this earth, life would be merely a coincidence. People would lose hope and fall into depression, or they would compensate by distracting themselves with pleasures, drugs, relationships, things and experiences until the day they die. Jesus literally is hope on earth. He bridges the gap between heaven and earth, so that we can have God's Spirit in our lives and throughout our days. God is infinitely creative. He created us, renewed us through Jesus and has good things planned for us. As we grow in the amazing knowledge of God's plan for our lives, people will begin to notice. They will see that we have a hope that is beyond this world. A hope that when our 70+ years on earth are over that we will live eternally in the presence of our Creator God. We can share this hope with others, so they too can recognize that they are masterpieces of God created to do amazing things for His Kingdom!

"For we were saved in this hope, but hope that is seen is not hope; for why does one still hope for what he sees? But if we hope for what we do not see, we eagerly wait for *it* with perseverance" (Romans 8.24-25 NKJV).

DAY 274
Been Brought Near

"But now in Christ Jesus you who once were far off have been brought near by the blood of Christ" (Ephesians 2.13 NKJV).

The Bible is filled with so many promises that it would take more than a lifetime to find and apply every single one. But we can start today finding and claiming these promises. One of the most profound promises is that we have been reconciled back to God. *Reconciled* is a religious word that simply means "*been brought near.*" We were separated from God in our sinful state, but through Jesus Christ we have "*been brought near*" Him again. In fact, the Bible says that we are in Jesus and Jesus is in the Father. So we are literally one with the Father through Jesus Christ. What a promise! No matter how ugly our situation or how horrible we feel, God is with us. He will never forsake us (Deuteronomy 31.6). We don't have to be discouraged or fearful because we have the God of the universe right by our side. He has the whole world in His hands, and our problem is no match for His great might. He will guide us in truth, peace and love, so we don't have to worry. We have "*been brought near*" to a God who saves! We have nothing to fear!

"On that day you will realize that I am in my Father, and you are in me, and I am in you" (John 14.20 NIV).

DAY 275
love of Christ

"May you experience the love of Christ, though it is too great to understand fully. Then you will be made complete with all the fullness of life and power that comes from God" (Ephesians 3.19 NLT).

We like to talk about God's power in our lives, but we sometimes miss where that power comes from. "The fullness of life and power…from God" is rooted in experiencing the "love of Christ." Though we will never understand Jesus' love in its fullness, we can gain strength from knowing that His love for us is so amazing and vast that it is beyond our comprehension. Jesus' love for us establishes God's expansive power in our lives. Jesus loves us so much that He not only died for our sins, but He also died to give us His power, strength and authority. That is the basic principle: fall in love with Jesus more every day and gain more of God's "life and power" every day. If we truly want to be Kingdom Builders and World Changers, our first priority should always be loving Jesus by getting to know Him more through Bible reading, prayer and meditating on Him. We don't have to worry about being strong enough or good enough—we simply need to trust and obey out of love. Once our love for Jesus becomes unshakeable, God can use us and our lives to do great and mighty things for His Kingdom.

"Truly, truly, I say to you, whoever believes in me will also do the works that I do; and greater works than these will he do, because I am going to the Father" (John 14.12 ESV).

DAY 276
Only One

"There is one body and one Spirit, just as you were called in one hope of your calling; one Lord, one faith, one baptism; one God and Father of all, who is above all, and through all, and in you all" (Ephesians 4. 4-6 NKJV).

Whatever clever and beautiful arguments people make about faith, there is only One hope, and that is through the Name and Person of Jesus Christ. Many people will implement their own understanding of God's mystery about the One and try to rewrite what God has established. They will divide the One Truth, into many truths to satisfy their need for human control and understanding. But the fact remains: there is only One body of Christ, which is the Church. There is only One Spirit in that Church, which is God's Holy Spirit. There is only One hope, which is our salvation and reconciliation to God through Jesus Christ. There is only One Lord, and every knee will bow before His presence and confess that He is Lord (Romans 14.11). We have one faith, one baptism, one God, one Father who reigns in and over all of us. Jesus is the only Way. Jesus is the only Truth. If we miss out on Jesus, we miss out on everything. There is only One.

"I would not give one moment of heaven for all the joy and riches of the world, even if it lasted for thousands and thousands of years." – Martin Luther

DAY 277
People of light

"For once you were full of darkness, but now you have light from the Lord. So live as people of light" (Ephesians 5.8 NLT).

Light changes our perspective on a situation. It brings illumination, clarity and objectivity. Light gives us the actual details of what is happening, which many times contradicts with how we are feeling at the time. Wrong feelings can distort how we see people and situations, especially if we are consumed with powerful emotions, like passion, anger, hurt, jealousy, etc. When our feelings and our understanding (guided by light) are at odds, we must always trust the light. We can't always trust our feelings. The Bible explains that the heart above all else is deceitful. But if our heart is submissive to the Holy Spirit, the light will expose our distorted feelings, and we can make godly choices instead of rash decisions. We don't have to walk around chained to negative feelings that rip apart our relationships and cause us to stumble. Jesus came to set us free from emotional-slavery. We can walk confidently and freely in the light, knowing that our steps are directed by truth, not by feelings that change on a whim.

"God is God. Because he is God, He is worthy of my trust and obedience. I will find rest nowhere but in His holy will that is unspeakably beyond my largest notions of what He is up to." – Elisabeth Elliot

DAY 278
Strong in the Lord

———— ❧ ✿ ❧ ————

"Finally, my brethren, be strong in the Lord and in the power of His might" (Ephesians 6.10 NKJV).

People talk a lot about being strong. Strength seems to be synonymous with someone who has everything together—all their ducks in a row. Strength helps people perform, advance and succeed in all areas of life. But what people don't realize is that human strength will not achieve the victory in God's Kingdom. Personal strength can only go so far, and most of the time God calls us to conquer things that are way beyond our current ability. The only way to thrive doing God's will is to rely on His strength, power and might. We gain a supernatural strength when we have a firm reliance on God's strength. As we become fully aware of how strong God is and how powerfully He can move in our obedience, we learn to tap into His might. We will never be strong enough to achieve the amazing things that God has planned for us, but God knows that. He bequeaths His strength to those willing to accept and wield it. God's strength is a gift that must be used in order to accomplish great and mighty deeds for His glory. Our arms may be weak, our emotions may be compromised and our perseverance may be floundering but God is consistent in His might. We simply need to step into a power that is rightfully ours through the Finished World of Jesus Christ on the Cross.

"So he said to me, 'This is the word of the Lord to Zerubbabel: "Not by might nor by power, but by my Spirit,"' says the Lord Almighty" (Zechariah 4.6 NIV).

DAY 279
Right Words

"And pray for me, too. Ask God to give me the right words so I can boldly explain God's mysterious plan that the Good News is for Jews and Gentiles alike" (Ephesians 6.19 NLT).

Many Christians fear not having the right words. We know that we are representatives of God and His Kingdom, so we want to discuss our faith in a way that would be pleasing and persuasive to others. We worry or fear being called on by people because we feel like we could possibly push them away from faith. Sometimes we can become so overwhelmed with thoughts of inadequacy or rejection that we don't even try to discuss our faith and the Good News of Jesus with anyone. But we don't have to worry or fear. All we have to do is ask God to give us the right words. If we are spending time with Him and reading His Word, He'll make sure to give us just what we need right when we need it. He loves His children more than we do, and He wants to reach them. He is more than capable of using our weakness to demonstrate His strength. We don't have to shy away from talking about Jesus. We can be open and honest with what we understand and what we don't understand about "God's mysterious plan," trusting that God will work His truth into our words.

"But when they deliver you up, do not worry about how or what you should speak. For it will be given to you in that hour what you should speak" (Matthew 10.19 NKJV).

DAY 280
On the Day

"And I am certain that God, who began the good work within you, will continue his work until it is finally finished on the day when Christ Jesus returns" (Philippians 1.6 NLT).

Our work for Jesus Christ does not end when we die. Actually, the seeds we plant and water won't be fully ripe and harvested until Jesus' return. This means that our work will continue beyond our single lifetime on earth. We won't fully comprehend the entirety of our obedience until all the earth has entered into heaven before the glory of God. Usually, we won't see the bigger picture of how God is using our seemingly tiny steps of faith. A single word of encouragement to a downtrodden soul may appear small to us, but it may have huge ramifications throughout time. Our words and actions guided by the Holy Spirit are like tools that God uses to shape His Kingdom on earth and bring it to fruition. When we get stuck on seeing immediate and big results, we may miss opportunities that look insignificant, yet play an important role in something beyond our comprehension. Many people forgo God's supernatural work in their lives because it looks trivial in the natural. But we must never underestimate God's will and plan. A small act of obedience given to God can be powerful enough to change the world.

"Plant what is right and good for yourselves. Gather the fruit of lasting love. Break up your ground that has not been plowed. For it is time to look for the Lord, until He comes and pours His saving power on you" (Hosea 10.12 NLV).

DAY 281
Working the Seed

"So then, my dear ones, just as you have always obeyed [my instructions with enthusiasm], not only in my presence, but now much more in my absence, continue to work out your salvation [that is, cultivate it, bring it to full effect, actively pursue spiritual maturity] with awe-inspired fear and trembling [using serious caution and critical self-evaluation to avoid anything that might offend God or discredit the name of Christ]" (Philippians 2.12 AMP).

Once we receive salvation through Jesus Christ and His work on the Cross, we are reconciled back to God. Our sins that separate us from God's Holy throne have been washed away, and we can boldly walk into His presence. This salvation is a supernatural seed that is planted within our spirits. But that seed needs to be "worked out" into every area of our being and lives. On this earth, we are becoming the people we will be for eternity. Our maturity in heaven depends on the choices and actions we commit here on earth. Yes, the salvation we receive is not based on our own merit, but this precious seed can produce a harvest for God's Kingdom if we are willing to cultivate it. If God only wanted to reconcile us, He would take us to heaven right when we receive salvation. But God has a specific design and destiny for us, and it will take a lifetime to come close to fully embrace and embody His purposes. Salvation is truly just the beginning of an amazing adventure with God. We will spend our lives allowing the seed of salvation to transform us into the image of Jesus, so we can produce an amazing harvest for His glory.

"For you have been born again, not of perishable seed, but of imperishable, through the living and enduring word of God" (1 Peter 1.23 NIV).

DAY 282

Mutilation

———•———❦———•———

"Beware of dogs, beware of evil workers, beware of the mutilation!" (Philippians 3.2 NKJV).

Paul is speaking to his fellow Believers, warning them to beware of three types of people. These people we can love with God's supernatural love, but we must tread carefully in their presence, staying cautious of their influence in our lives. They are not led by the Spirit, and at any time the enemy can use their actions to fight against God's purposes for us. The sad truth about these three types of people is that two of the three claim to be Children of God. The first group is "dogs," which is a metaphor for unbelievers—people who have not yet been cleansed by the Spirit of God through Jesus Christ. These people do not have the Holy Spirit and cannot be expected to knowingly participate in the things of God. The second group is "evil workers," which are Believers who think they are working for the Lord, but they are actually devising their own schemes. They stopped listening to the still, soft voice of the Holy Spirit long ago and are living out a self-directed life. The third group of people commit "mutilation." Mutilation is the counterfeit of circumcision. These people believe they are allowing God to circumcise their hearts, but in actuality they are mutilating themselves with self-righteous notions of human holiness. They have become their own lord and judge in the name of Christianity and cut themselves and others with "holy" condemnation. It takes time to allow God to purify us into the image of Jesus, and although self–guided religious mutilation may feel spiritual, it is actually damaging our spirits and preventing God's move in our lives. We must never put "confidence in human effort" and always "rely on what Christ Jesus had done for us."

"For we who worship by the Spirit of God are the ones who are truly circumcised. We rely on what Christ Jesus has done for us. We put no confidence in human effort" (Philippians 3.3 NLT).

DAY 283
Upward Call

———————————————

"I press toward the goal for the prize of the upward call of God in Christ Jesus" (Philippians 3.14 NKJV).

People can have many goals—get married, have children, earn a degree, create wealth, run a business, buy a big house, take a dream vacation, retire early—but those goals are fruitless if they are not seeded in the "upward call." Having a higher perspective, one focused on eternity, is a choice that doesn't come naturally. Our world and culture today are very goal-oriented. Books, TV shows, websites, magazines, etc., all provide information on how to set and achieve goals. However, these goals must be planted in the Vine of Christ in order to produce results that enrich God's Kingdom Plan on earth and heaven (John 15.5). There is nothing to fear, though. God would not place desires into our hearts only to torment us. We are citizens of heaven, and God has designed us with everything we need to achieve our goals on earth. And if the goals we have set don't come to fruition, God has something even better in mind for us. All we have to do is give God our goals and press on toward the "prize of the upward call" that God has ready for us. Switching from a self-focused call to an upward call is a simple decision that can radically change our impact on this world. We can choose to filter all our goals through the Holy Spirit, trusting that God has a plan for our good and for His great purposes.

"But we are citizens of heaven, where the Lord Jesus Christ lives. And we are eagerly waiting for him to return as our Savior" (Philippians 3.20 NLT).

DAY 284
Prayer Instead of Worry

"Don't worry about anything; instead, pray about everything. Tell God what you need, and thank him for all he has done" (Philippians 4. 6 NLT).

When thoughts are trying to consume us with worry, the only thing to combat our anxiety is to pray about everything. We can try to distract ourselves with books, movies, friendly chatter and other diversions, but we will eventually find ourselves full circle fraught with the same worries again. Paul says the only alternative to worry is prayer. God knows what we need, and He is more than able to provide for us physically, emotionally and spiritually. Anything that is plaguing us must be dealt with in the supernatural realm as we commune with God in prayer. He is the only One that can provide complete peace in our minds, hearts and situations. The longer we put off seeking God about our worries, the longer we will have to deal with our negative thoughts in our own strength. But our human strength will eventually run dry and we will either sink into despair or finally run to our Heavenly Father. It is best to prevent the destructive pattern of worry, anxiety and despair and turn to Jesus right away in prayer. When we finally seek God, He will give us His amazing peace, which will guard our minds and hearts from falling into a pit of despair once more.

"Then you will experience God's peace, which exceeds anything we can understand. His peace will guard your hearts and minds as you live in Christ Jesus" (Philippians 4.7 NLT).

DAY 285
All Things

"And this same God who takes care of me will supply all your needs from his glorious riches, which have been given to us in Christ Jesus" (Philippians 4.19 NLT).

As Christians, we may grow so accustomed to having an intimate relationship with God through Jesus Christ and His Finished Work on the Cross that we forget one very important fact: God is the richest, most powerful, most loving and most influential Figure in the universe. We think we understand God and we water down His impact on our lives because He has become too familiar in our limited understanding. And although God condescended Himself as a baby in a manger through the person of Jesus Christ and lowered Himself into our flesh so He could have a relationship with us, He is still the Creator, Owner and Master of all that is natural, supernatural and everything in-between and beyond human thought. Everything is under God's authority. We may have free will now, but eventually every knee will bow before the King of Kings and Lord of Lords (Romans 14.11). If God is this rich, powerful and influential, shouldn't we trust Him to meet all our needs—not according to what we deserve, but according to His glorious riches. We never have to worry about God not coming through for us. We simply need to match our faith to what we know is true from the Bible. God will "graciously give us all things" we need to accomplish His will.

"He who did not spare his own Son, but gave him up for us all—how will he not also, along with him, graciously give us all things?" (Romans 8.32 NIV).

DAY 286
Jesus, The Visible God

"He is the image of the invisible God, the first born over all creation" (Colossians 1.15 NKJV).

God can feel so distant and far away sometimes. In the middle of the night, fear can grip us by how lost or empty we feel. Is there a God? How can we reach Him? Why do we feel so alone? Questions like these can plague us and cause us to despair. How can we, mere humans, reach a perfect and holy God in a spiritual realm outside of our reach? But we don't have to lose hope. The feet of God walked this dusty earth. The hands of God touched broken flesh. The person of God lived thirty-three years on earth, interacting with His spiritual family wrapped in flesh. Jesus is God, intended to be the "first born" over all of us, and He entered our shattered world in order to have a relationship with us. We are not alone. God has the face of Jesus Whom we read about in the Bible. The Old Testament predicts Him, and the New Testament presents Him. He is Immanuel—God with us. We never have to feel alone again. God is not some remote entity in the great expanse. Jesus is the image of God on earth. Without Jesus, God is impossible to reach; but with Jesus, God is our Father, Guide, Friend and Savior. Once we have Jesus, nothing can separate us from an intimate relationship with God.

"And I am convinced that nothing can ever separate us from God's love. Neither death nor life, neither angels nor demons, neither our fears for today nor our worries about tomorrow—not even the powers of hell can separate us from God's love. No power in the sky above or in the earth below—indeed, nothing in all creation will ever be able to separate us from the love of God that is revealed in Christ Jesus our Lord" (Romans 8.38-39 NLT).

DAY 287
Maturity in God

"He is the one we proclaim, admonishing and teaching everyone with all wisdom, so that we may present everyone fully mature in Christ" (Colossians 1.28 NIV).

Accepting Jesus as Lord and Savior is the first step in our walk of faith. Jesus explains that we are literally "born again" spiritually. Therefore, we are newborns when we begin our journey of salvation on earth, and our relationship with God the Father is very fresh and immature. Just like a baby, a new Christian must be nurtured gently into the things of God. Once we have a relationship with God through Jesus Christ, we can walk through the process of becoming fully mature. This means we may experience our spiritual babyhood, terrible twos, childhood, adolescence, teens, twenties, midlife and seasoned ages with the Lord. There is no way that a person can skip from infancy to maturity overnight unless God puts him/her through a pressure-cooker of circumstance. Most of us wouldn't want to mature so quickly, and God would have to shower down His grace onto the soul who does. Rather, we want the experience of reaching every milestone in our Christian faith. Knowing that we will not become a spiritual powerhouse overnight relieves the anxiety of trying to be something we are not. It is better to have a true evaluation of where we are in our spiritual maturity, allowing the Holy Spirit to grow us according to His will for our lives. We are called to grow in maturity—not instantly become mature. We trust that God will be patient with us as we are becoming fully mature in Christ throughout every stage of our Christian walk. Also, we can rest in the yoke of Jesus, knowing that if we follow closely to Him, He will get us where we need to go and the burden of maturing will be manageable until the day we get to see Jesus face to face (Matthew 11.30).

"Jesus replied, 'Very truly I tell you, no one can see the kingdom of God unless they are born again'" (John 3.3 NIV).

DAY 288

A Head Disconnected

"Don't let anyone condemn you by insisting on pious self-denial or the worship of angels, saying they have had visions about these things. Their sinful minds have made them proud, and they are not connected to Christ, the head of the body. For he holds the whole body together with its joints and ligaments, and it grows as God nourishes it" (Colossians 2.18-19 NLT).

Staying connected to the Lord and His will for our lives takes a concerted effort. It is easy to get distracted and begin to live in our self-fulfilling, spiritually ignorant flesh. Even people in ministry can get sidetracked with the busyness of "doing" church and neglect to rely on the Lord and stay sensitive to His voice. They may wind up doing the things that make them look "pious," but they are not truly taking time to seek the Lord. We must take care not to head down this destructive detour; but if we find ourselves out of obedience with God's will, we can quickly repent and return to Him. Plus, we can use discernment when other people try to influence our lives, especially in spiritual matters. Are these people allowing God to be the head over their lives or has pride prevented them from staying submissive to the Lord? Jesus can only keep us secure and whole if He is in charge and the head over all we do. If He is not in His rightful place in our everyday thoughts, words, choices and actions, our lives will eventually fall apart. God is the glue that holds us together, and we can try to be in control for a while, but without the "Head" in our lives, we will wander around without eyes to see and ears to hear. Every moment of every day, we must choose to place God as the head, trusting that He will keep us secure in Him and lead us on the "best pathway."

"The LORD says, 'I will guide you along the best pathway for your life. I will advise you and watch over you'" (Psalm 32.8 NLT).

DAY 289
Things Above

"Since, then, you have been raised with Christ, set your hearts on things above, where Christ is seated at the right hand of God" (Colossians 3.1 NIV).

Physical baptism is a spiritual representation of what happens to us when we accept Jesus as our Lord and Savior. Our sinful self literally has been crucified with Christ, and a new creation has risen within Him. We are essentially tucked away in Christ, and we are now clothed in His righteousness, which gives us access to and a relationship with a holy God. We didn't do a single thing to undergo this supernatural transformation; we simply had to confess that Jesus is Lord, recognize our sin and ask Him into our hearts. But that is only the beginning step in our walk of faith. The next step toward working that salvation into every facet of our lives is up to us. Every day on this earth until we die and enter into God's presence in heaven, we have to choose to set our hearts on things above. We have to determine to place Jesus above all else, understanding that heaven is our true and eternal home. It is very easy to get swept away in the craziness of this life, allowing all sorts of distractions to knock our view on lesser things. But if we choose to keep our eyes on Jesus, seated as the right hand of God, the lesser things will become part of God's greater plan. God knows that we have responsibilities that must be done on earth, and He can make even the most tedious tasks—laundry, diapers, paperwork, lawn mowing—part of His grand design to grow us and His kingdom on earth.

"If only you would prepare your heart and lift up your hands to him in prayer!" (Job 11.13 NLT).

DAY 290
An Inheritance

***

"Work willingly at whatever you do, as though you were working for the Lord rather than for people. Remember that the Lord will give you an inheritance as your reward, and that the Master you are serving is Christ" (Colossians 3.23-24 NLT).

God created everything, and He has made us each a steward of His creation. We can work for people and receive awards allotted by them—paychecks, grades, fame, notoriety, etc. But these things will be fleeting because people can only share what they have been already given by God. When we work for God, however, we are not simply given rewards. We are given an inheritance of His Kingdom. We are granted an everlasting portion of God's fulfilling plan on earth and heaven that will never be taken or perish. We are in essence Children of God, showing ourselves faithful guardians of His supernatural agenda, so that in heaven God will give us dominion over our chosen inheritance. God will have us work for others on earth, but we serve them under the overlying theme of serving God. People may reward us, but our eyes are on the bigger prize—an inheritance from the Creator of the Universe. We can commit all that we say and do to the Lord, knowing that only He is the true and rightful master of everything. All that is created is under God's authority, and we will work diligently in obedience to Him and not to the changing whims of humanity.

"His master said to him, 'Well done, good and faithful servant. You have been faithful *and* trustworthy over a little, I will put you in charge of many things; share in the joy of your master'" (Matthew 25.23 AMP).

DAY 291
Laboring Prayer

"Epaphras, who is *one* of you, a bondservant of Christ, greets you, always laboring fervently for you in prayers, that you may stand perfect and complete in all the will of God" (Colossians 4.12 NKJV).

How many times have we "labored fervently" for someone in prayer? God knows that we are busy, and many times we can only whisper a short prayer on behalf of our family member or friend, but sometimes God divinely calls us to labor out our prayers. The image of laboring brings to mind words like sweat, exhaustion, toil and struggle. We can also picture a woman giving birth to her newborn baby. It is painful, difficult and filled with groans of difficulty, but the end result is new life! There are times when we must wrestle with our prayers because the need is so strong. When we feel the contractions of this kind of prayer coming on, we should never avoid them. God is asking us to step up to the challenge. There is someone who needs a breakthrough and our prayers mixed with our faith can help birth that breakthrough. What a reward we will gain if we willingly labor these prayers on behalf of others! We can be a part of bringing forth something new for the Lord! And when everyone beholds what God has done, we can know that our prayers made a difference. God has allowed us to carry a small portion of His kingdom plan on earth that will live out for eternity in heaven.

"Pray in the Spirit at all times and on every occasion. Stay alert and be persistent in your prayers for all believers everywhere" (Ephesians 6.18 NLT).

DAY 292
Joy Imitators

"You became imitators of us and of the Lord, for you welcomed the message in the midst of severe suffering with the joy given by the Holy Spirit" (1 Thessalonians 1.6 NIV).

Having an imitator may not sound like an enjoyable experience. Would we really want someone who behaves like us, mimicking our every move like a reflection of our lives? Every one of us has struggles, and we each have times where we fall short or even fall down. But when Paul tells the members of the Thessalonian Church that they have become "imitators" of him and the Lord, he was specifically pointing to one thing: They have welcomed the message of Jesus Christ with a joy given from the Holy Spirit. We may never be perfect in this life, and we will definitely have our ups and downs, but we can emulate our love of Jesus to the world and the joy that our relationship with Jesus brings us. No matter our hardships and struggles, we carry this joy with us every moment of each day. This joy isn't dependent on our circumstances, our moods, or the behavior of others. It is based solely on the Good News of Jesus Christ. We may have our personal struggles, but we can share the confidence that this joy brings us—confidence centered on the excellence of Jesus, not the flaws of our humanity. And, hopefully, the people around us will become imitators of this confidence, emulating the joy we all have in Jesus Christ.

"May the God of hope fill you with all joy and peace as you trust in him, so that you may overflow with hope by the power of the Holy Spirit" (Romans 15.13 NIV).

DAY 293
True Nature of Failure

—✦—

"You yourselves know, dear brothers and sisters, that our visit to you was not a failure" (1 Thessalonians 2.1 NLT).

Many times we think we have failed God because the results of our actions did not align with our own expectations. We believed God, worked hard and poured out our obedience only to be rejected, criticized or ignored. We were obedient with the call that God placed on our life, but the outcome of our faithfulness fizzled out and disappeared. We may be tempted to become doubtful and question if we truly heard God's voice leading us into defeat. But if we are truly trying to please God and not ourselves and others, then the results don't define our victory or failure. If we are obedient to God's call and faithful with His vision, then there is no need to question ourselves. God is pleased with the results, whether the world deems them as victorious or not. When Paul ministered to the Thessalonians, he didn't try to earn their praises or find victory in their eyes. He did exactly what the Lord had sent Him to do, and that is why he could say the following verse:

"We were not looking for praise from people, not from you or anyone else, even though as apostles of Christ we could have asserted our authority" (1 Thessalonians 2.6 NIV).

DAY 294
Really Living

"For now we really live, since you are standing firm in the Lord" (1 Thessalonians 3.8 NIV).

Timothy, Paul's spiritual student, has brought a report back to Paul that the Thessalonians are standing firm in their faith despite persecution. Paul has poured his life into these people, teaching them the Gospel through words, actions and deeds. So to hear that his obedience to God's call was making a difference on earth made Paul feel alive. He knows that his obedience, faith and work are bearing fruit in the lives of others. The word *live* is the Greek word *zao*, which means *to enjoy real life*. Although this word is short and simple, it offers a powerful portrayal of what it means to truly be alive. Paul says to really live we must be producing godly fruit in the people around us—fruit that comes from "standing firm in the Lord." When Paul sees that fruit—no matter the persecution and trials that surround him—he feels like his life has meaning and his obedience to God truly matters. Satan will try to seduce us with the riches, pleasures and even worries of the world to replace truly living, but only bearing fruit from our obedience to God will ever make us really feel alive.

"For to me to live is Christ, and to die is gain" (Philippians 1.21 ESV).

DAY 295

Work

"Make it your goal to live a quiet life, minding your own business and working with your hands, just as we instructed you before. Then people who are not believers will respect the way you live, and you will not need to depend on others" (1 Thessalonians 4.11-12 NLT).

Paul urges Christians to work, so they will not have to be dependent on others. This doesn't mean people shouldn't need each other. We are all unique parts of One Body (the Church), and we each rely on others to fulfill their purpose. We may fall behind in different seasons of life, and we may need our family and friends to help us back up. But as mature adults, we should be self-reliant. We each can have work (purpose) that we can commit to that makes us feel satisfied and accomplished. This doesn't necessarily mean we have to earn a paycheck. Mothers, missionaries and volunteers all work without getting paid or getting paid very little. In a sense, they do rely on others to meet their financial needs, but they are working for something greater than a paycheck. They are helping their families, communities and world by the work of their hands. God has a purpose for us on this earth and it undoubtedly involves some form of work. If we are consistent at our work and conduct ourselves honorably, people will respect how we live and sense that there is a supernatural force that is guiding us. Then maybe they will look beyond our work and into the heart of a God Who loves and cares for them.

"Be careful to live properly among your unbelieving neighbors. Then even if they accuse you of doing wrong, they will see your honorable behavior, and they will give honor to God when he judges the world" (1 Peter 2.12 NLT).

DAY 296

Test Everything

"Test all things; hold fast what is good" (1 Thessalonians 5.21 NKJV).

People like to share what they are learning, especially in their walk of faith. We are growing each day in the Lord, and with every struggle to understand comes greater wisdom imparted on us by God. Many times we hear the insights that people share and we agree with them. We can tell that God has truly revealed a powerful truth to them, and we immediately want to claim that truth for ourselves. However, when we try to share that truth only days later without really meditating on it, we are unable to articulate the revelation. We haven't fully made that truth our own, and we either water down or thwart the revelation with our words. Paul says to test everything. This doesn't mean we have to disagree with everything people say. It simply means that we need to make the revelations personal to us by really studying what has been shared. We must ask the Lord to reveal the truth to us in a personal way, so we can be better stewards of it. The Holy Spirit will allow that revelation to move from our minds into our hearts, and we will be able to explain what we learned with the authority of His power.

"What does this world need: gifted men and women, outwardly empowered? Or individuals who are broken and inwardly transformed?" – Gene Edwards

DAY 297

His Power

"So we keep on praying for you, asking our God to enable you to live a life worthy of his call. May he give you the power to accomplish all the good things your faith prompts you to do" (2 Thessalonians 1.11 NLT).

When God calls us to live according to His call, He will "enable" us and give us the "power to accomplish all the good things" prompted by our faith. We are not alone. If God plants faith in us to do something for Him, He will ensure that we have the strength, ability and resources that we need. We must not focus on our circumstances or ourselves because they will almost always display a lack of strength, a lack of resources and a lack of ability. Instead, we can move on faith, believing God's promise to provide for us to achieve His will. God sees what we cannot see, and He can shift things into our favor, but we must trust Him. We need to have more faith in His Word than we do in this world. We need to rely on His strength in us and not the strength of others or ourselves. God will give us the power we need to achieve anything our faith declares as part of our victory. A "life worthy of his call" is a life that believes God can and will accomplish His good work in us. We simply must grab onto the power that is rightfully ours as children of God and co-heirs with Jesus Christ and believe in the promises God has ordained for us before time began.

"Now if we are children, then we are heirs—heirs of God and co-heirs with Christ, if indeed we share in his sufferings in order that we may also share in his glory" (Romans 8.17 NIV).

DAY 298
Counterfeit

"The coming of the lawless one will be in accordance with how Satan works. He will use all sorts of displays of power through signs and wonders that serve the lie, and all the ways that wickedness deceives those who are perishing. They perish because they refused to love the truth and so be saved" (2 Thessalonians 2.9-10 NIV).

The only way to know a counterfeit is to know the real thing. People are easily deceived to accept counterfeit items if they've never really studied the authentic product. For example, if someone has studied, analyzed and memorized true currency, he or she will not be deceived when someone tries to give them a fake bill. This truth also applies to Jesus and our faith. When we get to know Jesus and really lean into our faith, we won't be easily fooled by Satan's schemes. When we know the heart and voice of God, even when Satan is trying to disguise himself as light, we will be able to see the deception. Everything must be analyzed according to God's Word because God will never contradict the Bible. The people that fall for the Devil's lies refuse to get to know Jesus and allow Him to be Lord over their life. They can even be Christians who have stopped listening to His voice and obeying His commands long ago. Without repentance, they may deceive themselves that they are actually following God, but instead they are following the Prince of Darkness, counterfeiting as light. Every day we can get to know the Lord more, so we will be better prepared to call out the enemy's attacks on us and those around us.

"For such *are* false apostles, deceitful workers, transforming themselves into apostles of Christ. And no wonder! For Satan himself transforms himself into an angel of light" (2 Corinthians 11.13-14 NKJV).

DAY 299
Teachers

"With all these things in mind, dear brothers and sisters, stand firm and keep a strong grip on the teaching we passed on to you both in person and by letter" (2 Thessalonians 2.15 NLT).

The Holy Spirit guides us in all understanding, and He will use people's words to teach us. He can teach us through sermons, books, circumstances, etc. He is not limited to one style of teaching, and He can use all of God's resources (both natural and supernatural) to lead us on paths of righteousness. Many times, the Holy Spirit will speak through others. God will appoint "teachers" in our lives who can mentor us in directions that may be new to us. Paul was an Apostle who loved to teach. He mentored individuals, like Timothy, and he mentored churches, like the Church of the Thessalonians. He willingly gave of himself to influence the lives of others. As Christians, we need to look for the teachers that God has appointed for us. We will never stop learning, and there is always someone God can select to pour Holy Spirit inspired words into our lives. Whether we listen to sermons, read Christian books, listen to Christian music or find mentorship from someone who is further along in their walk of faith—we can allow godly teachings to infiltrate our life. We can hold tightly to all that we have learned from our teachers, so we can stay firm in the Lord during the hard times and the good.

"If any of you lacks wisdom, let him ask God, who gives generously to all without reproach, and it will be given him" (James 1.5 ESV).

DAY 300
Separating Stone

"Take note of those who refuse to obey what we say in this letter. Stay away from them so they will be ashamed. Don't think of them as enemies, but warn them as you would a brother or sister" (2 Thessalonians 3.14-15 NLT).

Staying away from people we love is a difficult choice. If they are refusing to see truth and continue to behave against God's commands to love Him and love others, sometimes the most loving thing we can do is put some distance between them and us. They are not our enemies; however, they are not admitting and repenting to actions that are contrary to God's Word—actions that are hurting us, our family and our purpose. Only when we have done everything in our power to confront the issue in love and peace and they still refuse to heed the warnings, can we set a dividing "stone,' protecting us from further harm. We can still love them and pray for them, but they may never see their sin until they have lost all the people whom they care about. This separation may be their only hope to truly confronting their wounds, so that they may find healing. Hurt people will hurt people, but God wants to heal our wounds and repair our relationships. When God has us "stay away" for a time, we can continually pray and trust that God will offer healing and reconciliation to those who desire to atone for behavior that contradicts His heart.

"'See this pile of stones,' Laban continued, 'and see this monument I have set between us. They stand between us as witnesses of our vows. I will never pass this pile of stones to harm you, and you must never pass these stones or this monument to harm me'" (Genesis 31.51-52 NLT).

DAY 301
A True Child

"I am writing to Timothy, my true son in the faith. May God the Father and Christ Jesus our Lord give you grace, mercy, and peace" (1 Timothy 1.2 NLT).

No one knows for sure whether or not Paul had a wife and biological children. He doesn't write about them, which could either mean he didn't have a family or that the family was so much a part of his life that he didn't feel the need to point them out—almost like pointing out an eye or a hand is not necessary. However, we do know that Paul had a son by faith, Timothy. Having children is very much a faith phenomenon, not simply a biological occurrence. The position of a parent means that we have the ability to greatly influence the life of another human being. Unlike teachers, pastors or leaders who only have a limited impact on someone's life, a parental figure can greatly shape and grow a person's personality, design and purpose—much like the archer aiming his arrow in a chosen direction (Psalm 127.4). God gives everyone the ability to have a parental role in another person's life. We don't necessarily need to share similar genes with a person to have a powerful impact on them. Our true sons and daughters are those whom we share life with and to whom we impart our very presence. And once we are in heaven, regardless of whether we birthed biological children or not, we will have made a difference in the next generation moving God's Kingdom Plan into fruition.

"Jesus said, 'Who is My mother? And who are My brothers?' He put out His hand to His followers and said, 'See, these are My mother and My brothers! Whoever does what My father in heaven wants him to do is My brother and My sister and My mother'" (Matthew 12.48-50 NLV).

DAY 302
The Law of Love

"We also know that the law is made not for the righteous but for lawbreakers and rebels, the ungodly and sinful, the unholy and irreligious, for those who kill their fathers or mothers, for murderers…" (1 Timothy 1.9 NIV).

Abraham never received the law from God. He believed the Lord, so he was righteousness in God's eyes for his faith (Genesis 15.6). Abraham was not perfect by any means, but he loved the Lord and even in his flawed human state, he committed to follow and obey Him. The law was established after the Israelites demanded that Moses give them God's commands. They ignorantly believed that they could produce holiness by themselves without help from the Intercessor (Exodus 19.8). But the entire law and all of God's commands can be wrapped up in two commandments: Love God and love others (Matthew 22.37-40). If we can love God and His children, we will automatically do the things that please God. The law was given to the people who do not listen to the Holy Spirit and who do not desire to please God. They do not have the God of all truth leading them every moment of every day, so they need a set of parameters to keep them and others from harm. However, Christians have freedom in Christ because we lean on Him and obey Him, and He will lead us on paths of righteousness. To be sure the word "love" is not always easy, fun and sweet. Sometimes loving God means to be obedient even unto death—whether it be a physical death or a metaphorical death of our self-will. And truly loving others can be the hardest thing we ever do. Thankfully, though, we are free in Christ to do the best we can at loving God and others because we know that His grace fills in the cracks of our mistakes with His perfection.

"So Christ has truly set us free. Now make sure that you stay free, and don't get tied up again in slavery to the law" (Galatians 5.1 NLT).

DAY 303
One Mediator

"For there is one God and one mediator between God and mankind, the man Christ Jesus, who gave himself as a ransom for all people. This has now been witnessed to at the proper time" (1 Timothy 2.5-6 NIV).

We are separated from God because He is holy and we are not. God loves us and wants a relationship with us, but holiness cannot mix with even a touch of sin or it will be tainted. God cannot have anything to do with sin, so He needed a redemption plan to bring us back to Him. For this reason, He sent Himself into His own creation— a creation corrupted by our sin—and He redeemed all the earth and its people. When we accept Jesus' sacrifice for our sin, His blood—the very life-source of God— surrounds us, and we now are holy before God even in our sinful state, and we can have God's Spirit living within us. We are redeemed through the Work and Blood of Jesus Christ. Jesus is our Meditator to God. Jesus is God in the flesh Who was broken, so that redemption could flow freely onto the earth. God knew that we would fall short of His holy standard, which is why He already had the redemption plan ready during Creation Week (Romans 3.23). God completed all of creation by Day 6, so He rested on Day 7 knowing that Jesus was Lord over Sabbath. Jesus would do the work on Day 7 of redeeming the earth and bringing us back into fellowship with God. Praise God that we have a Mediator who was obedient even unto death, so that we could be saved.

"And being found in appearance as a man, he humbled himself by becoming obedient to death—even death on a cross!" (Philippians 2.8 NIV).

DAY 304

High Position, Low Character

"A church leader must not be a new believer, because he might become proud, and the devil would cause him to fall" (1 Timothy 3.6 NLT).

Most people know what happens to new Christians—or Christians newly committed to the Lord—when they get promoted too quickly. Usually, it's a recipe for disaster. Becoming a Christian leader puts us straight onto Satan's radar. We will now be tempted and attacked in every way possible in our personal and professional life. Satan knows that if he can make a leader fall that all those entrusted to that person's leadership will struggle or even scatter. Here's the truth of the matter: If a person is not willing to clean the floors in the background of a ministry, he or she should not be on the foreground bossing people around. There is no humility there and intentions may be rooted in self-projection and not in obedience to God. Usually, it takes a while before God promotes us. He keeps us in the wilderness of our dreams, so He can build our character to handle the burden and blessing of our promise. No wonder God makes us wait after He gives us our promises. He's preparing our character with humility, so we don't become proud and fall from our purpose.

"Do nothing out of selfish ambition or vain conceit. Rather, in humility value others above yourselves, not looking to your own interests but each of you to the interests of the others" (Philippians 2.3-4 NIV).

DAY 305
Prophetic Gifting

———•——≈—❈—≈——•———

"Do not neglect your gift, which was given you through a prophetic message when the body of elders laid their hands on you" (1 Timothy 4.14 NIV).

Although it would be nice, not all of us will have a body of elders lay their hands on us and speak a prophetic message over us about our gifting. God knows this, so He will establish a prophetic message about our gifting some other way. Many times, the Holy Spirit in us will whisper our calling into our hearts. Other times, a parent, pastor, teacher or mentor will recognize something special in us and call it out. Yet other times our own passions and desires will draw God's gifting out into the open. No matter how it arises, God has planted extraordinary giftings in each of us that will help us fulfill the purposes for which God has called us. Many times, this gifting will be our biggest struggle and our biggest victory, and at one point or another, we will want to give up. But Paul exhorts us not to give up on the gifting that holds the prophetic message to our destiny. We may be tempted to embark on a lesser, easier dream, but it will never satisfy the craving of our souls. Counterfeit callings will come and go, but we must stay strong in our prophetic calling. Also, we will watch others as they work out the prophetic gift inside of them, but we must stay faithful to the prophetic gifting that God has entrusted to us. We have only one prophetic destiny that will accomplish the best that God has planned for our lives.

"We are made for larger ends than Earth can encompass. Oh, let us be true to our exalted destiny." – Catherine Booth

DAY 306
A Trail Behind

"The sins of some are obvious, reaching the place of judgment ahead of them; the sins of others trail behind them. In the same way, good deeds are obvious, and even those that are not obvious cannot remain hidden forever" (1 Timothy 5.24-25 NIV).

The one thing that we never have to worry about is people getting away with doing bad deeds and others not being rewarded for doing good deeds. God sees everything we do, and He has placed a system of sowing and reaping into our world (Galatians 6.7). If people continually make choices that displease God, a trail of their sin will be right behind them. It may seem that they are getting away with their sin at first because they cut off relationships and responsibilities that keep them accountable, but eventually their bad choices will overtake them and affect their future. They can seek forgiveness, but the repercussions of their sin will have lasting consequences. However, the people who please God even in the unseen corners of their lives, serving and giving themselves to His will without seeking recognition will also be exposed and their good deeds revealed. It may seem that their efforts are passed over at first and that God doesn't seem to care, but eventually their good deeds will overflow onto the world around them. We don't have to worry our minds with trying to establish fairness. God knows everyone's good and bad deeds, and nothing will "remain hidden forever." God's ways cannot be bypassed or circumvented, and our actions will either plant a crop of blessing or destruction.

"For the one who sows to his own flesh will from the flesh reap corruption, but the one who sows to the Spirit will from the Spirit reap eternal life" (Galatians 6.8 ESV).

DAY 307
True Life

"In this way they will lay up treasure for themselves as a firm foundation for the coming age, so that they may take hold of the life that is truly life" (1 Timothy 6.19 NIV).

Paul is exhorting the people who are considered rich (abounding in material resources) to put their hope in God and not their wealth. But he continues to say that wealth can be enjoyed, but the people who have wealth should be giving and abounding in good deeds. This way they can store for themselves eternal treasures in our true, heavenly home. Although the spectrum of who is considered wealthy is vast, there are many people today considered "rich" compared to the rest of the world. These people have homes, cars, computers, food in the pantry, water in the faucet and beds laden with pillows and blankets. They are abounding with material wealth that they may be taking for granted. We can use these riches to find enjoyment, but we will only find a temporary fix to an eternal longing. God declares that to be truly living and fulfilling our purpose, we should be using our abounding material wealth to help, encourage and lift-up others. Yes, we can partake in the blessings that God has given us, but we also must use those blessings to bless others. It's hard to believe in our society of "take-as-much-as-you-can-get" that to give freely, we will actually receive more freely. When we encourage and help others, we too will be encouraged and helped. We can aggressively look for those in need who can benefit from our abundance, so that we can "take hold of the life that is truly life."

"One person gives freely, yet gains even more; another withholds unduly, but comes to poverty. A generous person will prosper; whoever refreshes others will be refreshed" (Proverbs 11.24-25 NIV).

DAY 308
Faith of Parents

"I am reminded of your sincere faith, which first lived in your grandmother Lois and in your mother Eunice and, I am persuaded, now lives in you also" (2 Timothy 1.5 NIV).

Parenthood is many times underappreciated in a culture that values prestige attached with wealth and fame. Being a parent garners no money or acclaim, and it is a service done in the quiet depths of the home. Satan aggressively devalues the ministry of parenthood in our world because it is so much a part of God's heart. God loves His children, and He cares about the little ones that can't care for themselves. When we as parents take the time to love and care for our children, we are taking part in something supernatural that money and fame could never achieve. We are imparting our faith into the existence of another person, which will shape the course of an individual life and God's Kingdom as a whole. The Apostle Paul saw the "sincere faith" that was passed down to Timothy by his mother and grandmother—a faith that was so strong it could thrive through three generations and into Timothy's influential ministry. These women didn't necessarily pass down money or fame to Timothy, but the faith that they imparted was far more valuable in the long run.

"But if anyone does not provide for his own, and especially for those of his household, he has denied the faith and is worse than an unbeliever" (1 Timothy 5.8 NKJV).

DAY 309
Deposits

———❖———

"For this reason I also suffer these things; nevertheless I am not ashamed, for I know whom I have believed and am persuaded that He is able to keep what I have committed to Him until that Day" (2 Timothy 1.12 NKJV).

God will "keep" or watch over the things that we give Him. We can trust that God will oversee all of the worries, responsibilities, mistakes and anxieties that we commit to Him until the Day of His arrival back to earth. We can also deposit our ministries, careers, families, health, goals, dreams and so on, resting in God's all-inclusive care. The Greek word for "have committed to" is *paratheke,* and it literally means to make a deposit, like at a bank. When we deposit our money at the bank, we can no longer touch it unless we literally take it back out again. But if we trust the bank, we know that our money will be faithfully looked after. This is the same way with God. We must make "deposits" every day into God's account, knowing that He's a better manager at overseeing the "currency" of our lives than we are. And once we finally release control and make deposits into God's care, we must leave them in God's secure vaults, trusting that He knows what is best for us. If we keep taking the deposits out, God cannot supernaturally move in our deposits because we are in essence slapping His mighty hand away. However, we can trust our God because He loves us, and we can let Him pour His glory into the deposits that we have committed to Him.

"We must cease striving and trust God to provide what He thinks is best and in whatever time He chooses to make it available. But this kind of trusting doesn't come naturally. It's a spiritual crisis of the will in which we must choose to exercise faith."
– Charles Swindoll

DAY 310
Strong in Grace

"You then, my son, be strong in the grace that is in Christ Jesus" (2 Timothy 2.1 NIV).

The world today demands that we be strong in all areas of our lives. We must be strong in our health, in our emotions, in our intellect, in our finances, in our relationships, in our careers and in our ministries. Even the Christian culture makes hints towards being strong in all areas of our lives, so we can be adequate leaders for the Lord. There is a great pressure for us to always be strong, so we can be pleasing to the Lord. However, Paul tells Timothy to do the opposite. We are to be strong not in ourselves, but we are to be strong in the pleasure that God has in us by grace. *Grace* is the Greek word, *Charis*, which means something that offers joy, delight and pleasure. Finding strength in the pleasure that someone has in us is completely foreign in our culture. We have grown accustomed to finding strength in our own merits, feeling confident in actions that please us and others. But we are imperfect people, and we will make mistakes. If we base our strength on our performance, we will eventually lose it. God wants us to find strength in a Source that never falters. Because of the cross, the grace that God has for us in always constant. Once we finally find our strength in God's grace, He will impart His continual strength to every area of our life. We will gain the ultimate strength that will never change or tire out. So let us today forget trying to always be strong enough. Instead, let us begin each day declaring that our strength is in the joy, delight and pleasure of God's grace!

"...Don't be dejected and sad, for the joy of the LORD is your strength!" (Nehemiah 8.10 NLT).

DAY 311
Chained

"Remember Jesus Christ, raised from the dead, descended from David. This is my gospel, for which I am suffering even to the point of being chained like a criminal. But God's word is not chained" (2 Timothy 2.8-9 NIV).

God's Word will never, ever be chained. No matter what predicament we find ourselves in, and no matter if we feel like our hands are tied behind our back, God's Word reigns freely inside and outside of us. We don't have to fear that our limitations and strongholds are preventing God's Spirit from moving in the world around us. Our chains— inabilities, mistakes, weaknesses—will never prevent the flow of God's Word. And it is usually when our strength is weak and our abilities are on lockdown that God shows up with supernatural might and fervor. When we are worn out and tired and find ourselves at the end of ourselves, God will take over and accomplish His glory with miracles and wonders only He can produce. Paul's chains spread the Gospel even further than he could ever imagine. Our chains will allow God to accomplish more than we could ever dream. We must never think that our limitations are preventing God's movements; in fact, they are probably propelling them!

"And because of my chains, most of the brothers and sisters have become confident in the Lord and dare all the more to proclaim the gospel without fear" (Philippians 1.14 NIV).

DAY 312
God-Breathed

"All Scripture is God-breathed and is useful for teaching, rebuking, correcting and training in righteousness, so that the servant of God may be thoroughly equipped for every good work" (2 Timothy 3.16-17 NIV).

Paul's words in these two verses to Timothy are renown. Paul summarizes the Bible in this one sentence. The Bible is spoken through God to us in order to teach, rebuke, correct and train us, so that we can accomplish all that God has planned for us. We will never accomplish our God-given destiny if we are not reading the Bible. We will not thoroughly grow in the Lord if we are not consuming His Word. When we become Christians, the Holy Spirit comes to live inside of us, and He will work in tandem with the Bible to shape us into the image of Jesus. Yes, the Holy Spirit can talk to us in other ways, but it is through God's Word that He reveals His Son, Jesus, and His Kingdom Plan to us. We need to be reading the Bible every day along with other Christian resources—devotionals, novels, sermons, articles, movies, music, etc.—so that we can be transformed and "equipped for every good work." Let us not neglect the One thing that will assure our victory—God's Holy Word!

"For the word of God is alive and powerful. It is sharper than the sharpest two-edged sword, cutting between soul and spirit, between joint and marrow. It exposes our innermost thoughts and desires" (Hebrews 4.12 NLT).

DAY 313
Itching Ears

"For a time is coming when people will no longer listen to sound and wholesome teaching. They will follow their own desires and will look for teachers who will tell them whatever their itching ears want to hear" (2 Timothy 4.3 NLT).

The Internet is a very useful tool. People can share the Gospel with others who live far away, and they can ascertain Christian resources that were once unattainable. But the Internet can also be very destructive. Both truth and lies can be found all over the various sites online. In fact, truth seems to be a changing idea based on the ebb and flow of people's thoughts, feelings and desires. Truth is no longer a moral standard established by God outside the corrupted human condition. It is now a standard established by individuals who are skewed by human fallibility. At any moment, we can search the Internet and find some "teachings" that contradict the Word of God. These teachings may suit our desires, but they actually go completely against the standard that God has established. We must ask ourselves a question when confronted with information that contradicts God's Word: Who has the authority? God or People? Just because we find a teacher or article that tickles our ear does not make it right. We should always go to the source of Truth first, which is God and His Word. Finding people to partake in our sin doesn't make our sin right. Instead of using others to justify our sin, we should allow the Holy Spirit to cut it away.

"But even if we or an angel from heaven should preach to you a gospel contrary to the one we preached to you, let him be accursed" (Galatians 1.8 ESV).

DAY 314
Eternal Life

"This truth gives them confidence that they have eternal life, which God—who does not lie—promised them before the world began" (Titus 1.2 NLT).

Everyone ages. Our bodies get older, yet our spirits do not age. A man or woman of 60 still has the life of a 16-year-old inside of them. Time doesn't affect the life of our inner being because it will live on for eternity. None of us wants our existence to end. Ask children what their greatest fear is, and many of them will undoubtedly say death. The Christian faith is based on one hope: We have eternal life. Where we spend that eternal life is up to us. We are not perfect, so we are separated from a holy God. We can't have a relationship with Him in our sinful state. Through the Finished Work of Jesus, however, we can have a relationship with God on earth. Jesus took our sin to death and left it there, wrapping us up in His perfection. The relationship we have with God on earth continues even after our physical death, and we live with God in heaven for eternity. If we don't have a relationship with God through the Work of Jesus Christ on the Cross, that lack of a relationship will continue, and we will be outside of God's presence for eternity in a place called hell. The choice is up to us. Christianity is the only religion that says we will never be good enough to make it into heaven alone, which is why we accept Jesus into our hearts as our Lord and Savior. Salvation is a gift that cannot be earned, but the importance of this gift gives us confidence and hope in our eternal home.

"For we know that if the earthly tent we live in is destroyed, we have a building from God, an eternal house in heaven, not built by human hands" (2 Corinthians 5.1 NIV).

DAY 315
Pretenses

"For there are many rebellious people, full of meaningless talk and deception, especially those of the circumcision group" (Titus 1.10 NIV).

Paul writes to Titus warning him that many of the circumcised religious people were rebellious with their words and their deception. These people were outwardly spiritual, yet their hearts were not circumcised by the Holy Spirit. Circumcision is a demonstration of obedience and separation—an outward confirmation of an inward transformation. Yet for these religious gossipers and deceivers, this symbolic conversion was literally only skin deep. It's a sad truth, but many religious Christians today have hardened their hearts to the Holy Spirit. They have fallen into the temptation to act and look perfect before others, but God sees our hearts. He knows that we each have our struggles, and we all make mistakes. God doesn't expect us to be perfect; otherwise, we wouldn't need the saving grace of Jesus. If we simply admit our mistakes and repent when the Holy Spirit convicts us, we don't have to constantly keep up spiritual pretenses. Christians who are always looking for flaws in others may be compensating for personal issues that they keep ignoring. This is a sure sign that they do not have a humble spirit and are not sensitive to the Holy Spirit. They use damaging words to make themselves feel better instead of dealing with their own problems. If they continue without repentance, they can cause chaos and division in themselves and in the people and places around them.

"They must be silenced, because they are disrupting whole households by teaching things they ought not to teach—and that for the sake of dishonest gain" (Titus 1.11 NIV).

DAY 316

Encourage and Rebuke

"Tell *them* these things. Encourage and rebuke with full authority. Let no one disregard *or* despise you [conduct yourself and your teaching so as to command respect]" (Titus 2.15 AMP).

Paul gives Titus a long list of leadership qualities that he can implement in order to shepherd his people. Paul finishes citing his assortment of leadership traits by telling Titus that he should both "encourage and rebuke with full authority." Many people are good at rebuking others when they see something wrong, but they may have difficulty encouraging them. Others can encourage all day long, but they avoid confronting problems. Paul says that we must do both with full authority. Whether we struggle with rebuking or encouraging those around us, we need to step outside of our personal comfort zones and do what God has called us to do. If we are leaders, God has given us the authority to serve the people around us, and we are obligated to encourage what's right and to rebuke what's wrong. It has nothing to do with us, and has everything to do with God's calling on our lives. We have to remember we all need to be rebuked and encouraged once in a while, so we may become wise and strong in the Lord. When we follow the Holy Spirit's lead with rebuking and encouraging, we never have to worry about overstepping our bounds. We can trust that God knows what He is doing, and He will use people to accomplish His greater will.

"Let a righteous man strike me—that is a kindness; let him rebuke me—that is oil on my head. My head will not refuse it, for my prayer will still be against the deeds of evildoers" (Psalm 141.5 NIV).

DAY 317
Government & Officers

"Remind the believers to submit to the government and its officers. They should be obedient, always ready to do what is good" (Titus 3.1 NLT).

Obeying our government and officers doesn't mean we have to like them, but we have to trust that God put certain people as our authority for a reason. Obedience is a difficult exercise of faith, especially when we don't feel like obeying or don't necessarily agree with the request. But as long as we are not going against God's standard, obedience will keep us on a path to victory and advancement. Yes, people with authority may abuse their power and persecute us, but God will use our struggle to make us more into the image of Jesus and to accomplish His Kingdom Plan. God did not create evil in this world, but He can use it as a tool to sharpen and mold us. As long as we are not doing anything that compromises God's Word and His Will, we should submit to the people and entities in authority. We can trust that God will redeem any situation in which we find ourselves the victim as long as we stay true to His call of obedience. Also, we can go beyond the call of duty of obedience and be "ready to do what is good." We can surprise people when we repay them good for the evil they use against us. And just maybe they will see something different in us and begin to look closely at the God they see in us. No matter what, God promises us a special blessing if we can keep our hope and joy in Christ even when the world seems to be against us.

"The authority by which the Christian leader leads is not power but love, not force but example, not coercion but reasoned persuasion." – John Stott

DAY 318

Divisive People

"Warn a divisive person once, and then warn them a second time. After that, have nothing to do with them" (Titus 3.10 NIV).

A "divisive" person is someone who enjoys stirring up conflict and causing division. This is a deep-reaching character flaw that can really cause a lot of problems in relationships, homes, workplaces and ministries. The difficult part about people who are divisive is that many times they don't realize it. They have so many emotional storms within them that they pour out those storms into the world around them, and they see this chaos and destruction as a normal part of life. But causing trouble and division is not normal. In fact, we are supposed to be keepers of the peace (Matthew 5.9). The only way to deal with a divisive person is to confront the problem head-on. Ignoring the issue will only make the storms spiral out of control, causing devastation and loss. Paul explains that we can warn a divisive person two times, but after that we have to separate ourselves from them. If we don't shield ourselves, they will be like a diseased body part that slowly sickens and kills the entire body. Much like gangrene found on the body's extremities, a divisive person can spread their devastation to the lives of those close to them. We can still love and pray for divisive people, but we must always keep them and their influence separated or contained if we want the health of our relationships, homes, workplaces and ministries to stay protected. And just maybe, they will see the relationships that they are losing, and they will finally allow God to calm the storms within them.

"I urge you, brothers and sisters, to watch out for those who cause divisions and put obstacles in your way that are contrary to the teaching you have learned. Keep away from them" (Romans 16.17 NIV).

DAY 319

Partnerships

"I pray that your partnership with us in the faith may be effective in deepening your understanding of every good thing we share for the sake of Christ" (Philemon 1.6 NIV).

We can have a variety of partnerships in life—marriage, friendships, business partner, co-workers, church leaders, etc.—and these partnerships are either moving us forward in our faith or causing us to stumble in our faith. Life is very short, and we must look at every single partnership in which we are committed. We need to ask ourselves if the partnership is drawing us closer to the Lord and our purpose or is it dividing us from God and our destiny. We are each on a journey, following a living God who is always moving and working His Kingdom Plan to fruition. If we get caught up with the slow movers around us, we will eventually fall behind. Of course, it is right to stop and help people who stumble along the way, but we must not allow ourselves to get so sidetracked that we lose sight of Jesus. We can trust that although Jesus is moving, He is still able to gather those who have fallen and are calling out to Him. We can lead by example, helping those around us but never losing sight of Jesus and the call He has placed in our lives. Then we can partner up with individuals who God uses to deepen our faith and understanding of His goodness and love.

"But Jesus replied, 'My Father is always working, and so am I'" (John 5.17 NLT).

DAY 320
Gentle Request

—————————— ❈ ——————————

"That is why I am boldly asking a favor of you. I could demand it in the name of Christ because it is the right thing for you to do. But because of our love, I prefer simply to ask you. Consider this as a request from me—Paul, an old man and now also a prisoner for the sake of Christ Jesus" (Philemon 1.8-9 NLT).

Studies show that when we ask for something instead of demanding it, people are more likely to give us our request. Paul could have demanded that Philemon obey his request based on the fact that he was a Christian leader and the request was the right thing to do. However, people have an inner defense mechanism that causes them to resist people who try to command them and force their obedience. Even if it was the right thing to do, Philemon might have denied the request simply based on how Paul presented it. The right idea can be enacted in the wrong way, causing a negative outcome. Instead of appealing to someone's sense of right and wrong with a critical tone, it is better to use love. It is especially important to not always demand from people whom we have authority over, like our children, employees, students, etc. We need to resist the urge to simply demand obedience just because we can. Instead, we can make our request known in love and empower those around us to make the right decision for themselves.

"What we need today is men and women who will take God by His Word and be persistent with it." – William Marrion Branham

DAY 321
My Very Heart

"I am sending him—who is my very heart—back to you" (Philemon 1.12 NIV).

One of the hardest things to do is to give someone up that you love. Paul was sending his friend, who had become his "very heart," back to Philemon. Paul wished that he could keep his friend with him, but he knew that the right thing to do was to send him back to where he belonged. Letting go of those we love can break our hearts if we do not trust in God. In fact, we may even be tempted to hold onto someone who God is calling away, thereby, disobeying God's will. But we must believe that God has His best purposes for those we care about, and we need to give up the control and allow our hearts to be open and obedient to the Lord. Yes, we will be sad by not having that person with us all the time, but we can be comforted to know that one day in heaven they will be present with us for eternity. God knows what He is doing, and He will accomplish great and mighty things through the people we care about. We can give God our hearts and the people we love, knowing that He loves us more than words could ever express. God gave us His Son, Jesus, to die for our sins, so we can give Him our loved ones, so they may fulfill their destinies.

"Getting over a painful experience is much like crossing monkey bars. You have to let go at some point in order to move forward." – C.S. Lewis

DAY 322
Radiance of God

"The Son radiates God's own glory and expresses the very character of God, and he sustains everything by the mighty power of his command. When he had cleansed us from our sins, he sat down in the place of honor at the right hand of the majestic God in heaven" (Hebrews 1.3 NLT).

We live in the New Testament age where we have God's glory radiating from within our dark world. God is like a great Sun—He can only be in the light of day and no darkness can be around Him. Therefore, Jesus is like a great Moon; He shines the Sun's light into the darkness when the light is gone because of sin. Jesus is the Light of the World, filling the lives of imperfect people with God's glory (John 8.12). Jesus left His rightful place by the Sun's light, so He could penetrate the dark areas of our lives and this world with His Truth. Now we can have light in the day and night, in joy and in pain, in victory and defeat. Jesus washed away our mistakes and imperfections, and He gave us His righteousness and holiness, so that the light would flood into the shadows of our hearts. We don't have to wish for an unattainable Holy God. We can now have God's Spirit, the Holy Spirit, in us because of the Finished Work of Jesus Christ on the Cross. And the wonderful news is that now Jesus' work is done. He is back in the Sun's light on a throne of glory, sustaining all of us by "the mighty power of his command."

"Everything was created through him; nothing—not one thing!—came into being without him. What came into existence was Life, and the Life was Light to live by. The Life-Light blazed out of the darkness; the darkness couldn't put it out" (John 1.5 MSG).

DAY 323
Redeemed Authority

"But we do see Jesus, who was made lower than the angels for a little while, now crowned with glory and honor because he suffered death, so that by the grace of God he might taste death for everyone" (Hebrews 2.9 NIV).

How could Jesus, Who is God, be made lower than His own creation? Jesus loves us so much that He willingly left His place as King of Kings and Lord of Lords, so we could be free from the slavery and the death of sin (Romans 8.17). If we are co-heirs with Christ, we are also kings and queens under the authority of the King of the Universe. And He gives us the authority to unleash God's glory on earth. We no longer have to taste spiritual death, which is an existence separated from God. We may experience physical death, but truly it is like a birth into our eternal, heavenly lives. Satan was able to steal our authority for a time because of our sin, but Jesus came to claim it back again. Today, not only do we not have to taste spiritual death, we also have the power to make a difference in this world. We can claim God's will on earth and watch it unfold in our heavenly destinies (Matthew 18.18). If we could only see and believe the authority we have been given through the death and resurrection of Jesus Christ, we would be an unstoppable force, changing lives by binding sin and death and unleashing grace and life!

"I have given you authority to trample on snakes and scorpions and to overcome all the power of the enemy; nothing will harm you" (Luke 10.19 NIV).

DAY 324
Enter His Rest

———————— ❀ ————————

"Therefore, since the promise of entering his rest still stands, let us be careful that none of you be found to have fallen short of it" (Hebrews 4.1 NIV).

What is God's rest and how do we make sure we don't fall short of it? During the first 6 days of Creation Week, God made all of creation with seeds to perpetuate life. The plants, animals and humans all have the ability to reproduce and continue. God was finished after the 6th day, so He rested on the 7th day. Jesus is Lord over the Sabbath day because that day was dedicated to the reconciliation of the earth and humanity back to God (Matthew 12.8). God knew that giving humans free will would corrupt His perfect creation, and His redemption plan through the Work of Jesus Christ on the Cross was already seeded and ready. God rested, so we could rest in Him on the 7th day, knowing that Jesus would accomplish the Redemption Plan. We celebrate Sabbath rest every week as a symbol of the True Sabbath Rest we have in Christ. We fall short of this Sabbath through unbelief. When we don't believe Jesus died for our sins, we fall short of God's eternal Sabbath in heaven. And even in our daily life, when we carry unbelief about God's goodness and His promises, we fail to enter into His daily rest. Failing to enter into God's rest every moment signifies that we are relying on our own weak strength, power and energy. We are exhausted and limited daily because of our unbelief. Let us not fall short of our eternal rest in heaven or our daily rest on earth because of unbelief.

"So we see that because of their unbelief they were not able to enter his rest" (Hebrews 3.19 NLT).

DAY 325
Learned Obedience

"Even though Jesus was God's Son, he learned obedience from the things he suffered" (Hebrews 5.8 NLT).

Learning obedience implies that there is an authority in which we are under. Jesus was the Authority with God, but He gave up His throne to enter into earth, submitting Himself to God unto death. He became less than the angels, and humbled Himself in flesh, so He could reconcile humanity by His death on the Cross (Hebrews 2.9 & Romans 5.1). If Jesus learned obedience to God through His suffering, so shall we learn through our own suffering. It is easy to obey God's commands when it feels good and it lines up with what we want. However, it is very difficult to obey when it does not feel good and it doesn't line up with what we want. But true obedience is seen only through suffering because we are staying obedient to God even when we don't want to. Jesus cried out to God to save Him from the Cross, but when God commanded His will, Jesus obeyed and allowed Himself to be the scapegoat for all humanity (Luke 22.42). He became sin, so we could be saved. We can follow Jesus' example. Instead of complaining when God's asks us to do something difficult, we can obey God even when it hurts. Only then will we begin to act as true Children of God, obeying their Heavenly Father and trusting His commands.

"For our sake he made him to be sin who knew no sin, so that in him we might become the righteousness of God" (2 Corinthians 5.21 ESV).

DAY 326
Wait Patiently

"And so after waiting patiently, Abraham received what was promised" (Hebrews 6.15 NIV).

God plants seeds of promise inside of us way before those promises come to fruition. Depending on how big the promise, the time before it is realized can last months to years to decades. There must be an in-between time after the promise is given and before it comes to completion. This delay not only prepares us emotionally, mentally and physically for our promise, but it prepares us spiritually. When our promise is given, we are not the people we need to be in order to maintain that promise. If our promise is fulfilled too early, it could cause us to sabotage our own destiny. So God must give us time to grow into the person who can carry such a weighty promise while still relying on Him every day. Many of us will work toward God's promise, but we may become discouraged when the promise almost seems to die. However, we must trust that God is the God of Resurrection, and He can breathe new life into our dreams when the time is right. Our job is to stay obedient to God and remain patient even as years pass by and everything seems hopeless. If we can hold tightly to faith and push away doubt when the natural situation to our promise is dead, God will unleash a supernatural miracle to bring our promise to life.

"Patient endurance is what you need now, so that you will continue to do God's will. Then you will receive all that he has promised" (Hebrews 10.36 NLT).

DAY 327
Hearts and Minds

"But this is the new covenant I will make with the people of Israel on that day, says the LORD: I will put my laws in their minds, and I will write them on their hearts. I will be their God, and they will be my people" (Hebrews 8.10 NLT).

During the Old Covenant, God's Spirit (Holy Spirit) could come upon people who were found faithful to Him. However, the Holy Spirit's movements in people's lives were temporary and selective. Today, in the New Covenant established by the death and resurrection of Jesus Christ, we can have the indwelling of the Holy Spirit always. We have been forgiven of our sin and are justified by the Blood of Jesus, and the proof of our righteousness by faith is the indwelling of the Holy Spirit in our lives. Now the Holy Spirit can write His words on our minds and our hearts. He is our constant Companion, Teacher and Guide, helping us every day with His promptings. We are not alone anymore. There is a God Who loves us, so He died to save us from our sins in order to be with us every second of every day. We can have an intimate relationship with God, and He can pour His Truth all through our innermost being if we remain open to Him. With God's Spirit in us, there is nothing too hard, too scary or too overwhelming that we can't have the victory over it with His help. We have been brought back to God, so we could be His people for eternity.

"And all of this is a gift from God, who brought us back to himself through Christ. And God has given us this task of reconciling people to him" (2 Corinthians 5.18 NLT).

DAY 328
Faith Assurance

———— ❖ ————

"Now faith is the assurance (title deed, confirmation) of things hoped for (divinely guaranteed), and the evidence of things not seen [the conviction of their reality—faith comprehends as fact what cannot be experienced by the physical senses]" (Hebrews 11.1 AMP).

Everything hinges on faith. We cannot have one plausible thought about heaven, salvation or victory in Christ without faith being the core of all that we believe and think. So much of our Christian walk is based on things we cannot comprehend with our five senses. God beautifully gives us physical symbols and metaphors to help us with the abstract truths of our faith. He gives us the Wine (God's essence mixed with flesh, the Blood of Jesus poured out to reconcile the earth), He gives us the Bread (the container that was broken to pour out the Wine, the Body of Jesus broken on the Cross), He gives us the Last Supper (the act of God's Children breaking the Body of Jesus and consuming His redemptive Blood), and He gives us so many more metaphors of spiritual truths that activate our faith: Tree of Life (Jesus), Tree of Knowledge of Good and Evil (free will), Garden of Eden (heaven and the presence of God), serpent (Lucifer or Satan) and so on. God relates to us in ways that we can understand, and our faith in these things gives us hope in realities we cannot see. God and heaven will become a reality to us if faith supersedes sight. We simply need to believe the unseen more than the seen and work our faith into all areas of our lives, making our trust in God a concrete fixture in all we believe, say and do.

"For we live by faith, not by sight" (2 Corinthians 5.7 NIV).

DAY 329
A Divided Mind

———❖———

"Therefore, strengthen your feeble arms and weak knees. 'Make level paths for your feet,' so that the lame may not be disabled, but rather healed" (Hebrews 12.12-13 NIV).

Satan is a liar (John 8.44), and his lies have no rhyme or reason except to take our minds away from God's Truth and His promises. Satan uses these lies to produce confusion and chaos in our lives to distract us from the "straight" path that God has set before us. When we faithfully seek the Lord, we will receive a definite word from the Holy Spirit. In that moment of confirmation, we are filled with God's favor for the promise and path that He has placed us on. We then transform our hope into firm faith, believing that His promises have already been accomplished in the spiritual realm. However, Satan knows that there is a delay until these promises manifest in the physical realm, so that's when he begins to implement his attack on God's will for our lives. Satan's plan is simple: if he can make us falter on our "straight" path—making us look left and right, questioning the still small voice of God spoken over us—we will lose our belief. Once we lose our belief in God's plan, our firm faith in God's promises diminishes. We cannot achieve God's awesome promises without faith. Disbelief hinders God's purposes coming to fruition, and Satan desires to sabotage our belief because he despises humanity, and he wants to bring all of us down with him. Hebrews 12.12-13 encourages us to rise up in strength and walk the ''straight" path that God has for us, so Satan won't be able to dislocate us from our place in God's will and the Body of Christ. In fact, when we continue down that path in faith, our "healing" (blessing, promise, provision, etc.) will surely be ours to claim, and we can walk in the greater Kingdom Purpose God has planned for us!

"Look straight ahead, and fix your eyes on what lies before you. Mark out a straight path for your feet; stay on the safe path. Don't get sidetracked; keep your feet from following evil" (Proverbs 4.25-27 NLT).

DAY 330
Gym of life

"Dear brothers and sisters, when troubles of any kind come your way, consider it an opportunity for great joy. For you know that when your faith is tested, your endurance has a chance to grow. So let it grow, for when your endurance is fully developed, you will be perfect and complete, needing nothing" (James 1.2-4 NLT).

Bodybuilders who walk into the gym bring with them a sense of excitement. They know that their struggle with the weights is what will tear the muscle fibers, which will eventually heal and grow stronger. When they enter the weight room, they understand that they will feel pain, exhaustion and brokenness, but that is all part of the sport. They will never become stronger unless they confront weights that are almost too difficult for them to move. They are getting ready for the day that they will present their bodies strong and powerful on stage. This truth is the same for Christians today. God is making us into the people we will be for eternity, and He knows that the struggles of this life are what will build us up, lean us out and make us stronger. If we never confront the weight of trouble, we would never mature and build strength in the Lord. This life on earth is like a gym, and we are preparing for the day we will be presented on the heavenly stage before Jesus. Will He say good job or will we have wasted away our life because we ran from every struggle that came our way? We must trust the process of brokenness and growth, knowing that the Lord doesn't want to make us weak; rather, He is trying to make us strong in Him.

"Finally, be strong in the Lord and in his mighty power" (Ephesians 6.10 NIV).

DAY 331
Blown and Tossed

"But when he asks, he must believe and not doubt, because he who doubts is like a wave of the sea, blown and tossed by the wind" (James 1.6 NIV).

God gives us some amazing promises and depending on our circumstances, our faith may go up and down. If we are struggling with discouragement and disbelief, the Bible says that we are like "a wave of the sea, blown and tossed by the wind." Instead of allowing the "winds" of circumstance dictate our belief, we must always rely on God's Word. If God has made us a promise, we should never doubt ourselves because of our circumstances. God is Lord over all, and He far surpasses our authority and the authority of this world. If He says it will happen, it doesn't matter if the thing we are believing for has died. He will resurrect it in His power and in His timing! We must never be "double-minded" when God has a call on our lives. It may take years and our Promised Land may look like a wilderness, but He will fulfill His promises. He can make streams form in the desert, and He can bring the dead back to life. There is nothing impossible for God to accomplish. God will delay His promise until we are secure in Him without any doubt in our mind that He can accomplish what He said He would do.

"God is not a man, so he does not lie. He is not human, so he does not change his mind. Has he ever spoken and failed to act? Has he ever promised and not carried it through?" (Numbers 23.19 NLT).

DAY 332

Complete Faith

———•———◦❖◦———•———

"You see that [his] faith was working together with his works, and as a result of the works, his faith was completed [reaching its maturity when he expressed his faith through obedience]" (James 2.22 AMP).

If we truly have faith in God's promises for our life, we will demonstrate that faith by being obedient to the process of fulfilling those promises. Although we in our own strength could never achieve the great things of God, our choices and actions reveal our belief in what God can do when we work alongside the Holy Spirit to the completion of His will. If we do nothing by faith toward experiencing God's promises realized, we prove that we lack faith in His Word because our actions are not being motivated by our belief. Faith and deeds go hand in hand. We can say we love someone, but unless our actions demonstrate that love, our words are superficial. Much the same way, we can say we have faith, but if our actions don't produce seeds in relation to our faith, our faith is also superficial. Our every thought, word and action should be motivated by what we are believing God for. When people look at our life, they should be able to see faith-steps leading toward a certain Promised Land. If our actions aren't lining up with our faith, we can choose today to stand firmly on God's Word and work diligently in obedience to the Holy Spirit, producing works that complete our faith.

"For in Christ Jesus neither circumcision nor uncircumcision avails anything, but faith working through love" (Galatians 5.6 NKJV).

DAY 333

Tame Tongue

"People can tame all kinds of animals, birds, reptiles, and fish, but no one can tame the tongue. It is restless and evil, full of deadly poison" (James 3.7-8 NLT).

Taming the tongue will be every Christian's constant battle. The tongue is very powerful; and when it is tame, it can move mountains (Mark 11.23). However, the tongue can be wilder than the wildest of animals. When unbridled and let loose, the tongue can cause havoc, devastation and death" (Proverbs 18.21). God has given us the authority to create with our words, and if we aren't purposeful when we think and speak, we will unintentionally cause our lives and the lives of others to be limited or even miserable. We must comprehend and utilize the power of the tongue every moment of every day. We should harness any word that speaks anything contrary to God's Word, and multiply all the words that speak God's Heart. Even in random clichés or everyday talk, "I'm starving to death," "I'll never lose weight," "I'm always broke," "You gave me a heart attack," and "No one loves me," we declare words that don't line up with God's will. Instead, we can say words that affirm that we are loved by God and that we are growing stronger in His mercy and grace. Let us recognize every word we speak and adjust our negative talk, so our words agree with what God says. He says we are more than conquerors and loved by a Holy King (Romans 8.37 & 1 John 4.10). Let's make sure our words speak this truth!

"Whoever guards his mouth preserves his life; he who opens wide his lips comes to ruin" (Proverbs 13.3 ESV).

DAY 334
Motives

"When you ask, you do not receive, because you ask with wrong motives, that you may spend what you get on your pleasures" (James 4.3 NIV).

Many times we don't realize that our motives are rooted in selfishness until God exposes them. Just like a child who operates in a me-centered mentality, when we first come to God, we will automatically exist in our selfish nature. It is a journey, walking hand-in-hand with the Holy Spirit, that grows us into mature Christians. God will give us promises, and when we first receive them, we will embrace them for selfish reasons that may appear "spiritual" because they are candy-coated with good intentions. God must peel away our wrong motives, uncovering our selfishness, so we can finally repent and embrace His promises with motives aligned with God's heart. Our default nature will always be self-centered, and we must choose each day to operate outside that selfishness and in the will of God. God will wait, holding our promises back, until we offer all our motives to Him. Only when we submit our intentions to God and lay our expectations at His feet, will we be able to "spend what we get" on God's pleasure and not our own. And when we please God, we will find that we have achieved our own ultimate pleasure in life—the pleasure of our Heavenly Father.

"A man's most glorious actions will at last be found to be but glorious sins, if he hath made himself, and not the glory of God, the end of those actions." – Thomas Brooks

DAY 335
Inaction

"If anyone, then, knows the good they ought to do and doesn't do it, it is sin for them" (James 4.17 NIV).

We usually think of sin as doing some sort of action against God's will, whether it be lying, stealing, cheating, murdering, etc. But there is more to sin than simply committing actions that displease God. Sin doesn't always have to be moving; it can also be stagnating. When the Holy Spirit convicts us to do something, like saying sorry, offer a helping hand, giving money, taking time to pray, etc., and we disobey His voice by doing nothing, we have now sinned. There are many Christians whose actions look perfect, but their inactions are leaving a trail of disobedience behind them. God has called us to be the hands and feet of Jesus. This doesn't mean that we should to do every good work that crosses our path—this too can be good works done in disobedience. It does mean, however, that when the Holy Spirit prompts us to act, we must obey. When we feel God motivating our spirits with a sense of urgency and need, we can step out on faith no matter the circumstance. Yes, we may be embarrassed and we may not know the outcome, but we will feel good knowing we didn't sin with our indifference and our complacency.

"But anyone who hears my teaching and doesn't obey it is foolish, like a person who builds a house on sand. When the rains and floods come and the winds beat against that house, it will collapse with a mighty crash" (Matthew 7.26-27 NLT).

DAY 336
Confess & Pray

"Confess your sins to each other and pray for each other so that you may be healed. The earnest prayer of a righteous person has great power and produces wonderful results" (James 5.16 NLT).

Confessing can be one of the most therapeutic and healing things a person can do. Sin and guilt carried within the mind, body and soul can have damaging effects on a person—not only spiritually, mentally, emotionally and relationally, but also physically. The burden of sin will eventually begin to cause our body to pay the price of the constant weight of sin it is carrying. We think we may be getting away with our sin because no one knows, but our own souls know and the consequences will eventually begin to show. Sin isn't always what we have done. It can also be what has been done to us. Although the fault is not our own, we may allow the effects of guilt and shame to remain active within us. Instead of allowing these negative emotions to fill our lives, we must give the pain to God. The best way to offer up these damaging feelings to the Lord is to confess them to people we trust. We may feel embarrassed and ashamed, but when we finally confess and let go, those emotions can have no more hold over us. We aren't accountable to what is done to us, but we are responsible for the negativity we allow to stay. It is better to receive healing by confessing to a "righteous person," and allowing him or her to pray over us and our situation. Only then can we attain the "wonderful results" that confessing and healing can bring to our lives.

"If we confess our sins, he is faithful and just and will forgive us our sins and purify us from all unrighteousness" (1 John 1.9 NIV).

DAY 337
The Value of Faith

———◦———⟫⟩✦⟨⟪———◦———

"These have come so that the proven genuineness of your faith—of greater worth than gold, which perishes even though refined by fire—may result in praise, glory and honor when Jesus Christ is revealed" (1 Peter 1.7 NIV).

Trials will come, but they are not to be feared, disregarded or circumvented. They are essential for the purity of our faith, which will be the one thing that gives our lives glory and honor once we enter heaven. We won't be recognized for our money, our fame or our position in life, but we will be applauded for the faith to which we clung, producing all kinds of good works for the Lord. Our faith not only guarantees salvation for our souls, but it also works that salvation into every part of our being. Faith is more valuable than gold. The world may bet its currency on the gold standard, but God establishes us with His gold standard of faith. God wants to refine our faith, and He will use the fires of life to purify our belief in Him and His promises. We must never walk away from our faith, and our resilience is only possible if we keep our focus on God and His Kingdom. Trials may try to weaken us, push us around or even take us out, but we can stand strong, joyfully knowing that God is increasing the bank accounts of our faith. God will not see the mistakes we made in this life because of the cleansing Blood of Jesus, but He will see our awesome faith, surrounded by the good works that it birthed.

"Cleverness is cheap. It is faith that He praises." – George Macdonald

DAY 338
Before Creation

"He was chosen before the creation of the world, but was revealed in these last times for your sake" (1 Peter 1.20 NIV).

The plan of redemption was enacted before God created the world on Creation Week. Our sin was no surprise to God. Much like a mother and father know that their children will one-day sin, the blessing of children surpasses the difficulty in raising them. Parents give birth to children not because they want perfect individuals, but because they want a family to love. God is all love, and He wants to share His love with His creation. He knows we will fall short of His holy standard, so He devised a plan to both love and save us. This way He could be our Heavenly Father even while we exist in our imperfect state. Our sin separates us from God, but God's grace and our faith bring us back into a relationship with Him once more through the Work of Jesus on the Cross. It's a miraculous thought, knowing that Jesus Christ was there before the beginning of time, ready to redeem and reconcile us back to the Father. It is even more wonderful to know that we live in the New Testament era where the Blood of Jesus Christ has finished its work. We can now have a relationship with God, and His Holy Spirit can now live within us. We have been perfected and set apart for God's good purposes. Jesus has been "revealed" to us in the "last days," and we are loved by a Father who would die to save us.

"But God showed his great love for us by sending Christ to die for us while we were still sinners" (Romans 5.8 NLT).

DAY 339
A Royal Priesthood

"But you are a chosen people, a royal priesthood, a holy nation, God's special possession, that you may declare the praises of him who called you out of darkness into his wonderful light" (1 Peter 2.9 NIV).

People act the way they believe themselves to be. Christians who don't read the Bible and truly soak up God's Word have no clue who they are in Christ. But Paul lays it out. He affirms that we are "a royal priesthood, a holy nation, God's special possession," and because of this knowledge, we will praise Him who calls us to such an elevated position in His Kingdom. We are royalty! We are priests! We are holy! We have been purchased by the Blood of Jesus! When the truth really begins to make its way from our minds into our hearts, we will start to behave accordingly. We'll walk in the position and the authority to which God has called each of us. The enemy doesn't want us to know who we are in Christ. This way Satan can make us think low of ourselves, so he can easily trip us up and destroy our destiny. But we must aggressively see ourselves through the eyes of God's grace every day. Our purpose and position in God is no longer hazy and blurred. Light has been shed through Jesus Christ, and we now know that we mirror the image of God. Jesus has cleaned and perfected us, and we can easily live a life that pleases God by faith.

"So God created mankind in his own image, in the image of God he created them; male and female he created them" (Genesis 1.27 NIV).

DAY 340
Inherit Blessing

"Do not repay evil with evil or insult with insult. On the contrary, repay evil with blessing, because to this you were called so that you may inherit a blessing" (1 Peter 3.9 NIV).

It is extremely difficult to be the recipient of someone's evil actions. Depending on how deep the wounds go, it could take months or even years to heal. Deep wounds are less frequent but can be very damaging. The Holy Spirit will have to work with us and through others in order for us to overcome our pain and find healing. More frequently, though, we will encounter insults, especially as Christians living for God. Satan has us on his radar, and he will use others (even Christians) to insult us and disrupt us from our destiny. It would be easy to sink to their level and insult them back, but the Bible says to "repay evil with blessing." This seems contrary to a world that is constantly defending itself, but God's ways are truth, and there is a promise found in this verse. If we repay evil with good, we will be blessed. The blessing can come in many forms, but it will usually show up in ways that money can't buy. God can give us peace, joy and hope—all things unattainable without the help of the Holy Spirit. When we obey by faith, God can move by grace. He will supernaturally transform evil into good when we offer a blessing for an insult.

"But I say, do not resist an evil person! If someone slaps you on the right cheek, offer the other cheek also" (Matthew 5.39 NLT).

DAY 341
Be Ready

"But in your hearts revere Christ as Lord. Always be prepared to give an answer to everyone who asks you to give the reason for the hope that you have. But do this with gentleness and respect" (1 Peter 3.15 NIV).

Many people use their service to God as an excuse to ignore the needs of the people right in front of them. They are so busy in their "ministry" that when a loved one needs a word of hope, they ignore the subtle plea for help and encouragement. We should never be so busy ministering that we can't minister to the people walking alongside of us. How many times have we looked passed an individual life because they didn't seem worthy of the "big" impact we believe we are making? Peter tells us to "always be prepared to give an answer to everyone who asks you to give the reason for the hope that you have." God places specific people into our lives who need hope. They are not the mass audience we imagine; rather, they are the teary eyes and the exhausted souls of people who cross our paths daily. These people should always come first. No matter what epic deed we are working on that we feel will impact the world, we need to be sensitive to the people we rub elbows with on a daily basis. God doesn't do things by accident. He knows exactly who will show up on our doorstep or call us on the phone. When we can, we should stop whatever we are doing and offer the hope we have in Jesus. In that way, we will truly make a difference in the hearts of God's children.

"Share each other's burdens, and in this way obey the law of Christ" (Galatians 6.2 NLT).

DAY 342
Being Good

"As a result, they do not live the rest of their earthly lives for evil human desires, but rather for the will of God" (1 Peter 4.2 NIV).

We've been told from an early age to "be good." When we were young, teachers, parents and other adults would explain that we needed to avoid being bad, so we could be good boys and girls. The world emphasizes the human standard of being good (which historically changes through time), yet people forget one very serious point: being good is impossible. Instead of telling us to "be good," Peter offers us something even better. He explains that the only way we can avoid following our "evil human desires," is do "the will of God." It's not about being good; it's about being obedient. It is so much easier to focus on doing God's will rather than trying to be good all the time. God is perfect and holy, and when we follow Him, we will automatically behave in ways that please Him. We may never be good enough, but we can definitely aim towards pleasing God by doing His will. So instead of constantly telling our children to shape up and be good, we can simply encourage them to do the will of God. As they obey God more and more, they will begin to become like Jesus.

"This is what I told them: 'Obey me, and I will be your God, and you will be my people. Do everything as I say, and all will be well!'" (Jeremiah 7.23 NLT).

DAY 343
Lifted Up

"Humble yourselves, therefore, under God's mighty hand, that he may lift you up in due time" (1 Peter 5.6 NIV).

God must bring us low before He can lift us high. He knows that humans by our default nature struggle with pride and self-glory, so He will not give us a platform to declare His Name until He works humility into us. If we are lifted high before humility becomes second nature, we will corrupt the very platform we use to exalt God. Every layer of pride must be exposed, so we can fully embrace a life of humility. The uncovering of pride takes years, and although we may always struggle with pride, we can come to the point where we surrender completely to the Lord. When we finally realize we can do nothing without God's help, we can let go of self-perfection and walk in the perfect grace of Jesus Christ. It is not about us and what we can do. It is about God and what He can do. If God has promised us a platform to declare His name, we must be ready for the process of being brought low. We will feel like God has stripped us of everything that gives us a feeling of worth. But we shouldn't get discouraged. God will place His worth into our bare souls, so we can confidently declare His glory to the world.

"Humble yourselves before the Lord, and he will lift you up" (James 4.10 NIV).

DAY 344
Knowing God

———•—✳—•———

"His divine power has given us everything we need for a godly life through our knowledge of him who called us by his own glory and goodness" (2 Peter 1.3 NIV).

Some people mistakenly believe that all they need is their emotions to love God. Studying God's Word and discovering His character takes a back seat, and their worship of God is centered on feeling good and alive. They think that having positive emotional feelings will guarantee a deeper relationship with Him. But this line of thought is just not true. It is difficult to love someone who we do not know or spend time with. There are four things that the Bible tells us we must use in order to grow in the Lord: our heart (emotions), our soul (personality), our strength (will) and our mind (intellect). The Holy Spirit will increase our love for God and deepen our relationship with Him in these four areas. And what we find is that when we grow in one area, we will also grow in the other three areas, strengthening our intimacy with the Lord. When we learn more about God by reading His Word and spending time with Him, our deepening knowledge of God will bolster our heart (intensifying our feelings for Him), our soul (molding our personality into His likeness) and our strength (increasing our obedience to His will). Peter explains that we achieve more of God's available power when we begin to know God more. It is impossible to claim something we do not know. Therefore, we must know God and all of His promises, so we can gain all His goodness. So if we feel like we are lacking what "we need for a godly life," maybe we should take time to open our Bibles and listen to God's voice today.

"He answered, 'Love the Lord your God with all your heart and with all your soul and with all your strength and with all your mind'; and, 'Love your neighbor as yourself'" (Luke 10.27 NIV).

DAY 345
Fall Away

- ❖ -

"So, dear brothers and sisters, work hard to prove that you really are among those God has called and chosen. Do these things, and you will never fall away" (2 Peter 1.10 NLT).

People fall away from the Lord when they forget the calling He has placed on their life. We all have been "called and chosen" to a destiny and purpose (Ephesians 1.11). God gives us authority to do a job on this earth; and if we do that job well, He will give us authority in heaven (Matthew 25.23). We meander from God's will when we get sidetracked from our purpose. However, Peter gives us a hint to help us stay on track. He explains that if we add a few things to our faith, we will "never fall away." The things include, goodness, knowledge, self-control, perseverance, godliness, kindness and love. Activating these attributes that are rightfully ours through the Holy Spirit will give us parameters in our calling that will prevent us from quitting. People quit for many different reasons, but if they are clinging onto goodness, self-control, perseverance, etc., they will not succumb to the desire to give up. Our journey to achieving our destiny will be littered with detours, pit stops and nay-sayers, but we can't let them distract us and cause us to give up. When we truly believe that God has given us a "holy calling," we won't stop for anything or anyone. People may fall all around us, but we will keep on working our destiny until the day we meet Jesus face-to-face!

"Who saved us and called us to a holy calling, not because of our works but because of his own purpose and grace, which he gave us in Christ Jesus before the ages began" (2 Timothy 1.9 ESV).

DAY 346
Not Free at All

"They promise them freedom, while they themselves are slaves of depravity—for 'people are slaves to whatever has mastered them'" (2 Peter 2.19 NIV).

Today there is much talk about our freedom of choice to do whatever we feel is right for us. People think they are freeing the world to do as they please, but in actuality they are enslaving the world to their own corruption and destruction. God's Words found in the Bible are true and right, and they lead to a life with meaning and prosperity. When we go against His Word—no matter how pretty and pleasing our actions seem to the world—we will trap ourselves in our own depravity. Humans are not able to achieve a moral compass alone. We need a source outside of ourselves to help guide us with Light and Truth. We walk in true freedom when we are surrendered to God's commands because only He can supernaturally open the road in front of us. God's path goes beyond this world and this life to an eternal life with Him. If we listen to ourselves and our own evil desires, the supernatural doors of God will be closed shut. He can't bless what is not committed into His hands. When we are obeying our own desires and not God's, we are in essence taking ourselves out of God's care. Freedom of choice outside of God's will may sound freeing, but the end result will be our own demise.

"But each person is tempted when he is lured and enticed by his own desire. Then desire when it has conceived gives birth to sin, and sin when it is fully grown brings forth death" (James 1.14-15 ESV).

DAY 347
New Earth

———— ❋ ————

"But in keeping with his promise we are looking forward to a new heaven and a new earth, where righteousness dwells" (2 Peter 3.13 NIV).

Heaven is not just a misty abyss with a few clouds and a smattering of angels. Heaven is the presence of God (with hell being the absence of God). God is a Creator, so heaven will be nothing short of amazing creations filled to the rim with the imagination of our Heavenly Father. When Jesus rose from the dead, He had a supernatural body that was also physical. He could appear out of thin air, but he had flesh that could be touched (John 20.19-29). The New Earth will be much the same—it will be supernatural yet physical all at the same time. We will have what we have on earth, only better. Just as exciting is that we will also have new bodies, which will be our bodies, only better! As Christians, we have so much to look forward to. Death is not the end; it is our true beginning. This life on this earth is much like a mother's womb, developing and maturing us into the people we will be for eternity. So let us not waste one single moment of our time on this earth. One day we will look back on our time here and realize just how quickly it went. God has promised us a New Earth and a New Home with Him through Jesus Christ. We can look forward to this promise by living each day to its fullest until we are finally called home.

"Then I saw a new heaven and a new earth, for the old heaven and the old earth had disappeared. And the sea was also gone" (Revelation 21.1 NLT).

DAY 348
Cool Spring of Confession

———— ❖ ————

"But if we confess our sins to him, he is faithful and just to forgive us our sins and to cleanse us from all wickedness" (1 John 1.9 NLT).

Our pride keeps us in the dark. Our humility releases us into the Light. "God is light; in him there is no darkness at all" (1 John 1.5). The most effective way to stay in God's light is to confess. We can be like King David when he asked God to "know my heart" (Psalm 139.23). The Holy Spirit excels at pointing out and cutting away sin in our lives, so He can move His redemption into those renewed areas. The more sin we reveal to God, the more God can move His will and authority into our lives. Confessing to God is a daily task that will guarantee His fullness in our lives every day. Sometimes, however, the Holy Spirit will want us to take our confession one step further by confessing to a trusted confidante. Confessing our struggles to another person is one of the most humbling things we can do, but it is an excellent way to pierce our pride so God's light can flood in. The Holy Spirit will let us know what to confess and to whom we should confess. And even though our pride will get badly bruised, we can trust that God's forgiveness and healing will wash over us like a cool spring over hot coals. We will draw closer to God and become more like Jesus in the process.

"Forgiveness is always free. But that doesn't mean that confession is always easy." – Erwin Lutzer

DAY 349
Walking in Light

"Anyone who loves their brother and sister lives in the light, and there is nothing in them to make them stumble. But anyone who hates a brother or sister is in the darkness and walks around in the darkness. They do not know where they are going, because the darkness has blinded them" (1 John 2.10-11 NIV).

If we are holding something against someone else, we have far much more of a chance of stumbling in our faith. Having negative feelings that are not of God towards another person places us in the dark and outside of God's light. If we are harboring feelings of anger, resentment, jealousy, criticism, etc., we must confess it quickly to God. Otherwise, we may become accustomed to living in the spiritual darkness, allowing offense to guide us instead of the Holy Spirit. This doesn't mean that we should ignore it when people hurt us, but it does mean we need to instantly give that hurt to God, so we won't step foot into the darkness. We can care for others while still maintaining a safe distance from them. We can separate ourselves from damaging people, but still pray for them. We don't have to excuse the harmful behavior of others in order to continue loving them. God is both loving and just, and we can learn how to love others but resist their destructive words and actions. We must not allow others to throw us out of God's will. God loves all of His Children, and He has died for each one of us. We can forgive others as God forgave us, knowing that we will live joyfully and peacefully in the light of God.

"Instead, be kind to each other, tenderhearted, forgiving one another, just as God through Christ has forgiven you" (Ephesians 4.32 NLT).

DAY 350

Passing Desires

———— ❖ ————

"And the world is passing away along with its desires, but whoever does the will of God abides forever" (1 John 2.17 ESV).

Sometimes a desire can come upon us so strongly that we need to stop what we are doing and really question if the desire is from God or not. If the desire goes against God's Word, we should automatically know that it is a worldly desire that will end in destruction. However, there are many desires that seem okay and that don't necessarily compromise God's Word in our lives, but we have to look closely before we follow through with them. Lots of things look good, but they aren't necessarily God's will for our lives. Selling the perfume that anointed the feet of Jesus to help the poor seemed like a good idea, but it went directly against God's will (John 12.5). The only desires that will have eternal results are the ones rooted in God. All the other desires we chase that are not rooted in God will fade away with the world. Life is short, and we only have this one lifetime to make a difference for eternity. We must be very careful how we manage our time, and chasing fleeting desires shows poor stewardship of the life we have been given. Every time a desire comes upon us, we must seek the Holy Spirit's guidance. God is more than willing to distinguish a shortsighted desire from an everlasting one.

"Take delight in the LORD, and he will give you the desires of your heart" (Psalm 37.4 NIV).

DAY 351
The Action of Love

"Dear children, let us not love with words or speech but with actions and in truth" (1 John 3.18 NIV).

Usually, it's easy for us to whisper, "I love you," to someone we care about. What is difficult to do is to show that "I love you" in our actions. Loving someone with actions has the power to speak louder than a million words shouted at once. Jesus showed His great love for us by dying on the cross (Romans 5.8). He didn't just say He loves us; He displayed it. We need to ask ourselves: What have we done today to demonstrate our love to those around us? How have we served, supported, encouraged and poured into the people we care about? If we are not cognizant of our actions, we will routinely do what only pleases us. It is easy to commit to actions that make us happy, but it takes determination to commit to actions that make others happy. Loving others moves us outside of our self-centered state and into a position of service, which pleases the heart of God (Hebrews 6.10). So let us take time today to show our love to the people that God has placed in our life, and we will realize that loving others through action will not only bless them, but it will bless us as well.

"Love is the doorway through which the human soul passes from selfishness to service." – Jack Hyles

DAY 352

Full expression

———— ❊ ————

"No one has ever seen God. But if we love each other, God lives in us, and his love is brought to full expression in us" (1 John 4.12 NLT).

We may not be able to physically see God on this side of eternity, but we can see His love in "full expression" when we love His Children. Ask any mother or father, and they will say that when their child is loved and blessed, they themselves feel loved and blessed. The same is true with our Heavenly Father. He wants to demonstrate His love in and through His Children. When we love one of God's People, we actually love the Father. The best way for non-Christians to "see" God is for them to experience first-hand God's Children loving each other. When Christians lay aside hurts and disagreements, so they can continue to love one another, people will take notice. They will see that there is a stronger love motivating Christians to act in ways that go against the world's expectations. The world has a selfish love, but God's love is unselfish, which can only be demonstrated when we continue to love even when we have reason to hate. Loving others is a choice, not a feeling. God can't command feelings, but He can command us to make a choice that pleases Him. Therefore, we must make the choice to love everyday, so that God can be seen in our actions and lives.

"So now I am giving you a new commandment: Love each other. Just as I have loved you, you should love each other" (John 13.34 NLT).

DAY 353
Water and Blood

"This is He who came by water and blood—Jesus Christ; not only by water, but by water and blood. And it is the Spirit who bears witness, because the Spirit is truth" (1 John 5.6 NKJV).

Jesus coming down to earth by "water and blood" leaves us with such a beautiful picture if we understand the metaphor each symbol represents. Water and blood can symbolize the baptism and sacrifice of Jesus, signifying the experience of every Believer of being reconciled back to God by Jesus' Finished Work on the Cross. However, water and blood can also symbolize God in the flesh. God is a picture of Living Water on the earth (Isaiah 44.3). When water rained down the first time in the Great Flood, everything washed away besides Noah and His family whom God placed in the Ark of His Salvation. God promises He will never flood the earth again (Genesis 9.11). But how can God pour His Spirit (water) onto the earth without destroying everything that does not match His standard of holiness? He pours His Spirit into His Son, allowing His Living Water to be mixed with flesh, which is represented in blood. Therefore, we have Jesus Who is the embodiment and God in the flesh. And His body was broken, so His blood (water mixed with flesh), could pour salvation onto the world, reconciling us all back to our Heavenly Father. Instead of destroying us, God saved us. So Jesus is God's solution to Get His Spirit onto the earth and into our lives. Instead of being carried in an Ark, like Noah and His Family, we have been carried in Christ's body—in His death and resurrection. Our sin has been cast into hell, and we have been made new creations in Christ (2 Corinthians 5.17).

"For we died and were buried with Christ by baptism. And just as Christ was raised from the dead by the glorious power of the Father, now we also may live new lives" (Romans 6.4 NLT).

DAY 354
The Chosen-Lady

"This letter is from John, the elder. I am writing to the chosen lady and to her children, whom I love in the truth—as does everyone else who knows the truth—" (2 John 1.1 NLT).

Some scholars claim that John was writing metaphorically to the church, not a specific lady. He is one of the major pillars of the Church and probably the last remaining of the original apostles. How could this faith giant waste his time writing to a single woman and her children? Culturally during this time, women did not have much power or prominence, and their worlds revolved mostly around the home. But the Apostle John, who invites us to love all God's children equally, does not play favorites. He brings women alongside men as important figures in God's Kingdom who have the right to learn, to work, to be rewarded and to be loved. John values the work that this woman has accomplished, and he writes her to make sure that she does not lose the rewards for her efforts. No one will ever know what work she had accomplished—whether it be as a mother, church leader, evangelist, etc.—but we do know that she has a purpose and a destiny, and she is working diligently for God's Kingdom. The fact that the Apostle John sees her deeds and cares about them says volumes about how much he values her and her work. For the Apostle John to take time to write to an individual and not just focus on writing to the masses shows that he didn't think so highly of himself that he couldn't stop to help a friend. Let none of us get to the point that we don't have time to love and encourage the individuals that God has placed directly on our paths, regardless of their gender, race, income or the degrees and acclaims they have received.

"A woman who walks in purpose doesn't have to chase people or opportunities. Her light causes people and opportunities to pursue her." – T.D. Jakes

DAY 355
Red Flag

"If anyone comes to you and does not bring this doctrine, do not receive him into your house nor greet him; for he who greets him shares in his evil deeds" (2 John 1.10-11 NKJV).

John is a huge advocate of love, but loving others doesn't necessarily mean we support everything they do. During John's time, when Christian preachers spread the Good News of Jesus Christ, they would stay in different homes of various church members as part of their missionary travels. John warned the Chosen Lady that many so-called teachers and Christian leaders were spreading false doctrine. Obviously, these individuals were not spending time with the Lord, and they had begun preaching what sounded good to them and to others instead of preaching the Truth from God's Word. John goes so far as to call these false teachers a type of anti-Christ, people teaching the opposite of what Jesus taught. John tells her boldly not to allow these people into her home or to support and encourage their work. Many times we feel obligated to support "Christian" work because the label "Christian" has been added to it. The people asking for help may have become so deceived by their own motives and actions that they seem really genuine in their requests. But we must look at the fruit of any Christian work before giving it our stamp of approval with financial and moral support. If the Holy Spirit puts up red flags into our spirit about individuals or ministries claiming to be doing God's work, we must carefully consider how we respond to them. We can continue to love them as we are called, but our love doesn't mean we must condone their work and open up our wallets to support them.

"You can identify them by their fruit, that is, by the way they act. Can you pick grapes from thorn bushes, or figs from thistles?" (Matthew 7.16 NLT).

DAY 356
Great Joy

"It gave me great joy when some believers came and testified about your faithfulness to the truth, telling how you continue to walk in it" (3 John 1.3 NIV).

Some friends went to visit the Apostle John, and they got to brag on another Believer in Christ. Instead of spending time gossiping or criticizing other church members, they expounded on this person's faithfulness. This message of someone's generosity and love towards others gave John great joy—so much so that he had to write about it. Many times we do need to be alerted to the negative actions of others, so we can deal with problems according to God's Word if we are called. Otherwise, we should be looking for the good in people and sharing the joy of all their accomplishments. Those who don't like when people do well are allowing their joy to be choked out by pride. They want to be "first," and can't stand when other people succeed. But what they forget is that when other Christians do well in love and truth, the message of Jesus Christ will thrive. As Believers, we want our brothers and sisters in Christ to accomplish great things in God's Kingdom. We know that when other Christians do well, the people of the world will take notice and wonder what is the driving force of their achievements. They will soon discover that Jesus Christ is the basis of all that is good in their lives, and just maybe they too will accept Him as their Lord and Savior.

"If one part suffers, every part suffers with it; if one part is honored, every part rejoices with it" (1 Corinthians 12.26 NIV).

DAY 357
Face to Face

━━━━━◦━━━━━✧❋✧━━━━━◦━━━━━

"I have much to write you, but I do not want to do so with pen and ink. I hope to see you soon, and we will talk face to face. Peace to you. The friends here send their greetings. Greet the friends there by name" (3 John 1.13-14 NIV).

John finished two of his letters to friends with the same closing statement, expressing that he wanted to see them soon face-to-face. John conveys that he had a lot to share, but he could not do it all on paper. Some words had to be expressed in person, eye-to-eye with his listener. In our high-tech, texting and social media world today, we can forget to visit people in person. We busy our schedules to the point that we may be tempted to do all of our communicating via the computer or phone. Although communicating with the written word can be efficient and useful, it will never achieve what a face-to-face visit can do. When we spend time with others, we can hug them and listen with our ears and eyes, catching body language and facial expression. Reading and writing are great forms of communication, but they are no match for speaking and listening with people we can see, smell and touch. It is awesome to read the stories about Jesus in the Bible, but how amazing would it have been to hear those stories from the very mouth of an apostle who walked with Him and lived life with Him for several years? Nothing compares to a personal, in-person exchange of ideas, affection and encouragement. If the Holy Spirit places people on our hearts to encourage, we should always first try to meet them face-to-face.

"And let us consider how to stir up one another to love and good works, not neglecting to meet together, as is the habit of some, but encouraging one another, and all the more as you see the Day drawing near" (Hebrews 10.24-25 ESV).

DAY 358
Do Not Understand

———— ❋ ————

"Yet these people slander whatever they do not understand, and the very things they do understand by instinct—as irrational animals do—will destroy them" (Jude 1.10 NIV).

Faith is one of those mysteries of life that we will never fully understand, so we must choose to believe what our minds cannot grasp. Our human intellect is too limited to comprehend and categorize the greatness of God and the wisdom of His plan on earth and heaven. God beautifully illustrates His spiritual truths in His Word, the Bible, with metaphors and images that we can seek to perceive and understand; yet we will never have the complete view of God until we see Him face-to-face in heaven. During our earthly lives, we can believe what we do not understand, for we know that our faith pleases God. People who choose not to believe because they cannot fit the mysteries of God and His plan into their short-sighted viewpoints may try to destroy the very things set in place to save them. Since faith and salvation don't make sense in the natural, they will walk to their deaths without having a relationship with God— not because God couldn't save them, but because they would not grasp onto faith in order to be saved. Not only do they destroy their own lives, but they also try to destroy the faith in the lives of others. They aggressively go after anything that does not fit into their preconceived notions of reality, never realizing there is more to life than what they can experience with their five senses. This earth and our lives are only a small glimpse of the supernatural world that we are actually a part of and will one day enjoy.

"And it is impossible to please God without faith. Anyone who wants to come to him must believe that God exists and that he rewards those who sincerely seek him" (Hebrews 11.6 NLT).

DAY 359
Wavering Faith

"And you must show mercy to those whose faith is wavering" (Jude 1.22 NLT).

A wavering faith means a growing faith. When we are first given faith, it is still in a seed-like, immature form. Our faith must grow, and the only way for it to grow is for it to meet up with resistance. During difficult times, our faith may flounder for a minute or even take a tumble, but if we cling onto God with all our might, our faith will grow stronger and more secure in the Lord. We should never feel badly if our faith waivers a bit. God is bringing us into deeper maturity in our relationship with Him, and our faith will waiver under the new weight of this intimacy at first. We must give ourselves and others time to strengthen their faith and be merciful to the ones under a new pressure in their Christian walk. The struggle shows that we are growing. If everything is always easy and nothing tests our faith, it will never grow or deepen. With every new level in our walk of faith comes new "devils," and the weight of adversity may shake us, but it does not have to break us. God will not give us more than we can handle, but when He does give our faith a heavy load, we must realize that He trusts us to stand strong under it (1 Corinthians 10.13). When we see someone struggling in their faith, the worst thing we can do is criticize them. It is better to encourage and strengthen their faith, knowing that someday we too will need the same encouragement for the faith that God is growing in us.

"When we get together, I want to encourage you in your faith, but I also want to be encouraged by yours" (Romans 1.12 NLT).

DAY 360
Church of Ephesus

"But you walked away from your first love—why? What's going on with you, anyway? Do you have any idea how far you've fallen? A Lucifer fall! Turn back! Recover your dear early love. No time to waste, for I'm well on my way to removing your light from the golden circle" (Revelation 2.4-5 MSG).

Relationships can fall into a show of predictability, veering steadily away from an outpouring of love. This is what happened to the Church of Ephesus. They did everything right, but they forgot to spend time with God. They hated wickedness, they did good deeds, they even demonstrated great discernment, but they stopped pursuing their love for God. When we begin to walk away from spending intimate time with God, loving and knowing Him, the effects might not show right away. But eventually our lack of intimacy will begin to reveal itself, and our once noble acts will become self-serving, removing us from the will of the Father. It is so easy to get caught up doing things for God that we forget to spend time with Him. We can become so busy with ministry that our relationship with God goes on the back burner. But ultimately that back burner will cool off, and our relationship with God will turn cold. Yes, we are still saved by grace by the covenant of Jesus' blood, but our love for the Lord has become stagnant. Our first priority should always be spending time with God, and our service to Him should spring from the wellspring of that intimacy.

"God loves each of us as if there were only one of us." – Saint Augustine

DAY 361
Church of Smyrna

———— ❧ ————

"Don't be afraid of what you are about to suffer. The devil will throw some of you into prison to test you. You will suffer for ten days. But if you remain faithful even when facing death, I will give you the crown of life" (Revelation 2.10 NLT).

The Church of Smyrna was in a great season of trial and affliction. They believed that they were poor and destitute, but their hardships were making them rich in faith and perseverance. The word, "Smyrna," can also be translated to the word, "myrrh," a substance used for many purposes, including medicine, embalming and perfume. There are two ways to extract myrrh. One way is to penetrate the tree containing the myrrh, letting the tree "bleed" the gum-like substance. Another way is to take the seeds of the tree and crush them, creating the myrrh perfume. Both methods of extracting myrrh call for a bleeding or a crushing, which was exactly what was happening to the Church of Smyrna. But if the people could only see what God saw, they would realize how rich they were in faith, anointing and strength. If they would only stand strong in persecution for a short season, they would be flowing with the "crown of life," and the powerful move of God in their church and lives. Many times we are called to a season of trial and affliction, but we must trust that our "bleeding" will pour out the Holy Spirit and our "crushing" will created a beautiful aroma to God. We can rejoice even in our pain and poverty because we know that God is pouring forth His Holy Spirit, and we are rich with God's presence.

"Live a life filled with love, following the example of Christ. He loved us and offered himself as a sacrifice for us, a pleasing aroma to God" (Ephesians 5.2 NLT).

DAY 362

Church of Pergamos

"But I have a few things against you, because you have there those who hold the doctrine of Balaam, who taught Balak to put a stumbling block before the children of Israel, to eat things sacrificed to idols, and to commit sexual immorality" (Revelation 2.14 NKJV).

Pergamos was an extremely wicked city filled with pagan traditions, which began to affect the Christians living in that area. Although the Church of Pergamos never renounced their faith in Jesus, they did begin to compromise their integrity in two areas: food and sex. Balaam was a prophet in the Old Testament, hired by Balak to curse the Israelites who were trying to secure their Promised Land. Balaam compromised himself as a prophet by going against the will of God. Balak was the King of the Moabites—a culture that feasted and had sex as part of their worship to their false God, Baal. Balak and Balaam tried to curse the Israelites, but God protected His People by turning the attempted curses into a blessing. However, since the Israelites traveled to Moab and lived closely with the Moabites, they quickly began to compromise their integrity by worshiping Baal. Part of this worship was having unsanctioned sex with the Moabites. God sent a plague on the Israelites, causing disaster to those who committed idolatry against Him (Numbers 25.9-10). Many Christians love the Lord, but they compromise in their sex life. They may boldly declare Jesus as their Savior, but their own acts against the Lord cause disaster in their lives. Following the example of compromise that the world deems as normal, Christians will incite the anger of God because their lifestyle choices are so damaging to their witness and their walk of faith. God does forgive through the work of Jesus Christ, but Christians living the sexual lifestyle of the world need to admit their wrongs, repent and separate from people who seek to make them compromise God's blessings in their lives.

"While the Israelites were camped at Acacia Grove, some of the men defiled themselves by having sexual relations with local Moabite women. These women invited them to attend sacrifices to their gods, so the Israelites feasted with them and worshiped the gods of Moab" (Numbers 25.1-2 NLT).

DAY 363
Church of Thyatira

———— ❈ ————

"Nevertheless I have a few things against you, because you allow that woman Jezebel, who calls herself a prophetess, to teach and seduce My servants to commit sexual immorality and eat things sacrificed to idols" (Revelation 2.20 NKJV).

The Church of Thyatira was thriving as a church, and they were accomplishing great deeds with the love and faith for which they were well known. However, they allowed one thing to disrupt their church—the Spirit of Jezebel. The Spirit of Jezebel is a very powerful, seductive, intimidating and self-righteous force. When we allow people into our lives who are manipulated by this spirit, we are inviting a twisted and disruptive entity to influence us. The sad truth is that at any given moment some Christians can be directed by this spirit because they are not completely submitted to the Lord. Satan can have free rein in areas of our lives that are not under God's authority. Self-absorbed people who always want to be in control are very vulnerable to being directed by this evil spirit. If we are not letting God have control, we are susceptible to letting the enemy have control. To believe we are in control ourselves is ignorant. People are created to be vessels, and either God's good or Satan's evil will fill us. When someone with a self-centered and controlling nature comes into our lives, we must be careful not to allow their subtle tentacles of power to wrap around us. They are looking for anyone who will put them first and establish their authority, and they resist people who seek to put God first and establish His authority. And many times, they have no idea that the Spirit of Jezebel is influencing them because they are so used to slapping God's hand away, so they can be first and in control. We are all susceptible to this spirit, which is why we need to remain submitted to the Lord.

"There certainly was no one like Ahab who sold himself to do evil in the sight of the LORD, because Jezebel his wife incited him" (1 Kings 21.25 AMP).

DAY 364
Church of Sardis

"These things says He who has the seven Spirits of God and the seven stars: 'I know your works, that you have a name that you are alive, but you are dead'" (Revelation 3.1 NKJV).

The Holy Spirit is always moving; and if we don't keep up, we will be left behind. Sometimes we get so comfortable with how we play "church" that we stop listening to the Holy Spirit and start living in our comfort zone. Our spiritual life becomes stagnant, and we commence performing Christian deeds out of a religious habit. Our spiritual life may seem "alive" to others, but in actuality our spiritual life has been neglected so long that it is dead. The spiritual life of churches can die just like the spiritual life of individual Believers can. Two things can cause us to die spiritually. First, if we have unrepentant sin in our lives, we severely restrict the flow of the Holy Spirit. Second, if we neglect spending time with God and obeying His commands, we deny God access to our hearts, souls and minds. God's presence is the heartbeat of our spiritual livelihood. When we take Him out of our daily life, we will spiritually starve to death and eventually die. We may look alive for the moment, but ultimately our roots will wither, and the enemy will pull us right out of God's will. People may look at the destruction and wonder how we could fall so hard, but they'll come to the conclusion that we were already spiritually dead—we just didn't show it until it was too late. Let us quickly wake up to our dying spiritual life, repent of our sin and turn quickly back to our Heavenly Father.

"Yet you have a few people in Sardis who have not soiled their clothes. They will walk with me, dressed in white, for they are worthy. The one who is victorious will, like them, be dressed in white. I will never blot out the name of that person from the book of life, but will acknowledge that name before my Father and his angels" (Revelation 3.4-5 NIV).

DAY 365
Church of Philadelphia

"These things say He who is holy, He who is true, 'He who has the key of David, He who opens and no one shuts, and shuts and no one opens: I know your works. See, I have set before you an open door, and no one can shut it; for you have a little strength, have kept My word, and have not denied My name'" (Revelation 3.7-8 NKJV).

As a Christian, there is one thing that will open the mighty will of God in our lives. This one thing allows us access to God and promotes us to His children, and it gives us the right as heirs to the Royal Throne, unleashing God's great promises for us. This one thing is the Key of David—Jesus Christ Himself. Once we realize that everything is possible through the resurrection power of Jesus Christ, nothing will be impossible for us (Ephesians 1.19-20). We will cling tightly to this Key, knowing that He is the Way to achieving our destiny. Our strength, resources, abilities and talents will never measure up to the promises that God has for us. We must learn to submit all that we have and all that we are to Jesus, trusting that He is Who opens doors that no one and nothing can shut. When we finally understand how to grasp the Key of David, we may have little strength left. The road to relying solely on Jesus is long, difficult and lonely. But Jesus knows our struggles, and He knows that we have persevered, holding tightly to His Word, His Promises and His Name. And even though our promises seem dead in the natural, He will come soon and resurrect what is dead in the supernatural. Finally, we will be awarded the victor's crown because we never gave up on faith and the hope we have in Jesus Christ.

"I am coming soon. Hold on to what you have, so that no one will take your crown" (Revelation 3.11 NIV).

DAY 366
Church of Laodicea

"I know your works, that you are neither cold nor hot. I could wish you were cold or hot. So then, because you are lukewarm, and neither cold nor hot, I will vomit you out of My mouth" (Revelation 3.15-16 NKJV).

When people are content in their own lives, they may cease to aggressively seek after the Lord. They have traded "God's best" for its human counterfeit "good enough." They may continue to go to church, but they aren't seeking anything from God. They have no expectations because they are physically comfortable, confident and successful. But what they don't realize is that they are spiritually poor, naked and blind. Because they have it so well in this life on earth, they forget to see through the eyes of eternity to their everlasting existence. They are not submitted or humbled to the Lord; therefore, they are acquiring absolutely no eternal rewards or treasures. In God's eyes they look destitute, but they can't see it over their own feelings of security. God can't bless those who don't know their need. God can't clothe those who don't see their nakedness. God can't heal those don't realize their blindness. These people are indifferent to the things of God—neither hot nor cold. God is unable to use them to further His Kingdom Plan on earth as it is in heaven, so His only choice is to leave them to their own fruitless and selfish devices. The only hope lukewarm people have is to realize their need and respond to God's discipline. They may have walked away from Him for a time, but He is always there, waiting for them to open the door to Him.

"Behold, I stand at the door and knock. If anyone hears My voice and opens the door, I will come in to him and dine with him, and he with Me" (Revelation 3.20 NKJV).

If you enjoyed this one-year devotional through the Bible, please consider writing a review on Amazon. You can find Alisa's other books on Amazon by searching *Alisa Hope Wagner*. Keep up with her current updates at her website, www.alisahopewagner.com. May God continue to bless your desire to know Him, love Him and be loved by Him. Always remember your Bible is your Sword, so slay your day!

www.ingramcontent.com/pod-product-compliance
Lightning Source LLC
Chambersburg PA
CBHW062033090426

42740CB00016B/2893